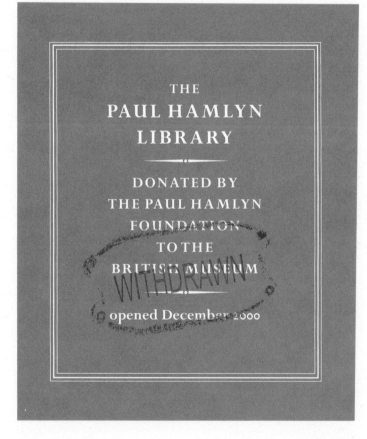

PORTRAITS AND VIEWS

Books by A. L. Rowse

Literature

Shakespeare the Man

Shakespeare the Elizabethan

Shakespeare's Sonnets: *A modern edition with prose-versions and notes*

Shakespeare's Southampton

Milton the Puritan: Portrait of a Mind

Jonathan Swift: Major Prophet

A Cornish Childhood

A Cornishman Abroad

Poems Chiefly Cornish

Strange Encounter: Poems

Poems of a Decade

Poems Partly American

Discoveries and Reviews

The English Spirit (*revised edition*)

The Annotated Shakespeare, 3 vols, with Introductions

The Poems of Shakespeare's Dark Lady

Christopher Marlowe

Matthew Arnold: Poet and Prophet

A Cornishman at Oxford

A Man of the Thirties

Poems of Cornwall and America

The Road to Oxford: Poems

Poems of Deliverance

A Cornish Anthology

Times, Persons, Places

History

The England of Elizabeth

The Expansion of Elizabethan England

The Elizabethan Renaissance: I. The Life of the Society   II. The Cultural Achievement

Sir Richard Grenville of the *Revenge*

Ralegh and the Throckmortons

The Elizabethans and America

The Cornish in America

Oxford in the History of the Nation

Windsor Castle in the History of England

The Tower of London in the History of the Nation

Heritage of Britain

Story of Britain

The Use of History

All Souls and Appeasement

The Early Churchills

The Later Churchills

Simon Forman: Sex and Society in Shakespeare's Age

Roper's Life of Sir Thomas More, with Letters: *edited with introduction and notes*

Homosexuals in History

The Byrons and Trevanions

PORTRAITS AND VIEWS

Literary and Historical

A. L. ROWSE

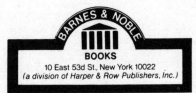

BARNES & NOBLE

BOOKS

10 East 53d St., New York 10022
(a division of Harper & Row Publishers, Inc.)

*First published 1979 in the UK
and all other parts of the world excluding the U.S.A. by*
THE MACMILLAN PRESS LTD
London and Basingstoke

First published in the U.S.A. 1979 by
HARPER & ROW PUBLISHERS, INC.
BARNES & NOBLE IMPORT DIVISION

British Library Cataloging in Publication Data

Rowse, Alfred Leslie
    Portraits and views
    I. Title
    082   PR6035.084

    MACMILLAN ISBN 0–333–27241–2
    BARNES & NOBLE ISBN 0–06–496018–8

LCN   79–53433

Printed in Great Britain

To
Evangeline Bruce
Good Friend of Britain
and of her Literature

CONTENTS

PREFACE

I welcome the opportunity of bringing together these essays and reviews, and of giving them more permanent shape, sometimes correcting to bring them up to date. For they have enabled me to portray various figures in our literature as I think of them, or to define my position with regard to significant historical issues, such as those of modern Germany and the two German wars of our time; or of the Russian Revolution, Marxism and Communism.

Macaulay thought that when the great days of Britain should be over – as they certainly are – she would be remembered for her achievements in literature. And, since the age of the voyages and colonisation – and as a direct result of them – English has become a prime world language. Dr Johnson held that a people was to be judged historically by its literature (to that I would add the other arts and sciences). Well, in this appalling time of universal confusion, anarchy and break-down, of the spread of violence, murder and rapine – with the people everywhere out of hand, except in Communist countries under force and military discipline – civilised persons may hope that Dr Johnson was right: I have no confidence that he will turn out to have been so.

These essays and reviews have appeared in various periodicals read by the intelligent minority: *Blackwood's Magazine* (going back, I am happy to think, to Walter Scott); *The Times* (which published my fellow-Cornishman, George Borrow, and the young Disraeli); and in publications of more recent origin, *History Today* and *Books and Bookmen*, the *Sunday Times* or *Sunday Telegraph*. To all of these I make grateful acknowledgment.

January 1979   A. L. ROWSE

I

JANE AUSTEN AS SOCIAL REALIST

For an historian to be asked to deliver the Address on the occasion of the second Centenary of Jane Austen's birth is a somewhat daunting undertaking – to confront embattled experts knowing everything about her and her work, where I have no qualification.[1] Or perhaps only one single qualification: I love both her and all her writing. Is that enough? If not, I also think that – when all is said, by the experts and the critics, she remains of all English novelists the most perfect artist.

As a human being, a remarkable thing about her, I find, is the degree of her moral perfection. That may not recommend her in the moral confusion of our own time – any more than the breakdown of standards in workmanship, craft, style, art of every kind recommends the perfection of her art: it renders her work the less intelligible to contemporary society. In America I am told that students at the universities no longer understand the complexities and subtleties of the articulated society she portrays. I can well believe it – too subtle, too refined and intelligent for them. But they can learn: a little intellectual effort is good for everybody.

As for us, everyone here will recognise the expectancy of enjoyment when we take up one of her novels to read it again: the enchantment, the challenge of her wit and sheer cleverness, the amusement, the sparkle like sunlight on the sea – and the disappointment when *Sanditon* breaks off unfinished, the author dead, at only forty-one. But what an achievement in the realm of art in that short time!

It is sometimes made a ground of complaint against her work that she does not deal with the heroic age in which she lived, the age of Napoleon and Wellington and Nelson, of Waterloo and Trafalgar. As it is sometimes remarked on with surprise that Shakespeare did not write about the Spanish Armada, the capture of Cadiz or Drake's Voyage round the World. Real writers write about what they know, what speaks to their imagination, what appeals to their instinctive choices. In fact, to anyone who knows about the subject and has the perception to see, a great deal of Elizabethan society is present in Shakespeare's work; as much – a larger spread than is generally realised – of the society of late Georgian England, its world of experience and manners, its thought and its standards, is perfectly expressed by Jane Austen.

In many quarters today, not only in Communist countries but in our own delightful society in deliquescence, in demotic America and Britain – particularly with the kitchen-sink school of novelists and dramatists – Social Realism is held up as the objective and the test in literature and the arts. An historian is struck by the remarkably firm grasp Jane Austen has of the structure of society, and the truthful realism with which she renders it. If anyone is a Social Realist, she certainly was.

Of course she had the challenge of a subtly articulated society, with its varying shades and shadows, its cross-rhythms and counter-rhythms, its conventions and rituals, to inspire her. A society of such a kind, hierarchical and ordered, but intricate and varied, offers immeasurably more inspiration, more character and colour, to a novelist than a monochrome society. The more it approximates to a one-class society the more boring it is to a real writer. This was the reason why Henry James left nineteenth-century democratic America for Europe with its richer material for a novelist's imagination to work on. It is one reason why the novel in nineteenth century America is so thin and unsatisfactory compared with the proliferating richness of the French novel, Stendhal, Balzac, Flaubert; George Sand, Victor Hugo, Dumas, Zola. Or compare nineteenth-century Russia, in the bad old days of the Tsars, with Tolstoy, Gogol, Dostoievsky, Turgenev, Shchedrin, Goncharov, with the bare cupboard under the enlightened rule of Lenin and Stalin.

Jane Austen had the articulated society of late Georgian or Regency England to write about – a more varied society, with far more shades and half-shades to it, than the disarticulated society of a Henry Miller or a Norman Mailer. An artist imposes his or her own limitations of choice on what they wish to write about – Jane Austen, a country lady of good family, tells us that she did not want to write about the sordid and the nasty. Norman Mailer called his novel of the War in the Pacific, *The Naked and the Dead*. Modern-minded and open-minded, we can agree that a butcher's shop offers a subject for art – Annibale Carracci depicted one three centuries ago. But does one want to live in a butcher's shop, eat and drink in a butcher's shop – let alone make love in a butcher's shop?

It is no valid objection to Jane Austen as a writer that she limits her field; limitation is the condition of good art (something that contemporary artists do not seem to understand – even the Prince

Regent's Chaplain was inept enough to suggest to a perfect artist subjects completely out of her way). One of her strengths was that she knew perfectly what she could do and what she could not. What the historian is suggesting is that her social range is much wider than is usually appreciated. She does not depict the nobility – but that constituted a very small section of society. All through modern English history, from the fifteenth century to the social revolution of our time, the backbone of English society has been constituted by the country gentry, in every county and parish, with their affiliated middling classes in trade and the professions; below them, the farming community and village life. Here is Jane Austen's field – from the point of view of social realism, the most significant territory for depiction, herself as a writer at the centre of it. So, from the point of view of the social historian alone – even apart from the perfection of her art – she is a most significant writer.

There can be no doubt about the realism. The chief difference between her and professed realists is that, where they are apt to be crude, she is discriminating and subtle. I find her sheer cleverness terrifying: she never misses a point in character or conduct, she saw – and saw through – everything and everybody. Of course, a subtly articulated society, with its codes and conventions, offers much more to observe or make fun of, it is so much more varied and interesting. She is never taken in, she has no illusions: we might adapt as epigraph for her the celebrated *mot* of an improbable contemporary of hers, the former Bishop of Autun, Talleyrand: 'Surtout point d'illusions'.

Take the rather *désabusé* beginning of *Persuasion*. Sir Walter Elliot is a baronet, of Somersetshire – the county communities are always clearly demarcated, by the way. His only book was the Baronetage, his favourite reading in it the pages describing 'the limited remnant of the earliest patents', followed by the story of his own family, when members of it served as high sheriff, members of Parliament, etc. The baronet has been living beyond his means; when forced to economise, he has no idea how to do so, 'without involving the loss of any indulgence of taste or pride'. Jane Austen well perceived the silly side of such persons in their social position: 'vanity was the beginning and the end of Sir Walter Elliot's character: vanity of person and of situation'.

Lady Russell, his neighbour, a good sort of person, sensible and well-bred, 'had a value for rank and consequence ... herself the widow of only a knight, she gave the dignity of a baronet all its due'. Sir Walter is under the necessity of letting Kellynch Hall to an Admiral Croft, though he is by no means favourably inclined to the Navy, 'as being the means of bringing persons of obscure birth into undue distinction, and raising men to honours which their fathers and grandfathers never dreamt of'. The Admiral, having made his fortune in the Navy, takes Kellynch; Sir Walter is consoled by the thought that ' "I have let my house to Admiral Croft" would sound very much better than to any mere *Mr.* A Mr (save, perhaps, some half dozen in the nation) always needs a note of explanation. An admiral speaks his own consequence and, at the same time, can never make a baronet look small'.

The hero of the book is to be another naval person, Captain Wentworth. Sir Walter mistook the reference to him for Mr Wentworth, the curate of Monkford: 'You misled me by the term *gentleman.* I thought you were speaking of some man of property. Mr Wentworth was nobody, I remember: quite unconnected: nothing to do with the Strafford family. One wonders how the names of our nobility become so common'.

Here, within a couple of pages, we see how firmly the niceties of the social structure, and the distinctions within it, are grasped – with no illusions as to its beauty: we are in fact told that Sir Walter was only half a fool. There is not only this in it, something very significant about the history of the time is suggested. We hear a great deal about how 'class-ridden' England was, in its great days, but in fact English society was always more flexible than on the Continent: one could move up in it, and also down.

The Navy was a grand way of making one's fortune; the Church was a good way; so were the other professions, the law and medicine. Sir Walter was quite right about the Navy bringing persons of obscure birth into notice – there was England's hero, Nelson, famous throughout the world: a poor clergyman's son. The father of the great Admiral Hawke was the son of a Cornish farmer. Sir Walter was much annoyed at having to yield precedence to a newly created Naval peer, whose father was only a country curate. In fact, many fortunes were made from prize-money in those prolonged wars, and I cannot recollect all the peerages: besides Hawke and Anson, Rodney and Nelson, there were two in the Somerset family of Hood (Bridport and Hood), St Vincent, Collingwood, Exmouth, Gambier, Graves (but that was only an Irish peerage).

As for the Church, we see that an ordinary clergyman stood in rather an equivocal position – Sir Walter did not rate a curate as a gentleman. In fact, the Church was intimately articulated into the social structure, and men from all ranks, from the aristocracy downwards, served in it. We need not cite the names that come to mind among the Georgian episcopate – Manners, Keppel, Cornwallis, Lyttelton, Barrington, North, Egerton, Percy; the point I am making is the flexibility that yet obtained within the class-structure. Jane Austen's Archbishop of Canterbury was that admirable man, John Moore, son of a Gloucestershire grazier. We all know the fortunes made at the bar, often from small beginnings; many doctors did well too. The Regent's own doctor, Sir William Knighton, was born in humble circumstances in Devon, his mother an impoverished widow; taken care of by an uncle who was a country surgeon, Knighton first achieved success as a man-midwife – to become one of the most influential men in England as the Regent's confidant.

With regard to marriage, we observe realism even to a fraction. Miss Maria Ward of Huntingdon was lucky to capture a baronet, Sir Thomas Bertram, with only £7000 – this was £3000 'short of any equitable claim': so she was three-tenths below par. Marriage is the essential social knot, and therefore the crux of all the novels – not the exaggerated preoccupation of a maiden lady. Jane Austen seems to have thought much as Shakespeare thought on the subject: Dr Grant says, conclusively, 'I would have everybody marry, if they can do it properly; I do not like to have people throw themselves away; but everybody should marry as soon as they can do it to advantage'. Mr Crawford considered that 'an engaged woman is always more agreeable than a disengaged. She is more satisfied with herself. Her cares are over, and she feels that she may exert all her powers of pleasing without suspicion. All is safe with a lady engaged; no harm can be done'.

On the other hand, it is his sister who doesn't mind if the man is taken in. 'Let him stand his chance and be taken in. Everybody is taken in at some period or other.' When her brother protests, she goes on, rather unreasonably: 'there is not one in a hundred of either sex who is not taken in when they marry. Look where I will, I see that it *is* so; and I feel that it *must* be so, when I consider that it is, of all transactions, the one in which people expect most from others, and are least honest themselves'.

We must not make a direct transference to Jane Austen, as if this were what she thought. We are on surer ground with the observation that 'Mrs Musgrove and Mrs Hayter were sisters. They had each had money, but their marriages had made a material difference in their degree of consequence'. For this is an observed social fact. Nor was her own attitude to marriage at all mercenary; she herself rejected a very eligible offer from a gentleman of estate whom she liked well enough, because – a sincere woman – she felt she could not love him. The facts of social life are what they are: in a settled society settlements must be provided for, with propertied persons property enters in, a necessary provision for subsistence. Of all her heroines, it is usually held that Anne Elliot, of *Persuasion*, comes closest to her creator, who says of her: 'she had been forced into prudence in her youth, she learned romance as she grew older'.

Jane Austen's view of society was that of the rational eighteenth century; it stirs the imagination strangely to think that, with a reasonable expectation of life she should have lived into the Victorian age, and what more she might have written!

As it was – no illusions. Ladies' schooling at the time? Here is *Emma* (dedicated to the Prince Regent). 'Mrs Goddard was the mistress of a School – not of a seminary, or an establishment, or anything which professed, in long sentences of refined nonsense, to combine liberal requirements with elegant morality upon new principles and new systems – and when young ladies for enormous pay might be screwed out of health and into vanity – but a real, honest, old-fashioned Boarding School, where a reasonable quantity of accomplishments were sold at a reasonable price, and where girls might be sent to be out of the way and scramble themselves into a little education, without any danger of coming back prodigies.'

This seems to have been Jane's own schooling, quite sufficient for the purpose – as Shakespeare's country grammar school was sufficient for him. Nothing mystifying about the matter – addicts of nonsense haven't the sense to see that men and women of genius educate themselves.

As for boys' schooling at the time, here she is on a July day in 1816 – on the Winchester boys going home for summer holidays: 'We saw a countless number of post-chaises pass by yesterday morning – full of future heroes, legislators, fools and villains . . .'. Then, 'Oh, it rains again; it beats against the window'.

One's heart stands still: one is in the room with her. Here is genius – that acute sense of life and its reflection in words.

And M.P.s, the legislators grown up – any illusions about them? We know what she thought of them, for she is speaking in her own person in her *Letters*: Mr Lushington 'is quite an M.P. – very smiling, with an exceeding good address and readiness of language. I am rather in love with him. I dare say he is ambitious and insincere'. And again, 'he puts me in mind of Mr Dundas'. Dundas, we remember, was impeached for bribery and corruption. We must remember that M.P.s were not paid in those days for their devoted services to the well-being of their country; on the other hand, how many of those who so distinguish themselves today do so 'with an exceeding good address'?

Here is the place to observe how much the *Letters* illuminate the author of the works – as Shakespeare's verse-letters, the Sonnets, do him; and how much Jane's letters are recognisably one with the novelist. We find the same firmness and precision, the infallible eye for people, every quirk of personality, every detail of appearance, gesture, character. No more sprightly letters exist in our literature, even Horace Walpole's are not more so; and his were written with an eye to posterity, hers were not. They are spontaneous and natural; herself humorous and witty, she couldn't help but be stylish in everything she wrote or did. Of course, between two ladies, Jane and Cassandra, a great many subtleties about women's clothes I do not much appreciate; but I do the ships' sailings and movements, the background to Trafalgar not only implied, but actually there. (We recall that Admiral Croft in *Persuasion* had fought at Trafalgar.) Dr Chapman is perfectly right in saying, 'Read with attention, they yield a picture of the life of the upper middle class of that time which is surely without a rival'. The historian can corroborate this expert Janeite – I could go on reading her letters for ever.

Critics have not always been so happy. Professor H. W. Garrod regarded them as ' a desert of trivialities punctuated by occasional oases of clever malice'. We observe as so often, what asses critics can be. Jane was too clever for him; for the malice was often cleverer than he, with masculine impercipience, could perceive: it was in inverted commas, half ironical, to amuse Cassandra and herself. The golden rule in criticism is for the critic to be on a level with the author – that is why the eighteenth-century Dr Johnson is still the grandest critic of Shakespeare, and also why we can ignore 99 per cent of the production of the critical industry. (No productivity troubles there!)

On the whole, Jane Austen, in our time, has been fortunate in her critics – in the admirable biography of Elizabeth Jenkins, and the scrupulously penetrating book of Miss Lascelles, on a par with their author in intelligence, unlike most critics. Even in her own day it was something to be appreciated by Walter Scott and Warren Hastings, and that remarkable connoisseur and man of taste, the Prince Regent – even if publishers were slow to publish. Very small editions of her novels were called for, and the general public couldn't see the difference between her and Mrs Inchbald. That was but to be expected: people never know.

Though the intimate correspondence between two sisters has been bowdlerised, we see at every point the realism of Jane Austen's mind, her outlook and her view of life without any illusions. She knew the facts of life as well as any Pinter or Sillitoe or Samuel Beckett. 'I am proud to say that I have a very good eye at an Adulteress, for, though repeatedly assured that another in the same party was the *She*, I fixed upon the right one from the first. She was highly rouged, and looked rather quietly and contentedly silly than anything else.' That is Jane at twenty-six. At twenty she wished to go to Greenwich to see one of her sailor brothers off, but had not heard whether the Pearsons could put her up, and 'if the Pearsons were not at home, I should inevitably fall a sacrifice to the arts of some fat Woman, who would make me drunk with small beer'. We see that Miss Austen was a Regency woman, not a Victorian. Can one imagine the portentous George Eliot writing anything so indelicate, though we know that the way she lived her life offered some points of contrast with the domestic life of Steventon and Chawton.

The so-called 'facts of life' make their appearance in the novels no less – in the Regency world they could be taken for granted; as the century progressed into the Victorian world, a writer had to be more careful. Illegitimate children occur, or are mentioned: they were more of a feature in upper-class society in Regency days than today. There are seductions, like Willoughby's seduction and desertion of Eliza Williams, or the sordid elopement of Maria Bertram, Mr Rushworth's wife, with Henry Crawford, which Miss Austen did not wish to explore further – it was not her subject – nor need we.

Our subject is the way the life of the age, the England of her time, is fully in our author – as the England of Elizabeth is in Shakespeare. The years between the outbreak of the French Revolution and Waterloo, coterminous with Jane Austen's active adult life, were an heroic period in our history, when first the revolutionary impulse from France spread beyond its boundaries and turned into aggression against other countries. A Liberal like Charles James Fox – a kind of aristocratic Aneurin Bevan – thought the outbreak of the Revolution the best news since Saratoga. Wordsworth, Coleridge and Southey, young men, saw in it the promise of a better world: they lived to be disillusioned. The person who had the imagination to foresee what it would all lead to was a man of conservative genius, Edmund Burke – i.e. to the military despotism of Napoleon. (Consider the Leftist hopes of the Russian Revolution in 1917, and what that has led to!)

No such nonsense in the Letters of this sensible young woman: Jane Austen was a good patriot. Nor was she at all the recluse of popular imagination: she led a very active family life, the constant comings and goings of her sailor brothers, her numerous relations, like the Knight of rather grand Godmersham; enjoyed her share of social life, especially dances and balls when young, her visits around the country, changes of scene and residence, and would have liked more. In 1801 she envies the wives of soldiers and sailors in being near the sea and moving about.

We have naval news a-plenty – of those fleets that ultimately broke the power of both French Revolution and Napoleon, and preserved the liberties of Europe. In 1798 we learn that brother Frank is at Cadiz; Lord St Vincent has left the fleet and gone to Gibraltar to fit out a privateering expedition against enemy ports, Minorca or Malta. The Letters are full of details of naval promotions, of the father writing on behalf of his sons to Lord Spencer at the Admiralty, Admiral Gambier, or the East India Company directors. Jane in 1798: 'The Lords of the Admiralty will have enough of our applications at present, for I hear from Charles that he has written to Lord Spencer himself to be removed. I am afraid his Serene Highness will be in a passion and order some of our heads to be cut off'. Shortly comes news of Frank's promotion to Captain – 'Frank is made', the contemporary phrase for it; while Charles is to join the *Tamar* in the Downs.

In December that year Cassandra was at Godmersham supping with George III's sailor-son, Prince William (later William IV). Jane equates that with the purchase of a new muslin gown, 'both delightful circumstances'. For herself she has changed her mind about dressing her hat: 'I think it makes me look more like Lady Conyngham than it did before, which is all that one lives for now'. (Lady Conyngham was the Prince Regent's Egeria.) In November 1800 brother Frank is in the *Peterel* squadron off Cyprus for provisions; he went from Jaffa to Alexandria 'to wait the result of the English proposals for the evacuation of Egypt'. That was the end of Bonaparte's dream of using Egypt as a springboard for the conquest of the gorgeous East.

Next year Charles spends three days in Lisbon, 'very well satisfied with their Royal Passenger – fat, jolly and affable, talks of Lady Augusta as his wife'. This was another of George III's all too numerous offspring, the Duke of Sussex. Enough of Jane's naval bulletins – suffice it to say that her brothers Frank and Charles had highly successful long careers in the Navy. They both became Admirals – after her death, alas; we know what joy that would have given her – in 1808 Frank 'wants nothing but a good Prize to make him a perfect character' – and the biographies of both have been written. What is more to our point is that their sister proudly cites the names of Frank's old ships, with several others, in her novels: the *Elephant, Cleopatra, Endymion*.

I wonder if people fully appreciate the part that is played by naval personnel in the novels. In *Mansfield Park* the very realistic account of the squalid home at Portsmouth of Fanny Price's parents, the seedy and drunken Lieutenant Price of the Marines, the description of the harbour, the berths of the ships, form a fine set-off to the inland grandeurs of the Park, Fanny's home with the Bertrams. In the second edition of the book a rather technical paragraph is inserted, about the sailing out of harbour of the *Thrush* and her sailing qualities, which perhaps Jane owed to one of her sailor brothers – as interested in her novels as she was in their ships. A speech of Admiral Crawford's niece, Mary, to Edmund Bertram should have been sufficient warning to him of the kind of woman she was.

'Do you know anything of my cousin's captain?' said Edmund, 'Captain Marshall? You have a large acquaintance in the Navy, I conclude?'

'Among Admirals, large enough; but' – with an air of grandeur – 'we know very little of the inferior ranks. Post-captains may be very good sort of men, but they do not belong to *us*. Of various admirals I could tell you a great deal; of them and their flags, and the gradation of their pay, and their bickerings and jealousies. Certainly my home at my uncle's brought me

acquainted with a circle of admirals. Of *Rears*, and *Vices*, I saw
enough. Now do not be suspecting me of a pun, I entreat.'

Edmund again felt grave, and only replied, 'It is a noble
profession.'

In *Persuasion*, though naval matters are more in the back-
ground, two of the leading characters are sailors, the hero Captain
Wentworth, and his friend Captain Harville; we have too Admiral
Croft and Lieutenant Berwick. We need go no further; the action
takes place at Lyme Regis, Bath and elsewhere. We are amused to
read in the Letters some years before, during Jane's visit to Lyme
Regis, a reference to a son and daughter-in-law of an Irish
Viscount, 'bold, queer-looking people, just fit to be quality at
Lyme'. At this same time Jane's aunt calls a sloop a frigate: 'never
mind, let them puzzle on together'. Charles will go to the East
Indies, 'and my aunt may do what she likes with her frigates'.

The Army makes no such figure in the foreground of her work –
though officers of the Militia play no very heroic part in *Pride and
Prejudice* – any more than it did effectively until the war began in
the Peninsula. Then, with Sir John Moore's heroic retreat, her
patriotism is aroused. In January 1809, 'the *St Albans* may soon be
off to bring home what may remain by this time of our poor Army,
whose state seems dreadfully critical'. Next, 'this is grievous news
from Spain. It is well that Dr Moore was spared the knowledge of
such a son's death'. Next, 'I am sorry to find that Sir John Moore
has a mother living; but though a very heroic son . . . I wish Sir
John had united something of the Christian with the hero in his
death'. There we are admitted into the privacy of her inner beliefs.
Her clerical brother wrote of her, 'she was thoroughly religious
and devout; fearful of giving offence to God, and incapable of
feeling it towards any fellow creature'. There is the ground of what
I have called, challengingly – and I challenge anyone to question
it – her extraordinary degree of moral perfection.

It is a sign of it that she never obtruded her firmly held beliefs;
she preferred to render the comedy of life, though she well
understood its tragedy – she had experienced it in her own most
intimate life, but never once mentioned it, let alone complained.
She had her own form of stoicism, a Christian stoicism. The front
that she turned to society was all gaiety and fun. Of a General – 'I
like his rank very much, and always affix the ideas of strong sense
and highly elegant manners to a General'. Nor need we be

surprised at her reading, in 1813, 'a Society octavo, an *Essay on the Military Police and Institutions of the British Empire* by Captain Pasley of the Engineers . . . which I find delightfully written and highly entertaining. I am as much in love with the author as ever I was with Clarkson or Buchanan, or even the two Mr Smiths of the City – the first soldier I ever sighed for – but he does write with extraordinary force and spirit'.

This reminds us how much wider her range of reading was than is usually appreciated. She was well read in history – a favourite from childhood – as well as in poetry, drama, and the novel, as we should expect. Nor need we be surprised that she does better than most critics in her defence of the novel, and definition of its aims, in just a paragraph of *Northanger Abbey* – after all, the best dramatic criticism in Elizabethan literature is that of the practising dramatist in *Hamlet*.

One of the best historians of the eighteenth century, Richard Pares – a great admirer of Jane Austen from his schooldays at Winchester – used to tease me by saying that the England of George III was, on the whole, a greater epoch than the Elizabethan age. Well? – there is much to be said on both sides. If Elizabethan music and drama are incomparable, its painting cannot hold a candle to Gainsborough and Reynolds, Raeburn and Romney, Constable and Lawrence, in whom Jane Austen's world is depicted. Nor can the Elizabethan novel be compared with that of her day, herself its master. If in naval and military exploits they draw fairly level, no praise is too great for a Warren Hastings, who saved and welded together a great Empire – one of the most remarkable achievements in history (we have found it easy enough to throw it away in our time). The greatest achievement was perhaps the Industrial Revolution – the foundation of modern civilisation, for good or ill – which was worked out and gathering momentum throughout Jane Austen's life.

It is no reproach to her that she didn't write about it, any more than it is to Shakespeare that he didn't write about the Elizabethan Voyages. They wrote about the society they knew – it provided them with all the material they needed; she could well afford to leave the Industrial Revolution to Mrs Gaskell and Charlotte Brontë.

I suppose, to be in the fashion, we might consider what a Marxist criticism of Jane Austen would be. A good deal of the action in the novels, socially considered, revolves round the struggle to keep up social position. Hence the concern to marry well, the importance of inheritance, settlements, etc. Otherwise you slip down the social scale; one has to keep up appearances, one's position in other people's regard. These are the necessary concomitants of a privileged society of *small* gentry – an aristocracy could afford to be more regardless and free.

The niceties of class-situation are never more crisply stated than in the opening pages of *Pride and Prejudice*. The Bingley young ladies

> had been educated in one of the first private seminaries in town, had a fortune of £20,000, were in the habit of spending more than they ought, and of associating with people of *rank*; and were therefore in every respect entitled to think well of themselves, and meanly of others. They were of a respectable family in the north of England: a circumstance more deeply impressed on their memories than that their brother's fortune and their own had been acquired by *trade*.

Similarly, the Bennets' neighbour, Sir William Lucas,

> had been formerly in trade in Meryton and risen to the honour of knighthood by an address to the King, during his mayoralty. The distinction had perhaps been felt too strongly. It had given him a disgust to his business and to his residence in a small market town; and quitting them both, he had removed to a house about a mile *from* Meryton, denominated from that period Lucas Lodge, where he could think with pleasure of his own importance, and unshackled by business, occupy himself solely in being civil to all the world. For, though elated by his rank, it did not render him supercilious.

We enjoy the shade of irony under it all; but I have never yet met a Marxist with much sense of humour, or any sense of social irony whatever. Yet what could be at the same time more firm, and more precise?

At the same time as the Bingley ladies had derived their wealth from trade, but in the generation before, they 'would have difficulty in believing [in regard to Mrs Bennet's brother] that a man who lived by trade, and within view of his own warehouses, could have been so well bred and agreeable'.

Jane knew well what fools people are. No wonder Elizabeth Bennet said,

> There are few people whom I really love, and still fewer of whom I think well. The more I see of the world, the more I am dissatisfied with it; and every day confirms my belief of the inconsistency of all human characters, and of the little dependence that can be placed on the appearance of either merit or sense.

In poetry Jane Austen's world can hold its own with the Elizabethans – the age of Wordsworth, Coleridge, Scott; and Byron, Shelley, Keats were not so very much her juniors. She died so young.

Elizabethan architecture is very grand at its best; it was challenging and experimental at the summit. But it did not achieve the classic perfection of proportion and integrated design of Georgian England. We need not bandy individual names like Adam and Soane, Nash, the Wyatts and Decimus Burton, or individual buildings like the Assembly Rooms at Bath or York, or the fantasy and exotic beauty of the Regent's pleasure-dome at Brighton. It is the *general* character achieved in Jane Austen's England that is so wonderful – and makes the heart ache to think of. In every county, practically every parish, there were going up those country houses, decent, well-proportioned, of restrained taste, sometimes magnificent palaces, often beautiful inside and out, with all their furnishings, portraits and paintings, their libraries and sculpture.

Theirs was an age of aristocratic taste: all taste is aristocratic; people in general haven't any, and never will have. All the lasting achievements of culture are the work of a small minority. So again it is not surprising that in a demotic age like ours they are being felled like ninepins; country houses have been destroyed in hundreds, their possessions, pictures, furniture, libraries dispersed, in the social revolution of our time.

In that age, all was still on the human scale; the beauty of the English countryside was incomparable, the countryside of Constable and Turner, Cotman and Girtin. A new school of landscape painters arose to depict its beauty, a new society of watercolour artists formed, whose exhibitions Jane Austen attended in London. We know how keen she was on Gilpin and the

Picturesque; the landscape improvements that were made by the country gentry all over England, the parks and gardens they formed, the plantations and woods they planned to decorate the landscape – all this is reflected in the novels.

The charm of those English villages – church, manor-house, well-proportioned houses of professional middle-class, farms and cottages – reflected an integrated society, all on a human scale: not one grotesquely out of scale, falling apart. Similarly with the towns of the time – the terraces of Regent's Park, the old Regent Street and the Adelphi we have destroyed, the Georgian squares of London we remember, Bath and Buxton – all was in keeping. Jane Austen's Bath, with its exquisite buildings, public and private, was new – she refers to its 'white glare'; to us, it is grey and peeling, and being pulled apart.

Constable's house in Hampstead had an uninterrupted view from Westminster Abbey to Gravesend, with the dome of St Paul's rising in the air, to remind him of Michelangelo's words on the Pantheon. Think of the skyscape of modern London – or any modern city – all confusion and chaos, all out of scale, out of scale with humanity. I remember reading that Constable, in all his life – he was Jane Austen's exact contemporary, born a year after her, but lived twenty years longer, still not old – can hardly ever have seen anything ugly, except perhaps an occasional human being. It is precisely the impression one would derive from her work.

The England that was so beautiful, with its pretty villages and small towns and cathedral cities, like Winchester – none of them large, except the capital itself, also beautiful – all on a small scale, but a society integrated and properly articulated like a body that functions well, may not perhaps have been the first country in Europe. We may leave that title generously to France, for the England of her day was the first in the world outside.

The England of Jane Austen was, as societies go, rise and fall, live and die, an efficient, highly successful, above all a *creative* society.

On this day, and in our time, we salute her memory with love and gratitude – and with grief.

NOTE

1. So I was told on the occasion by an unmemorable Eng. Lit. professor whom I had never heard of and whose name I cannot remember.

DR JOHNSON WITHOUT BOSWELL:
AN AMERICAN INTERPRETATION

'I am willing to love all mankind, except an American.' Considering this *boutade*, the Americans have been characteristically generous and forgiving to the Tory Doctor. Professor James Clifford gave us an admirable book on *Young Samuel Johnson*, to which this latest recruit to the industry has not much to add. But Professor Bate makes up for it in voluminousness and repetitiousness – I have noted some fifty repetitions.[1] American academics seem to think larger means better; I suppose it is an expression of the giantism endemic in American civilisation – airports and hotels so large one can't find one's way around in them. I recall a standard biography of Benjamin Franklin of some 900 pages, in the Preface to which the sanguine author said that he had 'cut it to the bone'. He evidently did not know what a bone was.

Professor Bate's good quality is sympathy with his subject: he evidently has something like love for the great bear with his bullying ways and his tender heart. A prime qualification, for it leads to real understanding of the complex nature of the man and a convincing portrait of the personality. Not to be able to admire Dr Johnson is a sure sign of lack of generosity of mind. Professor Bate has generosity in abundance. His chief defect, as with literary scholars (compare them on Shakespeare!), is a lack of historical grasp of the period, the proper perspective of a writer's life and work. To read Professor Bate one would think that Dr Johnson was almost a Whig. It is an American misunderstanding.

It is true that in the writing of seventeenth- and eighteenth-century history the Whig dogs have had the best of it. But, really to understand the background out of which Johnson came, a formative mould in his life, and even his political stance and opinions, one has to understand the strength of Toryism in the counties, and especially in cathedral cities. Though the Whigs were dominant in Parliament and in London, they were by no means so in the country at large, let alone the countryside. This is brought home to us by Boswell's surprise at finding a Whig in Staffordshire – Johnson's home county; to which the Doctor gave his reply, 'Sir, there are rascals in all countries'. In cathedral cities like Lichfield, where the bishops were apt to be Whigs – after their creator, Sir Robert Walpole – the atmosphere of Close and city was apt to be Tory, still more in the country outside.

In this Johnson was not minority-minded, exponent of a minority point of view. He first won attention and success with his poem, *London*, which was a whole-hogging attack on the Whig ascendancy under Walpole – and almost all the wits were in the Opposition, Swift, Pope, Bolingbroke, Prior, Gay. Johnson's Oxford was dominantly Tory, Johnson himself tinged by Jacobitism; he had a feeling of sympathy for the exiled Stuarts. This was how he wrote about the first Hanoverian: 'George I knew nothing, and desired to know nothing; and the only good thing that is told of him is that he wished to restore the crown to its hereditary successor'. This was manifestly unfair – George I was no fool, though a German boor and a Philistine; but it shows where Dr Johnson stood.

He became a friend of Dr William King, the leader of Oxford Jacobitism, the Public Orator whose *Redeat*, thrice repeated at the installation of a Jacobite Chancellor, brought down the house. This expressed acclaim, if no more than a pious wish, for the return of the Stuart Pretender. Johnson was present, and clapped till his hands were sore. When Dr King met the Pretender on a secret visit, he was somewhat disillusioned. Tories were able to rally to the young George III who had at least been born in England, 'gloried in the name of Briton', and spoke English like an Englishman.

A more important matter that connects up here is Johnson's hatred of war. Professor Bate appreciates the humanity of this but, not being an historian, does not understand the political import of it. The Whigs were the war-makers; the Tories were anti-war, or at least wanted to confine the wars, from William III and Marlborough's time onwards, to the sea. They disliked Continental entanglements (the Hanoverians were Continentals, entangled in German affairs) and the endless subsidies poured out to allies in the Whig wars for trade, empire, power in the world. Tories might be backwoodsmen, but it fell to them to foot the bill; the Whigs profited. For all that Johnson detested the revolt of the American colonists – were they not Whigs and rebels, the descendants of intolerable (and intolerant) Puritans? – he was no imperialist.

He equally detested slavery, the concomitant of economic imperialism. 'How is it', he asked of the American colonists, Whigs to a man, brought up on Whig doctrines, 'that we hear the loudest yelps for liberty among the drivers of negroes?' In grave company at Oxford the celebrated Doctor once proposed a toast:

'Here's to the next insurrection of the negroes in the West Indies'. Nor did he view with any sympathy the record of the colonists with regard to the American Indians, whom the Crown wished in vain to protect. We may say that the sceptically-minded, authoritarian, Tory Johnson was more sincerely devoted to the real freedom of men than the Whig doctrinaires of 'liberty', too often traders in humbug. (The cry, 'Give me liberty, or give me death!' of loud-mouthed Patrick Henry was pure humbug: nobody was going to give him death, though he required restraint.) And with regard to the great Whig aristocrats, the Revolution Dukes with their thousands of acres, Johnson was at one with the Tory Goldsmith in summing up their political objective briskly, as to

blockade the throne,
Contracting regal power to stretch their own.

Underneath Johnson's concern with social order and due obedience to authority to keep society together – Professor Bate is rather coy about 'subjection' – there is a wise scepticism about how much government can do for human happiness. The most we can expect of government is to provide a just and propitious framework. 'Most schemes of political improvement are very laughable things', said the humorous old bear with understandable exaggeration. He meant what the recent revolt against excessive taxation in California means – would that there were a similar revolt here! The English have always been the most taxable of peoples. An American citizen has put it to his representative in Congress: 'When you get to Washington, don't do anything for me: I can't afford it'. The slogan should be impressed upon the portals of Westminster. There is a profound wisdom in Johnston's rumbustious, 'I would not give half-a-guinea to live under one form of government rather than another. It is of no moment to the *happiness* of an individual'. There is the truth expressed against the intrusiveness of modern government: its proper concern is with external conditions. A man's happiness is nothing to do with them; it depends upon the subtler inner factors of his personal life, his physical and psychological make-up, family, religion, and so on. Governments that directly concern themselves with their citizens' 'happiness', like Soviet Russia or Communist societies in general, end with a shocking tyranny over the life of the individual.

The Tory Johnson would have men truly free; that and their 'happiness' depending more upon their religion. (I expect Solzhenytsin would agree.) Johnson's religion, like his politics, needs to be seen in the perspective of his time and Church. Here again Professor Bate, across all those miles of ocean, is still at sea. He does not understand Anglicanism, how important the Church was to Johnson, what a devout Anglican he was and the part this played in his life. The professor understands the psychological roots – psychology is his forte, indeed *fortissimo*: he has already been criticised for his heavy addiction to Freud. I agree pretty well with his diagnosis – though he does not obtrude upon us any explanation for the inveterate habit of lying long in bed and the continual expressions of penitence, consciousness of sin, etc. (What was this powerfully equipped man up to? He was not apparently 'much addicted to women'.)

It is Johnson's religious affiliations, the proper placing of him in his time, that are missing. He was in fact a High Anglican. Does the Massachusetts professor know what that implies? Johnson's fasting in Lent, the rigour of his Good Friday observances, his private devotions, all bear the stamp of his High Anglicanism. Of the two prime intellectual influences upon his early life, the High Church non-juring William Law was one. Johnson was never a Roman Catholic (unlike Gibbon!); but his custom of recommending the soul of a dear friend at Communion comes very close to a votive Mass. To the Puritan tradition of Harvard these things may not be so clear.

Professor Bate's express aim is to rectify the imbalance in Boswell: the first half of Johnson's life occupies only one-tenth of the biography. But there is no rectifying this quantitatively; the materials for Johnson's early life are exiguous, for the later overwhelming. Getting Johnson right depends upon subtler matters than quantity, mass and size – and, for one thing, Boswell who was a religious man himself, a prey to comparable tensions and depressions, understood Johnson's religion better than the professor.

There is even a paradox here, some contrast between Johnson's life and his expressed work. We can catch him out in a contradiction. He is for ever writing in terms of despair about life, this vale of misery, that satisfaction is not to be had on earth, we must look to another world for happiness and not expect any in this, life is empty, there is a *vacuity* in it, etc. All this is the subject of his most famous poem, *The Vanity of Human Wishes*. But it is not in accord with his evident gusto for life and capacity for enjoyment. He can easily be quoted against himself. 'The happiness of London is not to be conceived but by those who have been in it . . . When a man is tired of London, he is tired of life.' He gives Boswell a revealing piece of advice on the subject of indulging melancholy: 'Be well when you are not ill, and pleased when you are not angry'. And he polished off the nonsense of the Swan of Lichfield about death being but a pleasing dream, with robust sense: 'It is neither pleasing, nor sleep: it is nothing. Now mere existence is so much better than nothing that one would rather exist even in pain'.

Life is a precious gift, and depreciation of what it has to offer is not only ungrateful, but untrue in almost any circumstances. The explanation of the contradiction, I think, is fairly simple. Writers are apt to express themselves, even to write more, in moods of depression than when enjoying themselves. Thus the picture that arises from their writings is sometimes out of focus. Both Swift and Johnson had much to complain of from physical disabilities, and much they complained about life, yet each of them had tremendous gusto for living. It offers another reason, if a somewhat paradoxical one, why Boswell's biography, for all its concentration upon Johnson's later years, gives a better balanced portrait of the man as he was.

It is a tremendous tribute to Johnson that, with his physical and psychological burdens – scrofula (he was touched for the King's Evil as a boy by Queen Anne), deafness, semi-blindness, insomnia, at least two nervous breakdowns – he should have come through with so robust and commonsense a morality. I suppose he is the outstanding, certainly outsize, English moralist – much to be preferred to Old Moore, Russell and the Cambridge School. Nathaniel Hawthorne thought Johnson's morality 'as English an article as a beefsteak'. His observations may not have the wicked penetration of a La Rochefoucauld, they have rather the character of inspired common sense, commonplaces raised to a higher power by the precision of style.

Merit rather enforces respect than attracts fondness.

Many need no other provocation to enmity than that they find themselves excelled.

Among other pleasing errors of young minds is the opinion of their own importance.

The safe and general antidote against sorrow is employment.

He is no wise man who will quit a certainty for an uncertainty.

All censure of a man's self is oblique praise.

(So much for the humbug of modesty, we may comment.)

Johnson had a peculiar abhorrence of envy – 'the cold malignity' of it. He himself, with the decisiveness of his opinions, and the incisiveness of his wit, presented an obvious target. And because he wrote on diverse subjects the attacks were the more numerous. From the time that he achieved fame and something like a literary ascendancy they multiplied. (One is reminded of John Buchan's chastening remark: 'It is only when one is successful that one finds the world is not a very nice place.') Professor Boulton, in a useful book,[2] reminds us that Johnson was always a controversial figure; 'his work had to endure criticism which ranges from the crude to the sensitive, and his character to tolerate both savage denigration and panegyric'. Some of the attacks were 'vicious', others merely 'swingeing'; above all, his political views were misrepresented, and himself traduced for receiving a modest pension for his immense, single-handed accomplishment of the Dictionary. Into this field the mellow Professor Bate does not enter; it is overlooked today when Johnson has achieved the somewhat static monumentality of a classic.

In his own time things were different, and much more lively; as an early obituary of him said, 'few men could stand so fiery a trial as he has done. His gold has been put into the furnace, and really, considering the violence of the fire, and the frequent repetition of the process, the quantity of dross and alloy is inconsiderable'. He kept his head and spoke sense; he was a magnanimous, a big-minded man. 'It is advantageous to an author that his book should be attacked as well as praised ... A man whose business it is to be talked of is much helped by being attacked.' Moreover, there was fun in it; the melancholic who could hardly look upon a slope of ground without wanting to roll down it, was never afraid of a rough-and-tumble. 'There is no sport in mere praise, when people are all of a mind.'

All the same, it is fairly clear that he was thinking of himself when he wrote in one of his *Lives of the Poets*:

The incessant attacks of his enemies are never discovered to have disturbed his quiet, or to have lessened his confidence in himself. They neither awed him to silence, nor to caution. While the distributors of literary fame were endeavouring to depreciate and degrade him, he either despised or defied them, wrote on as he had written before, and never turned aside to quiet them by civility or repress them by confutation.

That consistent attitude, his obvious stance while he took no notice, was an added provocation to the inferior, who by definition abound. It was the right way for a first-rate literary figure to play the game; though the old professional occasionally comes out with an aside that shows what he thought. 'I wonder that so many people have written who might have let it alone.' How often one has cause, in reviewing the dreary multiplicity of superfluous books, to recall the comment! As for critics, supposing themselves distributors of literary fame, Johnson knew better: 'By the common sense of readers uncorrupted with literary prejudices must be finally decided all claim to poetical honours'. And then – no illusions about politics or glory, military or naval, or conquest or empire: 'The chief glory of every people arises from its authors'. Shakespeare rather than the buccaneer Drake (I cannot repress a weakness for him), Racine instead of Louis XIV, Walter Scott and Chateaubriand rather than Wellington and Napoleon. Johnson's was ultimately a more civilised scale of values: the old Tory was more in keeping with the pacific preferences of today than were the warring Whigs.

Johnson saw through all pretences, except those of the religious credulity he needed as consolation for despair. Thus he pinned down the silliness of critics' thinking they were displaying judgement in 'unwillingness to be pleased'. It is a curious fact that it is the third-rate – they should have more sense of humour about themselves – who are usually so difficult to please; it is so 'much easier to find reasons for rejecting than embracing'. Any fool can find fault, it is more of a challenge to elicit what is positive or substantive in an achievement. It is this, after all, that makes Johnson the greatest of Shakespeare critics; he was not afraid to tackle the vastness of the achievement: he was on a par with the subject. Then he suddenly says a curious and striking thing about Shakespeare: such is the intensity of his imagination that in reading him one 'looks round alarmed and starts to find himself alone'. *This is it.* But it is also a revelation of Johnson's own imagination, the sensibility behind the robust exterior of Boswell's depiction of Johnson in company. Boswell saw through to what was beneath, in a wonderful phrase, 'as truth itself'.

We are reminded that Johnson's origins were not so impoverished as, largely from pride, he made out; he came from good middle-class stock on both sides. And too much has been made of his straitened circumstances in early days in London, when occasionally he walked round St James's Square all night with Savage for want of a bed. What is more striking on reflection is the luck he had. He had good luck in his stable connexion with the *Gentleman's Magazine*. His poem *London* won immediate attention; his unplayable play, *Irene*, under the tuition of Garrick, ultimately brought him £300. *Rasselas* was translated into most European languages; the *Dictionary* brought lasting fame and a pension. The eight-volumed *Shakespeare* sold so quickly that a second edition was immediately called for. *The Lives of the Poets* were no less successful.

From the literary point of view Johnson had little to complain of; then, posthumously, came the finest stroke of all, from a quarter hardly to be expected, the greatest of literary biographies.

Professor Bate gives us some new information, if hardly new insights. Johnson wrote a great deal more journalism, did much more hack-work, of a miscellaneous character, reviewing whatever came along for the *Gentleman's Magazine*, for example, which kept him alive in Grub Street. He would probably have not been able to embark on a writing career at all if it had not been for his marriage to Tetty, a squire's daughter with a bit of a dowry – that is something new. We are surprised, too, to learn that Johnson wrote with such rapidity: intense concentration and sudden spirts of activity, and then long intervals of indolence. Mrs Thrale said that he gave the impression of having time always on his hands. His own preference was for biography: 'the biographical part of literature is what I love most'.

So much for the anti-biographical bias – 'the personal heresy', according to C. S. Lewis – which has dogged so much literary criticism in our time and rendered it both obtuse and dull.

Professor Bate knows better than that, and has given us a good biography of Johnson, though not the masterpiece it has been acclaimed in an unreliable quarter. There is 'a nimiety, a too-muchness' about him, as Coleridge said of the Germans: too much psychologising about Johnson instead of his religion, with an addiction to dreadful words like 'internalize', 'climactic', 'multifaceted', the English for which is 'many-sided'. We even have the ungrammatical 'more similar', and a proliferation of words compounded with 'self' – 'self-demand', 'self-experience', 'self-expectation', 'self-commitment', not only superfluous but pretentious. Pedestrianism is rather sad in a biography of one who was, above all, a master of style.

NOTES

1.   W. J. Bate, *Samuel Johnson* (Chatto and Windus).
2.   *Johnson. The Critical Heritage*, edited by James T. Boulton.

WELSH ORIENTALIST: SIR WILLIAM JONES

Of the scores of fine monuments in Oxford college chapels that go unregarded by the impercipient tourist, one of the finest is the Flaxman at the west end of University College chapel. It is a pyramidal pile with rounded gourds, a caduceus, a Welsh harp at the top; then a long Latin inscription, and underneath a scene in relief. A youngish Georgian figure with pleasant face is seated under a palm tree at a desk, writing down with his quill what an ancient Hindu sage on his haunches is reading from his books, two more Oriental figures behind him in attendance. Upon the seat is the motto: 'A nation should be judged by its own laws – Menoo'. Beneath the scene is inscribed: 'He formed a digest of Hindu and Mohammedan Laws'. That was his prime achievement, though he accomplished a great deal more than that, for this is the monument to the first Orientalist of his age: Sir William Jones. All that he did was in a short space of time, for he was only forty-seven when he died in 1794.

He was a Welshman, whose stock went back for unnumbered generations in the island of Anglesey. His father emerged from farming to become one of the distinguished mathematicians of his time, author of treatises, friend of Halley and Newton, Vice-President of the Royal Society. Becoming tutor to the Macclesfield family at Shirburn in Oxfordshire, he left his remarkable mathematical library to them: it is still there in that turreted castle reflected in the waters of its moat. The family procured a useful little sinecure for him, in the eighteenth-century manner: from this he was able to save enough to launch his brilliant son and leave him a competence.

The boy was sent to Harrow, where he made friends with Parr – later celebrated as the Whig Dr Johnson – and shared his Leftist convictions. (Jones did not become a bore about them, however.) More important, he became not only a good classic but added French, Italian, Spanish in the holidays from Harrow, and began on Hebrew and Arabic. Like a Red Admiral to a buddleia, or a death's head moth to a balsam-poplar, he was instinctively finding his way to his favourite feeding-ground: he had a *yen* for Oriental languages. The Welsh have a gift for languages; Jones's linguistic gift was phenomenal and brought him early fame. Not that there was anything pedantic about it: he didn't acquire languages as ends in themselves but as means to understanding peoples and cultures. And, quite young, he discovered for himself the proper way to learn languages – by speaking them with their practitioners, not by the dead grammatical grind of the public schools, killing what interest the boys might germinate. He commented how comparatively few of those Augustan gentlemen really knew Latin, for all the years they had spent on it. As an undergraduate at Oxford he gave board and lodging to a young Syrian to learn Arabic from him. In the end Jones came to know thirteen languages well, and to have a fair acquaintance with thirty more.

He was a young prodigy, but enchantingly naïf and spontaneous, full of high spirits, of enjoyment of everything – skating in Christ Church Meadow, excursions out into the country round Oxford to see Forest Hill, with its memories of Milton whom he worshipped (he was a Whig), dancing with the ladies at Bath. Everywhere he came his company was appreciated and sought after. Still young, he was made a member of Dr Johnson's Club, and became friends with, was accepted as an equal by, Burke, Goldsmith, Garrick, Gibbon. He has his place in the *Decline and Fall*, where Gibbon pays tribute to him as a scholar and 'a man of genius' – like having his name inscribed on the dome of St Paul's inside the cathedral he has another monument). But he has his reservations about the great Doctor: 'Johnson and I are very cool to one another. Can I be *cordial* with the libeller of Milton, whom of all men I most admire? Believe me, I cannot praise him; nor do I wish to have the good word of a man who abuses all the friends of Liberty.' Dr Johnson did, however, praise the young man's *Persian Grammar* – put together at nineteen – and sent it to the great proconsul, Warren Hastings. What a small world it was, but what a distinguished one! For his next book Jones had the Richardsons for his publishers, nephews of the novelist.

The fact was that Jones was extraordinarily precocious, but the clue to him was his recognisably Celtic nature, his ardent temperament, his enthusiasm and keenness, his *naiveté*. He will say things that no Englishman would say, especially an Augustan. Nothing damps his ardour – even the rebarbative study of law, in the condition it was in the eighteenth century! 'I do not see why the study of the Laws is called dry and unpleasant, and I very much suspect that it seems so to those only who would think any study unpleasant which required a great application of the mind and exertion of the memory.' He had not been at it long before he wrote his *Essay on the Law of Bailments*, which became the standard work on the subject in both Britain and America up to the middle of the nineteenth century. The simple truth was as Gibbon had said: Jones had genius.

And he was disarmingly simple about it. He went to the bar, 'since a legal career is the only way open for those who seek my country's highest honours. I am amazingly fond of both fame and hard work'. One can hardly hear a Georgian Englishman admitting that. 'But it is easy for me to put all these pleasures of life in second place to that one thing which I desire to distraction, glory. Glory I shall pursue through fire and water, by night and by day.' He thus unburdens his soul to his young pupil, who became the second Earl Spencer, at the end of a busy day in London in the autumn of 1771. 'You are now sleeping and, I hope, dreaming of your verses, or something agreeable. As for me, though it is midnight, the briskness of my fire, and the still silence of the house tempt me to sit reading an hour longer.' He was reading Middleton's Life of Cicero, and – 'I would willingly lose my head at the age of sixty, if I could pass a life at all analogous to that which Middleton describes'. Alas, the 'fire and water' he was to pass through – the climate of Bengal in eighteenth-century hygiene – was to bring him to his end at forty-seven. With so many of the plans he so enthusiastically adumbrated unexecuted – though what he did execute was astonishing enough. He planned to write a *General History of This Century*; later he meant to write a history of the American War. Both works would have been fascinating, especially coming from his point of view – for he was very much on the Left, wholly sympathetic to the American cause, as against the stupid George III and the arrogant English governing class, who brought the disaster down upon themselves. Jones was a patriot, but 'how much I have disapproved the conduct of the English, who were mad with pride'.

The eighteenth century, with its universalising tendencies, was not much given to thinking in terms of racial temperaments (unlike the sixteenth century), except for an occasional man of acute perception, like the poet Gray – with whom Jones had some marked affinities. So that Jones was not particularly conscious of himself as a Welshman, though he writes to young Althorp: 'I see you do not forget that I am half a Welshman, as you write to me on St David's day, and your letter came to me just as I was eating my Welsh rabbit, alias, toasted cheese, for my supper.' He did understand his own recognisable temperament: 'my nature is free and open, warm in friendship, anxious (perhaps to an extreme) for the welfare of my friends, consequently liable to be depressed by the disappointment of my wishes for their glory and happiness, nor less apt to be transported with joy at the completion of my hopes'. But his Celtic affinities and attractions were only half-conscious with him, though his nature was unmistakably so. It did not occur to him that his confidential clerk, whom he greatly cared for and took with him to India (where he promptly died), was a Pritchard; or that he chose a Welsh harp-player to teach him the harp.

But when he went on circuit in Wales, in which he had never set foot, he found himself immediately *en rapport* with the people, and in the end was surprised to find that all the cases came to him. He was as responsive as Gray to the beauty of the landscape: from Sir Roger Mostyn's house, 'we had the most magnificent view my eyes ever beheld, and almost the finest my imagination, warm as it is, could conceive. We had on one side a prospect of the isle of Anglesey, the ancient Mona, where my ancestors presided over a free but uncivilized people, and a very extensive view of the sea'. On the other was Conway Castle and the scene immortalised by Gray's Ode, 'The Bard'. He has excellent descriptions of his excursions, appreciating the scenery shortly to be explored by

Pennant and Gilpin in search of the Picturesque, and then to be painted by the painters. He gathers quantities of mushrooms on Harlech marsh, to dine on them with fresh herrings at Barmouth, canters over the sands at Aberdovey, crossing a dangerous tidal estuary to get to Aberystwyth. He enjoyed such outings, the picnics, the salmon out of unpolluted streams, the adventures, and recognised Wales as his native soil.

The first rift between him and Burke came when the latter, in the name of reform, wanted to abolish the Welsh judicature, making the people travel farther (and fare worse) for justice. Jones had a Welsh friend to visit soon after his arrival in Bengal: Richard Morris, who was publishing his uncle, Lewis Morris's *Celtic Remains*, and sought Jones's support. Morris's father had founded the Cymmrodorion Society in 1751. Jones replied, 'Need I say that it would give me infinite delight to promote your views? . . . As one of the Cymmrodorians, I am warmly interested in British antiquities and literature; but my honour is pledged for the completion of the new digest of Hindu laws, and I have not a moment to spare for any other study.' Who knows what he might not have accomplished in this field too, on retirement from India, if he had been granted the normal span of life?

Another Welshman was Jones's superior as Chief Justice in the Supreme Court of Bengal – Sir Elijah Impey. He was an appointee of Lord North, whom Cowper may well have had in mind in writing:

> But versed in arts that, while they seem to stay
> A falling empire, hasten its decay.

Jones was apprehensive lest 'the hot-headed Welsh Chief Justice should have power, by any turn in the political wheel, to procure my supersession on account of my Dialogue, which I shall never cease to avow and justify'. Jones had written this Left-wing work, an attack on authoritarian monarchical government and a strong plea for liberal constitutionalism, while in Paris in 1782 at the end of the American War, hobnobbing with Franklin whose admiring friendship he enjoyed. This tract had been circulated by the Society for Constitutional Information in Wales, where it was warmly welcomed and translated into Welsh. It is indeed significant that, in Britain as in America, Scots, Irish, Welsh, were the strongest opponents of George III and English ascendancy.

Jones's appointment to India was held up for five years by the Tory Lord Chancellor, Thurlow. A man of high principle and transparent sincerity, Jones had the usual Celtic independence of spirit and pride, and would not compromise with his convictions even for India and the supreme opportunity this would afford for his genius as an Orientalist. The consequences were unfortunate: had Jones gone out five years before, he would have been able to enjoy the full and enthusiastic co-operation of Warren Hastings in the prosecution and development of Oriental studies, and Jones would have completed his immense task, the Digest of Hindu Law as well as the Digest of Mohammedan Law he did complete. Hastings, like the great man he was, was the first patron of Persian and Sanskrit studies; Jones, with his enthusiasm and imagination, his linguistic genius, opened up a New World to the mind and literature of Europe. It was no less. Besides this, it provided the strongest impulse to the renaissance of Indian culture. Hitherto, under the dominance of the Moguls, Mohammedan culture and its classic language, Persian, held sway. Hindu culture retreated within itself, classical Sanskrit becoming fossilised, the knowledge of its sacred texts confined to the Brahmin priesthood. It was one of the long-term ironies of history that it was British rule that led to the revival of Hindu culture, the renaissance of India, consciousness of her identity and her past, the ultimate emergence of Indian nationalism.

Jones was equally sympathetic to both, and had already made a European reputation for his translations from Persian. A few of these into verse were in all the anthologies and had won him fame as a poet. This declined with the prevalent nineteenth-century conception of poetry, unsympathetic to that of the eighteenth. Some of his poems still survive, one or two of the songs of Hafiz, or the famous epigram:

> On parent knees a naked new-born child,
> Weeping thou sat'st when all around thee smiled:
> So live that, sinking in thy last long sleep,
> Calm thou mayst smile when all around thee weep.

When only twenty-three he had translated the History of Nadir Shah into French for the King of Denmark, characteristically refusing remuneration because he disapproved of the tyrant Shah – but it won him European *réclame*. On achieving his dearest wish, on his way out to the Orient, he was inexpressibly pleased to imagine himself almost encircled by Asia, a breeze from Arabia behind, Persia on the left, India ahead. He worked happily at his Persian and Arabic on the way out, jotting down some twenty-three Oriental desiderata he meant to tackle. No sooner was he settled at Calcutta than he founded the Asiatic Society, 'the mother of similar Oriental societies around the world'. The studies that he undertook himself and inspired in others were published in the *Asiatic Miscellany* he directed, and electrified Europe. Here *was* a New World of the mind: his example inspired Orientalists in Britain, France, Holland, above all in Germany.

To begin with, he found himself up against the opposition of the Brahmins, who did not want their sacred texts scrutinised by an infidel. But his enthusiasm won their confidence; he prevailed on the ancient sage who appears on the relief at Oxford to teach him Sanskrit, and thereafter spent his vacations from his hot and busy courtroom among the Brahmins at their ancient university at Krishnagar. In the end, they regarded him as a pundit. Never can they have had so apt a pupil or one who so richly repaid them. He began to do for the knowledge of Hindu culture what he had been doing since boyhood for Persian and Arabic – based largely on the Arabic manuscripts in the Bodleian, where he would work in the mornings all alone. (O blissful eighteenth century!) He began introducing the Hindu mythology, with its variegated deities, to Europe in hymns and odes, once imitating a stanza from Gray. He set on foot studies, and himself wrote essays, on Indian chronology, literature, language, inscriptions, religion, mythology. One might say that he was, among so many other things, a natural anthropologist. Most unexpected, perhaps, was his understanding and appreciation of Hindu music; and extensive contributions to Indian botany. He collected a thousand Sanskrit names for plants, then made minute dissections and descriptions of some eighty Indian plants, which his devoted wife – who shared his interests and edited his *Works* – then depicted by pencil or brush. He had the satisfaction of being the first to introduce to Europe the knowledge of the work of Kalidasa, and to translate the greatest classic of the ancient drama, the *Sakuntala*. Though Jones's sanguine hopes of a new inspiration for 'tired' European literatures were hardly realised – the Romantic movement found these within their own traditions – nevertheless, his translations had their influence upon Herder, their echoes in the poetry of Goethe.

All these activities were in a sense parerga to Jones's main preoccupation, always a human, and a humane, one. In term time he was up to his neck – or, should we say, wig – in the uncertainties and duplicities of administering justice according to imperfectly apprehended codes, Mohammedan or Hindu, at the mercy of native interpreters always ready to make profit out of the confusion. The Judge would rise before dawn for an hour of Sanskrit, and walk two or three miles to his court-room to administer justice in the sweltering heat all day; then return to the company of his Anna Maria and spend the evening at Kalidasa or Petrarch, or the delights of Indian botany. But his overriding objective was to be the Justinian of India, and provide her with a definite and sure digest of her own laws, Mohammedan and Hindu. Here is the relevance of the inscription upon Flaxman's relief at Oxford: 'A nation should be judged by its own laws – Menoo': Menoo or Manu being the legendary first lawgiver (if not Man), the Indian Solon.

The inspiration of his life became, as with thousands of Britons serving throughout the Raj, the well-being of India. Practical experience on the spot convinced this man of very liberal sympathies, an entire friend to the American Revolution: 'There are more virtues among our countrymen here than they have credit for at home, perhaps as many as Britain herself could exhibit, and, if the natives know their own good, they cannot sigh for the harsh and imperious domination of the Moguls.' Though more popular in his sympathies than Burke, whom he thought too 'aristocratical', he did not share Burke's maniac obsession against Hastings, who had not only saved British rule in India but was inspired by what was best for the Indians. If they were not capable of self-government, were the English of the eighteenth century? If the Americans were, as they insisted, it was a modern miracle that nobody expected – and they proved not particularly governable, even by themselves.

Jones devoted his energies, in the end life itself, to this massive and exhausting task. His marriage to the daughter of the Radical Bishop of St Asaph, another pro-American, had been a love-match, though Jones would not propose to her until his Indian appointment gave him the means to provide for her in the style to which she was accustomed. She entered into all his Indian projects and was a great help; but she was constantly ill in the climate of Bengal, and at length Jones prevailed on her to go home a year or two before his own retirement, to save her life. But the man it was who died. He stayed on a year after her departure, working for dear life against time on the great Digest. He had finished the Mohammedan section by 1792 – which provided the foundation for the administration of Muslim Law in India – but with regard to the Hindu was at length defeated, when in sight of the end. He died in Calcutta, April 27th, 1794, the vast work almost completed.

Actually the parerga were more fruitful. Everything that Jones touched he not only ornamented but illuminated, suggested new lines of thought, opened up new mines of scholarship and discovery – an image he used himself. His genius was essentially creative. Of course he was fortunate in the moment in which he came into Oriental scholarship, and in going to India as he so ardently wished. A new field was opening out for the European mind; the British were fortunate that the decadent empire of the Moguls collapsed into the capable and exploring hands of a Hastings and a Jones. This new world came in to redress the balance of the loss of the American colonies – and was far more rewarding intellectually. Not all his hopes in this field were to be fulfilled: he hoped that the themes and imagery of eighteenth-century poetry would be revivified by the impact of Oriental literature. And his own translations from Arabic, Persian and Sanskrit had immense *réclame* in their day, on the Continent where he was as well known as in Britain. As a poet he was overestimated, as, after the impact of the Romantic Movement, when literature, scholarship and law took on further dimensions, he has been underestimated.

It has been Professor Cannon's life's work to bring him back to us, to reinstate him as a human being; first with a biography,[1] now with a complete edition of his letters.[2] We can now see him alongside of his contemporaries, Gibbon, Burke, Dr Johnson, Blackstone, Warren Hastings, and in no way their inferior.

For, think what he accomplished, and consider its significance. His study of Sanskrit led him to perceive the similarity of its roots with Greek and Latin, and thus to postulate an original Indo-European from which both groups descended. His study of Arabic and Hebrew led him to postulate a Semitic-Hamitic grouping. He thus suggested families of languages, and became a founder of comparative linguistics. In India he was no less a pioneer of scientific archaeology. For practical purposes he devised a system for transliterating Oriental scripts into Romans: the Jonesian system thus pioneered an international phonetic alphabet. His inquiring interest in, and contributions to, the study of Indian chronology, mythology, music, botany, folklore, foreshadowed comparative anthropology. The keenness of his inquiring mind was inexhaustible. In the interstices of his time in Bengal we find him studying chemistry, and making suggestions as to the nature of kaolin, from which the Chinese made their hard china-ware. He was interested in both China and Tibet, and contributed an essay on Chinese literature to the *Asiatic Miscellany*, translating two poems from the *Shih Ching* which were much anthologised in Europe. What more might he not have accomplished if only he had lived to come home?

Now in his Letters we can see him fully as the man he was – the charm, the sincerity and high-mindedness, the good company he offered, the affectionate nature, the warmth, the intellectual vivacity, the endearing *naiveté* of the Celt. A young man, publishing his first works, he has a proper opinion of himself: 'if I retain my strength of memory and habit of application, I shall certainly have the success which I flatter myself your lordship wishes me'. Though for some years the tutor of the Spencers' son and heir, there was never any of the eighteenth-century sycophancy towards the nobility, and they, to their credit, treated him as a valued friend. Indeed, he risked his relationship with them by indulging a quite superfluous whim of independence. 'Now I have a competence independent of my profession, thanks to the wise parsimony of my father, and my own industry in College, where I have a profitable Fellowship. A consciousness of this has not a little supported me in that disposition which ... I think only a proper dignity of mind and a zeal for independence. True it is that I acknowledge no man as my *superior*, who is not so in virtue or knowledge, and if this be pride, I am not free from it.' Actually his feeling for young Althorp, the pupil to whom many of the earlier letters were written, was that of warm affection: 'my dear friend, whom I have loved without a moment's intermission from the first hour in which I knew you ... Again and again farewell, my best of friends, and believe me to be eternally yours'. It is rather like Shakespeare to young Southampton, in prose.

Jones fell properly in love with Bishop Shipley's daughter, but he would not marry into this family, socially superior to his, until he had financial independence. With his charm and early fame, he could have married several times over for money – the chances came his way; but, in spite of his early political ambitions (he stood as candidate for Tory Oxford!) he would never consider it.

No wonder a contemporary spoke of his 'ferocious integrity'. He is always sanguine, always keen. He assures his publisher that his first venture, the Persian history, 'from the peculiar circumstances of it, and the variety, as well as the novelty, of its subjects, will go off extremely well'. It did. Buying himself an Elzevir edition of Cicero in ten volumes, he intends to read them all diligently every year, 'nor do I despair of writing as many volumes myself'.

Something of the charm of life in Georgian Oxford comes through to us. We learn that the word 'Dons' is just coming in, in 1780, among young men; that the great judge, Blackstone, is 'a guarded man', who consulted all the judges on his *Commentaries* before publishing. We hear of 'the best of bishops', Shipley, 'taking exercise in the field'. 'My rank in college gives me two very good sets of apartments supplied with every convenience' – when today everybody is doubled up, and there are far too many (unappreciative) people in every college. Rarely can a Fellowship have been so richly justified as in his case, or been put to better use. There were his rooms always awaiting him, with a man-servant, and sometimes only one other Fellow to occupy space and share common-room with him. 'As for me, I pass the summer at Oxford, whence I frequently make a little excursion to the neighbouring places, and ride constantly every day upon my little grey horse. I study law and history seven hours a day, it is scarce creditable how much I read and write from seven in the morning till twelve at night, as I never go to rest earlier.' When one thinks of the tomes of stilted eighteenth-century correspondence, the supercilious Lord Chesterfield, the intolerable Mrs Montagu, the portentous letters of the poet Young (a Fellow of All Souls, too!) to the Duchess of Portland, here in Jones is a man after one's own heart. Because he is natural and spontaneous, gifted and transparent, he is a born letter-writer. He loves writing, and he writes not formally – except for his Latin letters to Continental scholars – but as he 'thinks and feels'. Hence their charm, and they touch eighteenth-century life at so many points and with far-ranging significance.

NOTES

1. Garland Cannon, *Oriental Jones* (Indian Council for Cultural Relations: Asia Publishing House, 1964).
2. *The Letters of Sir William Jones*. Ed. by Garland Cannon, 2 vols (Oxford: Clarendon Press, 1970).

THE ROMANTIC STORY OF CHARLES AUGUSTUS MURRAY

Charles Augustus Murray was a well known figure in the Victorian Age, as diplomat and man of letters; he is not only entombed in the *Dictionary of National Biography* but had an attractive, if overly discreet, *Life* of him written by a colleague, now hard to come by. The external facts of his varied and interesting career are there set out for all to read; in addition we have the verbal tradition of him at All Souls, of which he was a Fellow in the 1820s and 1830s, and at the end a sinister story, of which I may be the solitary repository left alive. So I must write it down, before I too am gone, and for the rest attempt to disentangle the College legend from the facts.

Murray's was certainly a romantic personality, going back to the age of Sir Walter Scott and Fenimore Cooper, both of whom he knew and was much influenced by as a writer; while the romance of his life – a singular love-story, well known in its day – brought together Scotland and America. On a visit to America he fell in love with a daughter of the celebrated James Wadsworth, who would not allow them to marry – and thereby hangs the tale, in part. The Wadsworths are now an aristocratic, senatorial family from upper New York State, and it is from one of their descendants, the late Countess of St Germans, that I heard the sombre end to the story.

Charles Augustus Murray was extraordinarily handsome, as anybody can see from the engraving óf the portrait of him that hangs in our Common Room at All Souls. He had a magnificent physique – hence the endurance of his life with the Pawnee Indians with whom he travelled for some months in the North Western wilderness of the United States, unvisited yet by White men, when Fort Leavensworth was the last military outpost of the United States. He survived cholera, and later on dysentery in Baghdad – to die a very tough old gentleman of eighty-nine in 1895.

He was equally charming and agreeable, with cultivated literary tastes and a strong Scotch religious vein to keep him, in Regency days, on the straight. For any number of people made up to him, understandably. As a young man he was a regular attender at the literary breakfasts of Samuel Rogers; the elderly bachelor-poet had an obvious *tendresse* for the handsome Scot, but nobody got any change out of him, outside his (ultimate) marital duties. He would seem to have been disappointingly strait-laced, in spite of his youth at Regency Eton.

Born in 1806, he was a younger son of the fifth Earl of Dunmore; his maternal grandfather was the Duke of Hamilton, his aunt by marriage the gifted daughter of William Beckford, who always conversed with her in French. Charles's paternal grandfather was – more to the point – the last Royal Governor of Virginia, who had had to take refuge ignominiously on a ship in Chesapeake Bay at the outbreak of the American Revolution. The Dunmores possessed title-deeds to property in Virginia, which they had been done out of, and it was partly with the idea of sounding out the prospects of recovery that the younger son originally went over to the now United States.

From the first the boy was surrounded by the best possible influences, and the grandest relations. His godfather was the Duke of Sussex, Queen Victoria's uncle, and Charles's own uncle by marriage; his father's estate-agent was the father of Archbishop Tait. The Dunmores were strong Whigs – like Queen Victoria to begin with; young Charles was an *habitué* of Woolbeding, that enchanting Whig temple (recently lost to the nation's heritage, alas!) devoted to the cult of Charles James Fox, after whom Murray named his elder son. He met the sensible (and liberal-minded) Lucien Bonaparte, who said the last word on Napoleon: 'I *know* him: I always said he would blow the bubble till it burst'.

As a boy Charles used to come south for Eton by ship from Leith; once the boat was blown over to Norway, and a fortnight later he arrived back at Leith. At school he developed a pretty turn for Latin verses, a highly thought-of accomplishment then, became a good scholar and made several friends for life. Always a good linguist, he came to read and speak fifteen languages – perhaps a bit too talented: if he had concentrated his abilities more, he would have left more of a mark.

He was less happy at Oriel, where he had Newman for tutor, whom he did not like. He presents a very different picture of that famous figure from the idealised portrait that has come down through his disciples of the Oxford Movement – and probably one more characteristic of the average normal man's attitude to the later Cardinal.

He never inspired me or my fellow-undergrads with any interest, much less respect; on the contrary, we disliked, or rather distrusted him. He walked with his head bent, abstracted, but every now and then looking out of the corners of his eyes quickly, as though suspicious. He had no influence then; it was only when he became vicar of St. Mary's that the long dormant power asserted itself, and his sermons attracted hundreds.

It is an interesting glimpse from the undergraduate's point of view: Murray never understood how it was that Newman became a great man.

He himself, after three years, crossed the High in 1827 to the more congenial atmosphere of All Souls, where the Fellows were traditionally 'bene nati, bene vestiti, mediocriter docti'. Murray certainly qualified for the first two – well-born and well-dressed, and for the rest had distinct literary leanings and gifts. Joining Lincoln's Inn to read for the bar, he was the pupil of Nassau Senior. In Scotland he met Robert Owen, of whom he disapproved: he tells us that, after half-a-dozen pregnancies among his girl-pupils, Robert Owen was driven out by the local people. Murray observed him again later in Philadelphia, but dimissed him simply as a charlatan. On a vacation in Germany he met Goethe at Weimar, and this led to an acquaintance with Carlyle.

After two unsuccessful attempts to enter Parliament young Murray decided on something more enterprising – the trip to America, which made name and fame for him, and shaped the romantic story of his private life. In 1834 he sailed in a new American sailing ship, the *Waverley* – such was the magic of Walter Scott's name. Old Sam Rogers wrote tenderly in May: 'He is now on the Atlantic. Well, he wears a talisman that makes everybody love him, so I don't care if he escapes shipwreck.' In fact, he very narrowly did: they met with appalling storms, the ship sprang a leak and nearly foundered. They made for the Azores with difficulty, where the vessel took a month to repair and Murray explored the islands in every direction. Altogether the passage took over fourteen weeks; people assumed that the *Waverley* was lost.

The British ambassador in the United States was Sir Charles Vaughan, another All Souls man; when Murray turned up in New York, Vaughan said – according to College tradition, in Regency language: 'God dam'ee, Murray, I thought you was dead'.

This was a prelude to a fascinating time in America, where all doors were open for such a young man – except for one that was resoundingly closed, as we shall see. Steaming up the Hudson, Murray had Fenimore Cooper as fellow-passenger, whom he had already met with Rogers. He found the Americans very touchy about Mrs Trollope – a 'vulgar woman' – and what she wrote about them. At Lexington he ran into the ubiquitous Miss Martineau, whom he was to encounter later in Egypt. He was the guest of the great, if oratorical, Henry Clay, who had twice run for President.

Murray was about to make the conventional tour, when an exciting chance offered itself. A steamer was making for the Upper Missouri, and the outpost of Fort Leavensworth, the life at which we read about in Parkman's classic, *The Oregon Trail*. There, on Independence Day, a party of 150 Pawnees turned up; Murray determined to join them, trusting himself to them with a nondescript German, of the inappropriate name of Vernunft, and his Scots valet. They all set off, riding in single Indian file, into the trackless prairie heading north-west – I suppose into what is now Kansas-Nebraska – to catch up with the main Pawnee 'nation' hunting buffalo.

We need not go in detail into Murray's experiences, original as they were for the time, one of the few White men to share Indian life and the first to write it up in his *Travels in North America*, which he published in two volumes in 1839, with a dedication to young Queen Victoria. The book won him some celebrity and went into three editions. It is sufficient to say that his experience of Indian life cured him of any romantic idealisation of the 'noble savage' *à la* Châteaubriand or Fenimore Cooper. Murray experienced the real thing. He found that, with some exceptions, 'truth and honesty are unknown or despised by them'. One young brave sprang at his brother and bit his nose clean off; the brother bore the pain stoically, but that night stalked the offender and shot him dead – and was made chief of the tribe for his prowess. Another young brave, angered at his horse's obstinacy, leaped at it – a fine specimen – and buried his knife in its eye. On one occasion Murray found himself being stalked, but his magnificent physique stood him in good stead.

When he had had enough of these amenities and his curiosity was slaked, he led his little party back through the wilderness with the aid of a compass towards the Kansas River. They underwent a good many hardships and much exposure, Murray himself keeping watch at night, finding the value of his Highland plaid and repeating Aeschylus in the starlight. On his way back he hunted with the Winnebagoes in the Wisconsin territory and visited the early lead-miners there, appalled by the drunken Irish (he says nothing about the Methodist Cornish, whom I have described in *The Cornish in America*).

He spent Christmas at New Orleans, crossed the Gulf to Cuba, returning via Charleston and Baltimore – as a good Whig, disapproving of Slavery – to his favourite Philadelphia. Thence to Lake Otsego and upper New York State, where he met his fate at James Wadsworth's place, Geneseo, though Murray kept silence about what befell there. Wadsworth was a remarkable man, if rather a hard one. He had taken up an immense tract of land in the Genesee Valley, towards Buffalo, had broken it in and organised it, settling it with tenants and farmers – I remember reading somewhere of their drives to kill off hundreds of rattle-snakes, which made such an impression on the European mind as characteristic of America. Wadsworth had built up a splendid estate and equipped it with a fine country-house, still there, in the English style.

But Wadsworth was far from being pro-English: he had some of the animus of Revolutionary days and was not particularly partial to a Scotch younger son without a post or prospects for son-in-law. Wadsworth had a son and a daughter, Elise: she and Murray fell hopelessly in love. The story is – though the biography does not say so – that her father at first gave permission for them to marry, then withdrew it: this was what made what happened so cruel. Murray did not want to become an American; Wadsworth would not allow his daughter to live in England. In the end he forbade all communication between the lovers, and forced a promise upon both that they would neither write, send or receive messages from each other. On their side, the lovers promised each other that they would remain faithful and marry no-one else.

Murray returned to England heart-broken; then, after a third attempt at a seat in Parliament, he got a rather exalted post, at first groom-in-waiting to the young Queen, who very shortly made him Master of her Household. There is an All Souls story, which Lytton Strachey got hold of, to the effect that, one evening at whist at Windsor, old Lord Melbourne dropped a card, to see under the table the tiny foot of the young Queen resting on the broad patent-leather shoe of Charles Augustus Murray. And decided that it was time to find her a husband, from Coburg.

This may be merely *ben trovato*. But the rest of the tradition is true enough: there *was* a lady-in-waiting who was madly in love with the handsome Scot, and all to no purpose. One of the Queen's German relations fell for him too. The daughter of the Grand Duke of Baden had a romantic *schwärmerei* for Scots, and had heard so much of Murray's looks that she set her heart on marrying him. Charles would not even consent to meet her for the purpose, but was ultimately overborne by the remonstrances of his uncle, the Duke of Hamilton. However, he saw to it that nothing came of it: he regarded himself as absolutely pledged.

In 1839 his *Travels* came out, and received an accolade from one of the greatest living writers, Châteaubriand, who had been foremost in putting America across the imagination of Europe in various works. The great man – who was a Celt and a tremendous egoist – had read the young Scot's work with 'le plus grand plaisir'. A kind friend said, in the way kind friends have: 'C'est le seul ouvrage qu'il aura lu avec le plus grand plaisir qui n'est pas écrit par lui-même'.

Murray remained Master of the Queen's Household for six years, from 1838 to 1844, taking his part in the wedding arrangements, the festivities and visits of those gay early years. His letters from Windsor Castle and Buckingham Palace give interesting accounts and provide a not fully explored source. One naturally didn't know from the Queen's Letters, for example, that on the Tsar Nicholas I's visit, he insisted on an immense sack of fresh straw for his bed.

Charles kept up his literary and political contacts, rather contemptuous of Disraeli's 'Young England' antics and disapproving of his attacks on Peel. He brought out a pamphlet anonymously defending the Coburgs as good Protestants and smoothing the way for the marriage – which was not exactly popular: Uncle Leopold, who would have been Prince Consort had Charlotte lived, was such a gold-digger. But, often enough, Charles attended the festivities and observed Victoria's radiant happiness with an aching heart. 'How often it has ached at that table!'

What could he do, under sentence of no communication with Elise from that gaunt old patriarch at Geneseo?

Charles decided to send her a message in the form of a novel,

The Prairie-Bird: a message that she, and she only, would interpret
– that he still remained faithful and would always remain so. The
book came out in 1844, and became a best-seller. It was suffused
with the Fenimore Cooper spirit, to which schoolboys in my youth
were still addicted, *The Last of the Mohicans*, and all that. In the
book Murray described the Genesee Valley country, he himself
was in large part the hero, but the *Prairie-Bird's* name, Oolita, was
known only to him and Elise: it was that which he had given her.
She got the message and, like Charles Murray, rejected the
various offers that came her way in these long waiting years.

By 1844 he had had enough of his gilded servitude at Court,
though those of his letters published show his talent for description and what an intelligent observer he was. Unfortunately, his
too discreet Victorian biographer omitted most of them as 'forbid-
den fruit'. Some dedicated American researcher should get after
them, both in Scotland and at Geneseo.

Murray had intended to write a history of Windsor Castle, but
his duties there got in the way of research; all he could manage
was his novel, and charming *vers de société*, like those from
Nuneham on a visit to the Archbishop of York, another All Souls
Fellow in those old grand days. Actually his letters give a charming nostalgic impression of bachelor-life in College, especially his
correspondence with Sir Charles Vaughan – but that is not my
subject here.

Murray followed his senior into the diplomatic service, went off
as secretary of legation at Naples and two years later, in 1846,
became Consul-General in Egypt, under the régime of the famous
Albanian adventurer, Mehemet Ali. In a later novel, *Hassan or the
Child of the Pyramid* (1857), Murray gives a striking portrait of this
redoubtable buccaneer. In the engraving of Charles at All Souls,
there is a little dusky attendant from this time looking up at his
master, handsome as Apollo, wavy golden hair, regular features,
moustached, holding a hookah, dandyish in striped dressing
gown. While serving in Egypt, Murray made zoological history by
securing the first baby hippopotamus to come to Europe and
arranging its safe transit to the Zoo, where it lived in comfort till
1878.

Then, one day on vacation at home in Scotland, Charles and
Elise met, apparently quite accidentally, and found that they were
as much in love as ever. The old tyrant at Geneseo was now dead,
leaving Elise rich, and the lovers could marry. In 1850 they

married – after fourteen years of waiting in silence; they had one year's blissful happiness, but Elise was no longer young for child-bearing, and in child-birth next year she died. On her death-bed she made Charles promise that, since they had known such all-too-brief happiness in marriage, he would marry again.

Elise left a son. Not for another eleven years did Charles marry again – to find happiness once more and beget another son, whose end was so mysterious.

I do not mean to follow Murray's subsequent diplomatic career in detail, or his writings. It is interesting that, Whig as he was, he was not overcome by the Victorian – and very Cambridge – cult of Macaulay. Murray thought Macaulay's History should be called 'A Defence of the Whigs' rather than a 'History of England'. Moving on from Egypt to Persia, Murray became a target of attack, which led to a little local war. It was really the fault of the Home Government which, in the Victorian zeal for economy – would that we had a little of it today! – refused to rival the French and Russians in making lavish presents, or indeed any at all, to the Shah's Grand Vizier.

This started a peck of troubles. The Grand Vizier retorted by making 'odious' charges of a sexual kind against Murray – completely out of character with him. There were silly questions in that wise assembly, the House of Commons, and *The Times* – the 'Thunderer' of those days – thundered unfairly against Murray. The bombardment of Bushire and the dispatch of a small force, which cost £3 millions – far more than a few discriminating presents – settled the matter. Murray was vigorously, and rightly, defended by Palmerston, as one would expect, but the ill-success damaged his further prospects in the service.

He was not advanced to first-rate posts, but to the smaller capitals, like Copenhagen – where he made the friendship of Hans Andersen – to Dresden and Lisbon. A gifted linguist, he consoled himself with languages, particularly Oriental, and writing. In 1874 he retired to Windsor, to 'The Grange', which he built for his second wife and son – he was a rich man, having inherited his first wife's fortune, upon the death of her brother in the Civil War. In 1883 he published another novel, *Nour-ed-dyn*, or the *Light of the Faith*; while *A Short Memoir of Mohammed Ali* was published posthumously, in 1898.

In 1895 Murray died, full of years and with a due modicum of honours – we need waste no time on those, it is the story that counts. Apparently the younger son, by the second wife, had been born in 1865 and gave some concern to his father. The official biography by Sir Herbert Maxwell speaks of Murray's 'tender solicitude' for the youth and his care to nurture him in the classics, in literature and in sound religion. Sir Herbert mentions laconically, in a footnote, 'Mr. Cecil Murray died at sea, under most painful circumstances, on June 3rd 1896, the first anniversary of his father's death.'

There must have been something wrong. The story, as it came to me, was that the young man was difficult, perhaps a psychological case. His father had paid a return journey to America in 1883, some fifty years after his first acquaintance with it, to attend to the business affairs that had, after all, fallen to him there – if not the Dunmore inheritance in Old Virginia.

Now the family decided to send the young man out, in the charge of a tutor or bear-leader. On the way out, in mid-Atlantic – where his father encountered those storms long ago – the son had a mental storm, and swallowed the acid which he used in the photography that was his hobby. He was buried at sea.

The family lawyer was sent to Liverpool to meet the returning tutor-in-charge. In the first-class compartment reserved to themselves, the latter told his story. At the point at which he said, 'you should know that Mr. Murray made a will in my favour leaving me everything', the lawyer rose and crossed to the opposite corner of the compartment.

No further word was exchanged. The story as it came to me was that the family suspected the tale the tutor told as to the youth's end, though nothing could be proved against him. Rather than provoke a public scandal, it was decided to compromise the matter – and share the inheritance. I should have thought that, if true, a quasi-admission, in itself a suspicious circumstance.

The mystery was never resolved: perhaps somewhere, in some remote Scottish archive, an answer may be folded away.

POST-KILVERT: A MORAL TALE

The discovery and editing of Kilvert's Diary just before the Second German War added a charming and endearing figure to Victorian literature. It is not easy to account for the spell that Kilvert puts upon his readers – partly nostalgia, partly escape into the more settled and restful nineteenth century, before the world had moved out of the human scale and when the English countryside was at its most beautiful; before it was broken up and the integration (let alone the integrity!) of its society was destroyed. Then, too, Kilvert had such an exquisite response to life, natural, unaffected, poetic – to the beauty of nature and human beings, their characters and stories, their joys and sadnesses – along with an observant gift for writing, translucent and pure.

Some evidence of the spell he exerts is to be seen in Mr Le Quesne's book.[1] Kilvert so occupied the author's mind that he went to live in the house at Clyro on the Welsh Border, where Kilvert had lived a century ago, and devoted himself to following in the young curate's tracks in the villages, valleys and hills around, piecing together memories and relics of the life he lived there. Out of it, not wholly 'innocently', he has made a book of his own, recording the scene, changed and unchanged, passages from the Diary along with his own descriptions and comments. It was an interesting idea; the book is faithful to Kilvert and has caught something of his charm, though not the spell.

All those of us who have fallen under it recognise the symptoms. I have myself, though not a member of the Kilvert Society, been to see the places where he lived his so moving life – not only following in his tracks at Clyro, the church and parish he served, the places he knew, his grave not far away at Bredwardine, but also his home where he grew up, a son of the rectory at Langley Burrell in Wiltshire.

The story of the Diary itself is very curious. Some twenty-two small volumes of it turned up at Jonathan Cape's, the publisher; William Plomer selected about a third for publication in three volumes, and then the only typescript was accidentally destroyed. Meanwhile the original manuscript had gone back to the family, and – in the idiotic manner the imperceptive have – it too was almost all destroyed. Already, it seems, the last volumes of the Diary, which described Kilvert's courtship and marriage, had been destroyed, probably by his widow. Really, ordinary people have no imagination, sense or understanding; as Henry James says, 'Nobody ever understands *any* thing'. Kilvert himself, simple, natural, endearing, was an elect spirit, with the touch of genius upon him.

I had an example of the obtuseness of the ordinary person in this connection myself. I was travelling back in the train from Hereford (having had some small part in spreading the Kilvert gospel) when – who should my companion turn out to be but the nephew of Daisy Thomas, the farm-girl with whom Kilvert had been more than half in love. (He was, with his sensitive, ardent, responsive temperament, extraordinarily inflammable, only just under control.) This Herefordshire farmer put to me the question, in all puzzled sincerity, why did people fall so much for Kilvert? What ever accounted for it? I did my best to enlighten him.

But, of course, such people – perhaps people in general – never can understand. Mr Le Quesne has difficulty himself in explaining what it was that drew him back, from Australia, to live in Kilvert's house, draw the threads of life there and in that neighbourhood together again, all so strongly marked for him by the memory of a curate living there a hundred years ago. It wasn't only the idea of writing it up in a book; he gets nearer to it when he says that it was not only a nostalgia of place but of time. The mystery of time passing is really the subject – just as much as with that most characteristic work of our century, Proust's *A la Recherche du Temps Perdu*. 'What is the meaning of this nostalgia that slips so easily between our eyes and the reality of that old landscape?' What *is* it indeed?

I think I know something of the answer. It is the sense of the transitoriness of our own lives; Kilvert had the gift, that goes with genius, of catching life on the wing. One notes it again and again; he saw through to the other side and, without effort – though all the same with discipline, for he trained the faculty – expressed it as few can. Of course the Diary was consolation and companionship, an outlet for his sensitive but repressed sexuality.

On a more usual level Mr Le Quesne devotes himself to observing what has changed, and what is unchanged, of Kilvert's countryside. Of the houses that he visited, then full of the life he enjoyed and observed so acutely, 'Llanthomas was destroyed years ago. Hay Castle is now the abode-cum-warehouse of the largest second-hand bookseller in the world. Cae Mawr is intact and privately owned by a naturalised Yugoslav potter of Polish extraction. Mrs Venables' grandson still lives at Llysdinam. Wye Cliff was burnt down ten years ago; Clyro Court has been a secondary modern school for twenty years. The gentry are here still, but they have left their palaces and they reign no longer.' The social revolution has taken place, we see.

The author's taste is not infallible: 'palaces' is not the word for their decent country houses, which offered a saner and more balanced way of life than any known to history. Clyro Court is described as 'graceless and coarse and pretentious' – he evidently doesn't know what is what about Victorian architecture; a photograph shows the house as well-proportioned and rather fine. 'The heir killed in the First World war, his sister struggling on till after the Second, the estate then broken up and the house sold. . . . The gentry garrisons have evacuated their decaying fortresses.' I do not like the noun 'gentry' used as an adjective, but it is commonplace among historians today. (The author is an Oxford historian.)

'At Maesllwch Castle and Garnons, two-thirds of the old houses have been demolished since the war.' Around Clyro 'Kilvert's woods have long since gone; the woods in the dingle now are only young and untidy fir plantations'. In Kilvert's time the gardens at Cae Mawr employed six men, and larger country houses more. By 1969 the grander walled garden at Clyro Court was a wilderness, the cottage of Cooper, who had tended it for the Baskervilles, 'squalid in its dereliction'. Is that any improvement?

That is the story everywhere in the country today, except for the dreary gardens of public institutions and the better ones of the National Trust. The fact is, as those of us who live in the country know, working people do not want to garden, or do much work anyway, unless seated in some machine to propel them to it. Half of England is suburbia: a kind of Black Country creeping across the landscape; and three-quarters of the population suburban, with suburban tastes – far too large a population for so small a country, without any immigration from abroad. We all know that the immigrants were brought in simply because the whites won't work. Nor, shortly, will our visitors either. The point is made succinctly: in Kilvert's time 'one postman did all the local deliveries on foot – and you still got the post earlier than you do now, when there are three vans'. Well, we all know how trade unionists and civil servants, local and central, put away their time. And our society is a trade-union bureaucracy. Any improvement on Victorian society?

The author is in two minds about this; his dilemma runs interestingly through his book, giving it a certain tension – absent in Kilvert, who accepted the Victorian age as it was. (What more could he have done about it, except do his duty faithfully in the station to which he was called, and that he did nobly? He was a faithful priest, who loved his flock and did his best for them; he seems to have been loved in return by them.) On one side, the author, meeting with friends, admits 'All four of us, at bottom, *hate* the present'. What man of taste and discrimination does not? He then asks, 'Is it typical of our age, our class, or what?' One thing is clear: most people of taste and discrimination do not say openly what they think about it – any more than in that blueprint for modern civilisation, Soviet Russia.

The author sees the facts well enough: 'We live among ruins, as Kilvert did not. He did not have, as we have, a whole lost order of things before his eyes.' On the other hand, the author – like so many middle-class people – has a guilt-complex; he has the sense that Victorian Clyro offers 'an indictment that must be ans-wered'. Why ever? The moralising strain, and the expression of a twentieth-century moral superiority towards the nineteenth, are the least pleasing features of a nice book. What has the twentieth century to be so morally superior about? – the most destructive, the most evil and violent century in history, that has seen hate, violence, genocide on a global scale, whole peoples obliterated, millions eviscerated around the planet. The author's perspective is not merely insular, but parochial; yet it is fairly general among educated middle-class people and partly accounts for the feeble-ness of their reaction to the nauseating features of contemporary demotic society. They feel themselves spitted on the horns of a dilemma.

They have a feeling of guilt about the treatment of the working-class up till quite recently, and this reduces them to silence. Perhaps, as a working-class product, I may speak out. The main indictment of Victorian society is on the score of the poverty of the poorest class. Let us confront the issue squarely. It is perfectly true that in our village in Cornwall, before the First German War, there were people who did not have enough to eat. This was true mainly of the 'unrespectable' fringe, whom we respectable work-ing people looked down on, for not working, drinking their substance away and neglecting their families, or simply having too many children to support properly. It is bad for a society to make this low-grade fringe the main object of its concern – this turns it into an eleemosynary society; to set the standards by the slackest and the stupidest undermines and kills initiative – the greatest internal danger to society today. Everybody who knows about the evolution of man knows that it has been through competition, not co-operation, that human progress has been achieved.

With all the resources of modern industrial production available, there is no reason *now* why poverty should not be entirely eliminated – and people could enjoy even better standards of living throughout society, if only they would work, do an honest day's work for pay – instead of perpetually slacking and striking for more pay and less work. With all our resources of increased wealth – mechanisation, oil and gas on tap, electrical power – there is no reason why the constructive achievements of the upper classes should have been eroded and destroyed – country houses pulled down in hundreds, contents, pictures, furniture, books, archives, family possessions scattered, sold abroad, gardens left derelict, woods cut down, landscape ruined. Let alone destroying newspapers of quality: everything of quality goes – as in Soviet Russia; for what do they care about quality, or culture, or even education? You can see their interests from their appalling newspapers, the muck they do read.

There is no reason for all this destruction of things of value, or why all should not prosper, if they set their hands to it. In the Victorian age it was simply not possible. So why stand superfluously in a white sheet for what, largely, could not be helped?

The author should see this point well enough, since he writes: 'December 1970, the cold made the threat of power-cuts more alarming – they were widespread, and the go-slow was the universal topic of conversation (and execration). It does seem wrong that a small body of men wanting more wages should be able to inflict so much inconvenience on the whole country.' 'Seem' is not the word for it: it *is* wrong. The point is that these men *do not care*, either for the country or for their own less well-paid comrades, let alone the poorest for whom the author expresses most sympathy.

This is simply a question of material well-being, wages – which is all these people care for – whether their industry in particular or the country as a whole can afford it. Pure, blind selfishness, of course. So we need not take too seriously the author's moral squeamishness about manual work. He expresses the view that

'None of the assumptions of his [Kilvert's] society is more alien to us than its assumption of the easy availability of cheap human beings to look after the necessities of your existence – to cook, to wash up, to clean the boots, to bring hot water to your bedroom'. Really?

Here we have the middle-class guilt-complex in all its finery. Bishop Frere, aristocrat and scholar, used to clean the shoes of his guests at Lis Escop at Truro; Sir Maurice Powicke, eminent historian, used to spend a lot of time washing up; several of my scholar-friends are good cooks. What is wrong with working people doing these jobs? – it is much more in keeping with their talents than it is mine. Actually I do quite a lot of manual work about the house and garden. The only thing that is wrong is misdirection of energies – that a person who can do rarer and more important work should waste time and energy on what any fool can do. If it comes to the point I could do any of those jobs; ordinary people could never do mine.

So these are matters on which we should be hard-headed and practical, not softies. The middle classes have lost their courage, their confidence undermined by the dominant ideology of the day, coming mainly from third-rate intellectuals at the universities. They have got their priorities wrong, instead of putting first things first; no wonder society is topsyturvy – janitors better paid than teachers, and so on.

And this is to say nothing of finer moral issues and sentiments. The author notices the readiness of the poor to help each other in Kilvert's day, the frequent charitableness and kindness at all levels, not to mention 'charity' – I suspect, a dirty word with him. In place of it we have the constant scuffling of the best-paid workers at the expense of the less well off. Life in today's society has lost half its savour.

Mr Le Quesne concludes, 'There is much less suffering and much more comfort in the village now than in 1870.' That is something to the good, though we cannot strictly estimate 'suffering' – some of which is unavoidable, some not dependent on material conditions; while 'comfort' is relative. W. P. Ker, that great scholar, preferred to read by candlelight, and refused to have electric light in his rooms at All Souls; nor would he use a bathroom, he preferred to be spartan with a cold hip-bath. Even in the matter of bare feet, I remember the eminent Aristotelian at Oxford, Professor J. A. Smith, telling me that he had grown up barefoot in the north of Scotland: he did not seem to be the worse for it.

The author allows: 'The questions about beauty, truth, and goodness may still remain – but only if you have the right to ask them.' That qualification shows the guilt-obsession, the *bourgeois* inferiority-complex peeping out again . I do not share it: we all have the right to ask these questions: beauty, truth, goodness – they are the right questions to ask of a society and the proper standards by which it is ultimately to be judged. We do not remember fifth-century Athens for its sanitation, or Renaissance Florence for the education of the hardly educable, or Elizabethan England for its softness towards criminals.

By the absolute standards of historic civilisations, we can only regard demotic society as unworthy and discreditable.

Perhaps a further interest of Mr Le Quesne's sociological observations is in that they reveal the attitude of mind of his generation and class – of a middle-aged, middle-class university man reflecting on contemporary society. His mind is confused, his view obscured, really by sentimentality. Nor are other observations particularly penetrating, especially when compared with Kilvert's, which were always sharp and just. He is taken to task for remarking on the ugliness of a Dissenting chapel: 'A building which was very ugly, high and boxy-looking and of course white-washed, the usual conventicle.' This is put down to Kilvert's prejudice as an Anglican – but wasn't he in fact right? Victorian Dissent was inaesthetic – the ground of Matthew Arnold's dislike too, who as a school-inspector had a widespread acquaintance with it.

The author is a historian, so perhaps his literary sensibilities are not quite up to the mark. On Tennyson, for example: 'It would be a commonplace of criticism to add that in any case Tennyson had only his rhythms to give; for an autonomous way of seeing the world, Kilvert had no choice but to go back to Wordsworth.' This is simply obtuse: the best criticism knows that Tennyson has an exceedingly close observation of nature – the blackness of ash-buds, for one, is a well-known example to be pin-pointed. 'Ineffably dismal peasants out of a Hardy novel' – this is very second-rate, when some of the marvellously humorous talk of Hardy's peasants is available even in anthologies. 'Readers of Macaulay – if there are any' – a historian should know that all elect persons have read Macaulay; it has no significance that the mass of people do not, for they read little of any value. Real standards are not mass-standards; and mass-culture is not culture.

NOTE

1.   A. L. Le Quesne, *After Kilvert* (Oxford University Press).

KIPLING: A NEW APPRECIATION

It has taken a whole generation, and more, for liberal intellectuals to come to terms with Kipling; less than a generation ago Eliot came alongside of his poetry – but he was really a Tory. We may regard Angus Wilson as a liberal, in the best sense of the word: he has always been a stalwart in favour of progressive causes (as I have myself). He tells us that 'the critical resuscitation of Kipling's work in academic and intellectual circles' began with a much-publicised essay by Edmund Wilson. 'Critical resuscitation' be damned: who cares tuppence what academics and intellectuals think? And Edmund Wilson's essay is wrong-headed, like almost everything he wrote. Liberal 'critics' always hated Kipling's guts for the home-truths he told them and the contempt in which he, rightly, held them. Critics might fuss and fume, but Kipling held the devotion of readers all over the world; and it is ironical to think that in Soviet Russia he is the most widely read of all foreign writers – except Jack London.

This Mr Wilson, Angus – admirable novelist and short-story writer himself, when Edmund Wilson was neither of those things – makes a much better job of portraying Kipling.[1] The clue to it is Angus Wilson's generosity and perception, for the two go together. Good literary criticism should always be generous, as today criticism hardly ever is. (But, then, it is hardly ever good.) And that for a psychological reason: generosity of mind goes with sympathy, and hence perception. Then, too, Angus Wilson is a creative writer himself; in consequence his book is most illuminating on Kipling's creative processes, the genesis and value of the short stories. He confines himself to Kipling's prose on the whole, and does not deal, except incidentally, with the other, equipollent, half of his amazing body of work, the poetry and verse. A remarkable amount of conscientious research has also gone into this book, so that it is as good as we are ever likely to get. Kipling's spirit, looking down from heaven, must be assuaged as well as surprised at the tribute and understanding from such a source.

Mr Wilson is right to emphasise the *strangeness* of Kipling's genius – there has been nothing else quite like it in our literature, though plenty of other writers are like each other, or are comparable, or have much in common. There is nobody the least bit like Kipling. Mr Wilson speaks generously too of his 'unparalleled variety' (what about Shakespeare?); but I see what he means – the ground Kipling covers, the sheer spread of interests, the knowledge from close experience, the local knowledge: India and the Far East, South Africa and all the Commonwealth, Australia and the Pacific; the United States and Canada; France and England. And that, too, beside extent in time – the historical interest in *Puck of Pook's Hill*, the poems, the History of England he wrote with C. R. L. Fletcher.

Altogether, Kipling was a meteoric apparition, quite unpredictable, and quite as strange. He himself thought – with public-school 'modesty' – that his originality as a writer consisted in his closeness to action. That was one aspect of it. Where most writers are armchair commentators, Kipling went out, like a good journalist, to collect his material from all over the world, observing it close at hand – North-West Frontier, South African war, the Grand Trunk Road, the bazaars of the East no less than the slums of London. And all done in the railway and steamship age – no alighting anywhere easily from a plane: hence the authentic local colour.

Mr Wilson attaches even more importance to Kipling's life-long worship of children. One side of his spirit was very close to them: hence his genius for telling them stories. (They are for adults too, for most people are only grown-up children.) In his house at Burwash is a revealing photograph of him, crouched down, squatting on his heels, and a group of children mesmerised by the primitive wizard weaving his spell. His daughter Elsie used to tell me that the earlier stores were all read to the three children; and she thought that the later stories were less good because the children, Kipling's audience, had grown up and were no longer there to try them out on. I did not agree with her – though I differ from Mr Wilson on such a point with some diffidence. The late story, 'The Gardener', is one of the most moving ever written: and the late stories are more adult in experience; about pain and grief and suffering, they have layer upon layer of meaning. True, they are more difficult, because they are often elliptical and Kipling has deliberately removed the clues. He was always highly stylised and mannered – what a strange mixture he was! – but these late stories are, in my view, quite as fine as, though less popular than, the earlier ones. I am in hope of converting Mr Wilson to this view, on a further look into the matter

To dig deeper down into the man – Mr Wilson thinks that a source of anxiety (genius is always associated with tension) was the problem of identity, that Kipling could find no satisfactory ans-wer to the question, Who is Kipling? I am not sure that there is not a modish cliché here. Lionel Curtis, who knew Kipling well, told me that he was two men: on one side an inspired prophet, on the other a grousing reactionary. (Curtis told me some funny stories about the second aspect, for which I have not space.) But there is no doubt about the intuitional, and Kipling's reliance upon it: he tells us so in his autobiography, *Something Of Myself* (so reveal-ing about writing). And Kipling was undoubtedly psychic – he had the second-sight of a Highlander. G. M. Trevelyan told me something odd about Kipling's story of the Centurion on the Roman Wall: Kipling had plumped for a certain legion being there at the time. Later, a coin turned up which showed that indeed it had been so. Trevelyan wrote to Kipling to tell him of the find.

Mr Wilson thinks that there was a tension between Kipling's need to put down roots and the need to get out on the trail. This is getting nearer to the clue. An element in Kipling's inner tension may have been due to the strain he was under in identifying with the English, when he wasn't of that 'race'. He was a great figure all over the English-speaking world, regarded as the spokesman for English values, standards and prejudices, almost a prophet of the 'race' (as if there were one). Hostile people called him a Eurasian, for he looked exactly like one: small, very dark, rather squat, hair sprouting from nose and ears, very primitive-looking. As indeed he was. One side of his family, the Macdonalds, were Highland; on the other side, Elsie Kipling told me, there was a distinct Welsh strain. Kipling never said anything about it, and Mr Wilson has missed the clue – but Kipling clearly belonged to the racial type in this island who were here before even the Celts, the old Iberian stock.

That he knew about the difference these things make is clear from his poem about the Celts:

> The Celt in all his variants from Builth to Bally-hoo,
> His mental processes are plain – one knows what he will do,
> And can logically predicate his finish by his start;
> But the English – ah, the English! – they are quite a race apart.
>
> In telegraphic sentences, half nodded to their friends,
> They hint a matter's inwardness – and there the matter ends,
> And while the Celt is talking from Valentia to Kirkwall,
> The English – ah, the English! – don't say anything at all.

In short, Kipling was always an Outsider, and like many Outsiders – fell in love with England, the old England. (I have done so myself before now. But not today.) And he made himself the chief proponent, doctrinally and imaginatively, of what English standards were. Mr Wilson perceives 'what service to the Empire (and indeed the preservation of civilised society) demands'. Service to India, for example, which Kipling understood from his childhood and young manhood, was not at all the cheap and vulgar caricature which Marxists, or even liberals like E. M. Forster, have put across. Hard work, responsibility, upright standards of justice, incorruptibility in administration, the well-being of the people in so far as peace could be kept in the internecine conflict between Hindu and Moslem. Are things any better in India now that British rule has ended? Just look at the picture it presents today!

Mr Wilson understands the *love* for the Indian people which inspired Kipling's greatest work, *Kim*. E. M. Forster told Raymond Mortimer, who quoted it to me, as if it had any authority, that Kipling's knowledge of India was not extensive. What a give-away of thoroughly superficial judgement! As if mere extension in space it to be compared with the *depth* of Kipling's inner, intuitional knowledge of India from infancy: it was where he was born; his first language was the local language from his ayah, so that when he came into his parents' drawing-room he had to be reminded to speak English. Childhood and adolescence shape a writer; India entered his heart and engaged his mind and intuitions. Radakrishnan, first President of India, told me that, of all Western books, *Kim* was the one that best understood India.[2] Not, certainly not, Forster's *A Passage to India*, absurdly overestimated by second-rate intellectuals because it is written in their terms. Actually Indians do not care for its patronising tone – and Forster himself, honest man, knew that he was not a great novelist.

Mr Wilson, though a liberal, understands well how fatuous are the liberal intellectuals' dismissal of Kipling's political ideas. Societies depend for their survival on discipline, and that rests on self-discipline – as among the handful of civil servants from English manors and Scottish manses who kept the great mass of India together, diminished famine, enabled its population to live in peace and multiply, with the minimum exertion of force. So much for British, as against Russian, imperialism – the British record in India, to an informed historian, is one of the most astonishing achievements in history. Whatever superficial liberals may say, with their fatuous illusions about human beings, the Indians themselves recognise it. On one side there is the recognition of *Kim* as their classic; on the other side, Pakistan has inscribed on the great gate at Peshawar, leading to the Khyber Pass, verses from Kipling.

More widely, Kipling understood in his bones what Mr Wilson describes as 'the fragility of the human condition, his apprehension of the threat to order'. But, of course. Like Shakespeare, he knew how thin is the crust of civilisation, and how easily, when order and discipline are undermined, societies can plunge into what dark waters beneath, what chaos. Look round the world today, or within our own society – and see how right he was. Indiscipline, disorder, murder, political assassination on every hand, holding to ransom not only industrialists but political leaders – so that it is difficult to see how democratic societies can continue to be governed, or where it will all end. So much for liberal illusions – the Communists have an answer. The plain evidence shows that from the Far East to the Middle East, from Italy to Northern Ireland, in the breakdown of hierarchical order, the people are everywhere out of hand. For, of course, the masses are always and everywhere idiots, as Communist psychology presupposes and acts upon. No one knew the truth about human nature better than William Shakespeare; Kipling did not put it quite so drastically, but when he was alive the break-up and the rot had not gone so far. But he saw it coming.

Knowing what he did and that he was right, why shouldn't he portray intellectuals as the fools they were, nibbling away the heart-strings of society, depicting them as the chattering monkeys of the Banderlog? Mr Wilson – as a professor at one of the five new universities now recognised to be superfluous (*pace* Lord Robbins!) – does not like to face this home-truth. Kipling's view, he thinks, was 'vitiated by his too persistent belief, that educated minorities have no real force or influence in society'. I suspect that Kipling thought that they have had all too much influence, and on the whole a deplorable one. I am sure that Communists would agree that it has sapped the entire strength of our society. For more than a century the dominant trend of intellectual opinion – against which Kipling struggled in vain – has been liberal, in favour of throwing the British Empire away, among other things. Has it been any advantage to civilisation that its place has been taken by the brutal imperialism of Soviet Russia? Or has it been any advantage to the suffering blacks of Africa to have thrown over Lugard's idea of trusteeship on their behalf (in *West* Africa, Mr Wilson, not East) for the bloodstained military dictatorships that have taken its place all over Africa?

Let us take an example nearer home. Mr Wilson sheds tears, as everybody does, at what happens in Kipling's late, post-war story 'Mary Postgate'. Everybody deplores it. But it is too easy to deplore and set oneself up as holier than Kipling. In the story the spinster woman's nephew has been killed by the Germans; in her village she sees the children at the inn killed by a bomb. The German plane that dropped it falls in her garden; she leaves the dying German airman to his fate. She says, in German, 'No. I have seen the dead children'.

All holier-than-thou English liberals have screamed against this story, and reams have been written against Kipling on this score alone. I am not going to argue the ethics of it. I shall merely point out, as a historian, that the leading German historian today, Fritz Fischer, acknowledges that the two wars of 1914–18 and 1939–45 were but the crests of the long wave of German determination to expand and dominate Europe, at whatever cost to others or even themselves. *Welt-Macht oder Niedergang.*

As we all know, they got *Niedergang*, with Germany divided from top to bottom – very rightly, for – as a German–Swiss professor said to me recently – the rest of Europe couldn't live with a united Germany. But at what a cost! At least 20 million lives in Europe. The Germans have, in fact, ruined the twentieth century, reduced modern civilisation to the shambles it now exemplifies.

As a historian, I gravely blame the English for being so easy-going and liberal-minded as to forget what the Germans were responsible for in 1914–18. It was in my view, as in Kipling's, immoral to overlook what they had done – for it made it easier, and gave them the chance, to try it all over again. As they did. Kipling did not live to see that, but he knew too well what lily-livered (Shakespeare's word for it) English liberalmindedness would enable the Germans to do. It was not only that they had killed his only son, and broken his heart – read 'The Gardener', the most heartbreaking story ever written, written when he went to see his boy's grave in France – but that he understood and intuited the consequences of that lightmindedness, the wrath to come.

The Celts are good haters; the English are not. Kipling was a Celt. There is something to be said on both sides of this equation, *con* as well as *pro*; I hope I have the justice of mind to admit that. But where the German record was concerned, and their potentiality for further evil, it was an absolute dereliction of duty between the wars not to remind the British people of what the country had suffered, in the lost lives of a whole generation in 1914–18, and not to keep the warning alive.

All Kipling's warnings were ignored – as mine have been; and we are where we are today. I hope people like it (well, the third-rate do, for it is a society which was always intended for the benefit of the third-rate).

Mr Wilson does get so far as to recognise that aesthetic matters are not settled by ethical judgements: they are different and to be distinguished. Perhaps he would not go all the way with me and say that hatred is just as valid a subject for art as love. Sometimes it is more interesting – as Iago is a more interesting character than Othello. It is not a question of approving or disapproving (we disapprove of both, humanly speaking), but of watching the work of art, observing its operations. Mr Wilson, as a creative artist, sees that critics refuse 'to face the difficult truth, that aesthetic satisfaction is not one with ethical satisfaction, although the critic has every right to distinguish the moral impulse which disgusts him from the story which is such a wonder to read'.

How diplomatic of Mr Wilson! Still he comes down on the right, or intellectually respectable, side. Less diplomatic, I take no holier-than-thou line, and I do not burke the issue: I, of course, approve of 'Mary Postgate', as of most of what Kipling thought and wrote.

My old friend Quiller-Couch, best of liberals but a good critic, appreciated the importance of this distinction, as lesser critics do not. He used to say of Kipling: 'I detest his opinions; but I worship his genius'. Myself, I worship his genius, while, after as before his death, events have shown that his opinions, and even his prejudices, were largely right.

NOTES

1. Angus Wilson, *The Strange Ride of Rudyard Kipling. His Life and Works* (Secker & Warburg).
2. I fear Mr Wilson has not read my foreword to the American paperback edition of *Kim*, or he would have noticed this authoritative judgement.

A GREAT WRITER? – THE CASE OF E. M. FORSTER

E. M. Forster was a delightful writer, an original short-story writer, an entrancing essayist – but not a great novelist. An honest and transparently sincere man, he knew that and stated it unequivocally: 'I am sure I am not a great novelist'.

Then why has he been treated so solemnly as if he were? The reasons are obvious, and throw some light on the condition of contemporary literature. The confirmation may be said to have been solemnised by Professor Lionel Trilling in America devoting a whole book to Forster's greatness, and that started the cult. The Americans, in the goodness of their hearts and like a herd of buffs, followed the trail; circulation soared and Forster became at least quite rich.

Trilling's admiration, no doubt sincere, is easily accountable: Forster was an academic liberal, Trilling a liberal academic. Their standards and values, their moralism and dominant ethicality, were similar; a professor of Eng. Lit. needs a subject to write about, here was one that fitted as smooth as a glove. The smoothness did not last. The Trillings brought their son to see the great man at King's, by this time revered almost as a saint, certainly a guru. At tea the liberal boy said he would have some more cake; to which Forster replied severely, 'You will have some when you are offered it'. I sympathise with him; but Mr Furbank records that 'the Trillings, who had been greatly attached to Forster, thought the snub intolerable and could never feel quite the same towards him again'.¹ How hard it must be for a saint to keep the devotion of such sensitive devotees!

Then, too, Forster has always had a Cambridge *claque* – not so at Oxford, as one of them still clacking away has recently noticed. Poor Leavis, however, who regarded himself as an authority on greatness, was not one of them.

To be a great novelist one must obviously have greatness: not only width and depth of range but force of imagination, a powerful grasp of human nature expressing itself in memorable, indeed unforgettable, characters like Anna Karenina or Pierre Bezhukov, Père Goriot or the Baron de Charlus. Forster had eminent and distinguished qualities, but none of greatness: his range was restricted; in place of a powerful imagination he had careful observation and fancy; instead of passion he had sentiment, sentimentality – as he truthfully observed of himself – and whimsy. His distinction of mind revealed itself in his style and his interests, particularly his devotion to music; his odd turn of mind, emerging from a character verging on the eccentric, gave him unexpected tricks of humour, which appear at their funniest in his 'unpublishable' stories, piously published after his death. He had become such a venerated sage, such an institution – with the B.B.C., the PEN Club, an O.M. hung round his neck – that all that naughty, and much the most amusing, side to his life and work had to be suppressed.

A First World War general, who apparently shared his interests, noticed 'how Morgan's friends always drop their voices when they talk of him, as if he were Jesus Christ'. Christopher Isherwood writes ineffably, 'Morgan is so accustomed to the Presence of God that he is unaware of it: he has never known what it feels like when the Presence is withdrawn'. Really now! I am amused at the way Forster cheated the conventional – imperceptive as usual – who regarded him as a saint when his personal life was far otherwise: bisexual policemen, 'my boy in blue', willing sailors, semi-criminals, jail-birds – all the *tohu-bohu* not of honest working-class life, but the highly dubious fringes of it.

A Marxist approach would appreciate the class circumstances that peculiarly conditioned Forster's life and work and the class restrictedness of his novels. No one was so restricted as the Victorian *upper* middle-class person, obsessed with gentility, living a rather suburban life on the edge of country and county, with so many people outside, above and below, whom one couldn't know. This inhibiting fact, obvious in all the novels and stories, is explicitly acknowledged in *Maurice*, the most autobiographical of them. Maurice is a wishful extrapolation of Morgan himself as he would have liked to be; he is going to stay with his upper-class Cambridge friend at his country-house home. 'County families, even when intelligent, have something alarming about them', we are told, 'and Maurice approached any seat with awe.' There follows a pertinent observation. His friend's family did not dislike Maurice: 'They only disliked [*sic* for 'disliked only']² people who wanted to know them well – it was a positive mania – and the rumour that a man wished to enter county society was a sufficient reason for excluding him from it'.

The restrictedness of Forster's outlook was reinforced by the peculiar circumstances of his family life. His father died when he was young, leaving the baby to be watched over and fought over for possession by a doting mother and grandmother. He lived with, or shared much of his life with, Mother till he was a man of sixty-eight, and was in a way her victim. For the first half of his life he felt that he was expiring from the stranglehold – D. H. Lawrence's intuition at once gave him the impression of 'cramp'. Forster in the end took various courses to escape, but his spirit retained the indelible stamp.

Neither an aristocrat nor a working-class writer is so restricted socially or, so to say, spiritually; compare Tolstoy or Byron on one side, or D. H. Lawrence on the other. And contrast the proletarian force and passion of Lawrence, with Forster's delicate sentiment and fussy moralism. Ethics provides the element in which the upper middle-class lived and moved and had its being. Forster's later life was a courageous breakaway from the inhibitions imposed by it, and the inanition which drove him to despair. It began with the visit to Edward Carpenter: 'He and his comrade George Merrill [the one a Cambridge ex-clergyman, the other a working man] combined to touch a creative spring. George Merrill also touched my backside – gently and just above the buttocks.' At that moment *Maurice* was conceived; it is borne in upon one that Forster's spirit was essentially feminine, though very much that of a lady. Forster wrote to the other Lawrence, T. E. – all three had much of the feminine in them – 'But when I die and they write my life, they can say everything.'

Mr Furbank has proceeded to do so. His first volume was rather pallid, like Forster's life up to halfway; the second volume is much more variegated and interesting. Actually one volume would have been enough for the subject; a good deal that is trivial, particularly the dispiriting details of family life with Mother and the minutiae of ludicrous court-life with the Maharajah, which we already knew from *The Hill of Devi*, could have been omitted with advantage. However, we are grateful to Mr Furbank for telling us everything: nothing to shock, much to laugh at.

In considering the question of 'greatness' or no, *A Passage to India* is crucial; it has always been regarded as Forster's masterpiece, though he thought *Howards End* his best novel. *A Passage* has a significant theme historically – the relations between the British and Indians in India. Forster was in a good position to observe his subject, through his two Indian visits and his emotional friendships with Indians. All the same he was an observer, seeing things from the outside, for all his sympathy with Indians; one cannot say that India had entered into his bloodstream, lit up the inner life of the imagination as with the author of *Kim*.

Forster himself always recognised, as his *claque* does not, how faulty his book is. Not only in mistakes of detail – Forster acknowledged the criticisms of those people who knew so much better: 'The novel is full of mistakes in fact – naturally, for I've only been twice to India'. He accepted the criticism of an Indian civilian who had spent thirty years in the service: 'Frankly your Collector is impossible. There is not a Collector in India – not an English Collector – who would behave as he does. No Collector in his senses would go to the railway station to witness the arrest of a native assistant-surgeon.' An 'Anglo-Indian', who had spent his life in the education service, also regarded Forster's portrait of

Turton, the Collector, as quite unreal: 'This man is not an Indian civilian, he is a college don, and ridiculous enough at that.... And what is one to make of the women, so inhuman are they without exception? And if these people are preposterous, equally preposterous are the scenes which they enact.'

As for Forster's women, his misogyny peeps out in all his work; and this was a further restricting factor in his experience and outlook. He understood women, of course, for he was largely one himself; but he had not a *man's* experience and understanding of women. Compare a great novelist, like Balzac or Turgenev or Tolstoy.

Forster admitted the hard impeachment; he wrote to a friend, about his 'Anglo-Indians': 'I loathe them, and should have been more honest to say so'. He said that he preferred being with Indians – and every man according to his tastes. But what did he really think of them? He wrote to a Moslem friend: 'When I began the book I thought of it as a little bridge of sympathy between East and West, but this conception has had to go: my sense of truth forbids anything so comfortable. I think most Indians, like most English people, are shits'.

This is worse than undiscriminating; in my view it is positively unbalanced in its harshness. The great bulk of human beings, of whatever nation or colour, are *not* shits, that is, bad; they are merely simpletons, as much greater writers than Forster have always known. (What price democracy?) Forster went on to confess, 'I am not interested whether they [the English and Indians] sympathise with one another or not. Not interested as an artist; of course the journalistic side of me still gets roused over these questions'.

That is precisely my criticism of the book: too journalistic, faulty as a work of art. Naturally, literary journalists cannot tell the difference. But when I read *A Passage to India* I find the way that 'Anglo-Indian' insensitiveness, condescension and rudeness to Indians is brought up on page after page is inaesthetic; it becomes a bore and spoils the book.

Mr Furbank notes that other critics had observed the flaw, the mix-up, that these bad manners were pre-1914 and had changed in the post-war India Forster purported to describe. Such manners are at any time insufferable, but I have a deeper sociological, or even philosophic, point to make. The collective reactions of all groups – not merely 'Anglo-Indian' – are apt to be stupid and rude, and are not to be taken (intellectually) seriously. The English say harsh things about the Irish, the Irish about the English; I have heard intelligent French people say the most appalling things about the Americans, and the Americans say some pretty unintelligent things about the French. And so on; it is a universal phenomenon, and Forster was quite unphilosophic and unfair in constantly harping on this silly aspect of 'Anglo-Indians' in much of his work, as if it were not true of all humans collectively. I suspect that the Indians said as much back about the 'Anglo-Indians'.

The philosophic person takes no notice of what people say collectively about other human groups. The ordinary person is really very 'ornery', to use an American term. I never pay the slightest attention to what they think, for – in the strict sense of the term – they do not know how to think. Only the elect do, and they, as we see in Forster's case, not always fairly. Actually his scepticism did not reach down far enough, it got arrested halfway, somewhere in the region of his prejudices. He did learn, however, and became more disillusioned with experience.

The central flaw in *A Passage to India* is, as perceptive critics have seen, the mysterious happening in the Marabar cave from which the English lady gets such a shock, upon which the action depends and from which explosive consequences ensue, blowing up such tenuous good will as there was between English and Indians. What exactly happened in the cave? Nobody knows. Forster called it 'an unexplained muddle', and when asked what happened, replied, '*I don't know*'. This is not good enough; it is a crucial defect artistically when all the significant action of the novel depends upon it – no advance upon calling the god Pan in as a *deus ex machina* in the early stories.

I confess a personal preference: I prefer all Forster's later work, including *A Passage to India*, to his earlier work. I respect more the writing that came after his initiation into life than the old-maidish earlier novels with their claustrophobic atmosphere. I think his short stories in general better than his novels, especially such a fine late story as 'The Other Boat', with its atmosphere of eroticism and tragedy. Some of these later stories, like 'The Obelisk', have an uninhibited sense of humour – far more genuine and true to life than the trivia of lady-like frequenters of foreign *pensioni* with their liability to visions of the god Pan, or the absurd 'goblins' that occur in *Howards End*. Alongside the short-story writer I place the essayist and biographer – he was a delicious essayist with his own idiosyncrasy and unexpected turns of phrase. I had a pleasant exchange of letters with him over *Marianne Thornton*, the deft skill of which I could admire, to make up for my lack of appreciation for his etiolated political views, the devitalised liberalism of *Two Cheers for Democracy* for which I could raise only 'Two Cheers for Mr Forster'. I fear I was not his type – Sebastian Sprott, J. R. Ackerley and Christopher Isherwood were – and not made for a reverend disciple.

Forster's values were Cambridgy, or – perhaps to make a refinement – very much King's, 'the most civilised place on earth', according to the gospel. This meant a strict addiction to the Truth, as those of King's saw it, which we may take for granted; a certain unworldliness (here Keynes was an exception, disapproved of by pure Bloomsbury on this score); tolerance of oddities and eccentricities, though very intolerant of ordinary conventional people; refinement and cultivation, along with superciliousness towards lesser breeds without their law; an absorbing ethicality, ever ready to sniff and condemn; an excruciating concern with personal relations, derived from the slightly absurd figure of G. E. Moore, of whom they made a cult, for want of religion.

Forster, to his credit, stood slightly at an angle in all these matters: he was not wholly Bloomsbury, he had too much pragmatic common sense to be absolute or so arrogant. He had not read the prophet Moore – no less. He did not take up the extreme, and nonsensical, position of Bertrand Russell with regard to the First German War of 1914–18; indeed he did not have Russell's passionate wrong-headedness and wicked perversity. Forster wanted to lower the temperature: 'I do not believe in Belief'; he stood for 'tolerance, good temper and sympathy' – which Russell never did, and who did a great deal of harm in different directions.

But Forster had the virginal attitude to Power, usual in liberal thinking – fatal to the understanding of society and politics, for the struggle for survival is the fundamental condition of all life on the planet, for human beings as well as other forms. He came to understand by the time of the Second German War: 'I realise that all society rests upon force'.

What bad guides those Cambridge liberals were on the crucial issues of the 1914–18 War (as Keynes had a disastrous influence with *The Economic Consequences of the Peace*): with their political innocence perhaps it was no wonder that the next generation at Cambridge – not only Maclean and Burgess, but Julian Bell and Cornford and many others – should have turned to Communism. It is revealing that the only politician Forster really hated was Winston Churchill, and the poor political judgement breaks out like pimples all over the place. 'If the present order breaks, Communism seems the only hopeful alternative.' To this piece of highbrow Cambridge silliness, a man-in-the-street replied, 'It might be dangerous for Mr Forster to imagine the amount of civil liberty that he would enjoy in a Communist society'. While Gide, whose sympathies and interests Forster largely shared, declared at one of those fatuous International Conferences of Writers both of them figured at, 'individuals and their peculiarities can best flourish in a Communist society'! (His own 'peculiarity' has been particularly proscribed by it.) We have had to wait for the insufferable Sartre to proclaim – after all the experience of Stalin and the great Purges, Gulag and Soviet Russia as we know it to be – that the U.S.S.R. is the incarnation of human freedom!

What idiots these intellectuals are – they disgrace the name of intellectual; but what beats me is that people should ever take their views seriously. It is fair to state that Cambridge did not have a monopoly of them: Oxford had its Ralph Fox and Christopher Hill, its Tony Crosland and Denis Healey, each of whom saw the Red Light before the end.

Forster, more sceptical, was better than this; all the same, the poor psychology upon which intellectual liberalism rests reveals itself again and again in bad political judgement. He thought that the First German War would end in a stalemate of 'exhaustion and nausea'; he thought that in the Second German War Britain would be defeated; that in order to defeat totalitarianism we should become totalitarian ourselves – whereas the wonderful thing in that crisis of Britain's existence was the way in which she maintained essential freedom. Why not be generous and admit these things? If there were 'injustices and brutalities' in the British Empire at times, they were chicken-feed compared with Soviet Russia – or even with the white record against the blacks in the U.S.A., let us not forget. Forster thought he sniffed anti-Jewish feeling in England: 'A nasty side of our nation's character has been scratched up – the sniggering side,' he wrote. Well, there are always some nasty people; but do not overlook that the nation took in Jewish refugees from Hitler – and greatly Britain gained from *those* immigrants, as she deserved to do.

Forster objected to the 'obedience' necessary to win the war – or even, we may add, to keep order in the nursery and society in running order. He thought order (today breaking down) might be well enough, 'if we were sure it wasn't the Kylsants who were giving the orders'. Liberal illusions again – it never is the Big Bad Businessmen who order society; it used to be the politicians, today it is the bureaucrats and the trade unions. Do we note a marked improvement?

Excessive ethicality is the bane of liberal illusionism. Forster was a moralist through and through – moralising appears on every other page of *Howards End*. Alas, it does not speak to me, a working-class man and, for the rest, an aesthete: it ruins the aesthetic effect of the book. To consider morals for a moment, if with some reluctance. Forster confesses that he had not been straight with his publisher, Arnold: 'I have not been straight with him, *but do not mind*'. Uncouth proletarian as I am, ethically under-educated, never having been middle-class, I consider that one ought to be straight with one's publishers, though I have sometimes been taken advantage of by them. Literary sincerity raises awkward questions. In his Cambridge lectures, *Aspects of the Novel*, Forster publicly credited Percy Lubbock's book on the subject with 'genius and insight'; privately he thought the book not much good, 'a sensitive yet poor-spirited book'. (He was similarly disingenuous with, and over, Virginia Woolf.) I do not think that the saintly Moore (G. E., not Sir Thomas) would have approved of this double-talk. On one occasion Russell asked the Saint, a close personal acquaintance: 'Do you like me?' After some reflection Moore said: 'No'.

That was strict Cambridge ethics, from which Forster somewhat deviated. He publicly propagated Russell's *Principles of Social Reconstruction* (which misled me when young) as 'splendid and brave', while admitting to Russell that he did not much hold with it. Mr Furbank bravely provides several instances of this kind of thing. I sometimes find Forster's behaviour quite unethical – those hysterical rages, throwing himself against the furniture: fancy giving way to such childishness! He behaved similarly to the squire of Abinger and his family, though here class-consciousness kept breaking in, for Mother had been a governess in that family and this made the Forsters uncomfortable (so middle-class of them). I wouldn't have minded; but when the Farrers took back the lease of the Forsters' house, the eminent guru put every obstacle in their way and created the maximum nuisance in obstructing their lawful rights. No – he was not a pure G. E. Moore man!

In the end, disillusioned – like Wystan Auden and the rest of them – he came to believe in aristocracy (I do myself). 'I believe in aristocracy. Not an aristocracy of power [of course], based upon rank and influence, but an aristocracy of the sensitive, the considerate and the plucky.' We note that those are not precisely aristocratic values: courage, yes; considerateness, no. Since I believe that works of art and intellect are what redeem mankind from the slime, the aristocracy I believe in is that of taste; and, anyway, aristocrats are better and more interesting than bureaucrats.

We return to the novelist, his qualities and what constitutes greatness.

Forster thought *Howards End* his best novel, 'approaching a good novel', he wrote truthfully. He knew it was not a great novel. When one thinks of a great novel one thinks of *Crime and Punishment, The Possessed, The Brothers Karamazov*: terrible and appalling as they are, what depths of human nature they reach down into! In consequence, the characters – even the atmosphere – go on and on in the mind; one cannot forget them. In Forster's novels one cannot remember them: they have no power, and so do not impose themselves; one does not even care what happens to them.

Forster's favourite, however, was *The Longest Journey*, for flawed as he knew it to be, in it he put the Cambridge values by which he sought to live and tried to express the role they might be thought to have in 'the world' – their small, *bourgeois* world, I should gloss. Professor Trilling wrote of this work, ineffably: 'perhaps the most brilliant, the most dramatic, and the most passionate of his works'. We see that this is a prime example of lack of critical discrimination; for Forster is never passionate, nor is he dramatic. The plays he wrote were no good as drama. Nor was he really brilliant; he was certainly clever, and sometimes he gently scintillates and often amuses. No: he would never himself allow that he was brilliant.

Forster and Furbank together give a more truthful – and, critically, more honest – account. An encounter with a shepherd-boy on Finsbury Rings *à la* Richard Jefferies 'swamped his first design', and made him fanciful and mystical – Pan again; 'the novel became the queer, ardent, fumbling affair that we know as *The Longest Journey*'. Forster himself said that 'it spoiled it as a work of art': that is the point, and answers the question posed by this essay. 'Only connect' was Forster's much-publicised message to the world, repeated *ad nauseam* by the disciples. (Disciples have not much sense of humour – the Freudian suggestion of the phrase, of which they are unaware always makes me laugh.) I suggest as motto for my gospel, 'Only reflect'.

Maurice was written in 1913–14, but not published until after his death. By then he had become the Grand Old Man of letters and the book was reverently trumpeted in America. The *New York Times* hailed it as 'a major novel – a wonderful novel to read, rich, beautifully controlled, deeply moving ... a timeless story, a complex work of art'. It is, of course, nothing of the sort; all his English friends knew that it was inferior to his best work. He himself, honest as usual, pointed to its central fault, inspired by wish-fulfilment, suffused in the sentimentality of its subject, insufficiently distanced – or, we might say, ejaculated – from the autobiographical. It bears much the same relation to Forster's *œuvre* as *Lady Chatterley's Lover* does to Lawrence's, and Forster's gamekeeper is as much a wish-fulfilment fancy as Lawrence's. Once more the characters are not created out of the silent depths of the imagination, as with Hardy, but fancied. This is not to underestimate Forster's courage in tackling such a subject at such a time and he was understandably proud of having been so early in the field. Moreover, as Mr Furbank admits with candour, 'Forster had relatively few fictional patterns and was content to use those he knew again and again'. Here at least was something refreshingly new.

We are now in a better position to sum up his qualities and answer our question. Forster had natural distinction of mind, and was clever and cultivated, musical and well-bred. His moral discrimination was fine, even exquisite – both from his growing up among upper middle-class ladies (himself one) and his Cambridge training. This is reflected in his style – always what is most personal: his felicity with words, his deftness and skill, his unexpected turns of phrase, his humour and fantasy, a streak of poetry, even a little surrealist in *The Hill of Devi* and his feeling for odd characters like the Maharajah and Masood, Cavafy, Ackerley and Sprott with their jail-birds.

His public concern made him a somewhat improbable guru – really because leftist liberals were, and are, in control of the mass-media. All the same his liberalising influence was a good thing: natural human brutality, ignorance and imperceptiveness needed his contribution, his light and enlightening touch. He had public spirit and, for so essentially private a person, he showed courage and a sense of responsibility.

By the same token his gifts were *not* those of greatness, that is, power and force of imagination, passion, probing into the depths of human nature. But we have reason to be grateful for his contribution, original and idiosyncratic, humorous and charm- ing, laughing and lovable – when greater spirits are apt to be less so. Forster, too good a critic to be dominated by mere prejudice, admired Kipling and said that he was one of the few men whom he deeply regretted never to have met. Alas, we may be sure that the author of *Kim* would not regret never to have met the author of *A Passage to India*.

NOTES

1   P. N. Furbank, *E. M. Forster. A Life*, two vols (Secker & Warburg).
2.   Surprisingly for a good stylist, Forster regularly misplaced the word 'only', which should come before the phrase it governs. Particularly noticeable in *Howards End*.

IN JUSTICE TO BELLOC

I have never done justice to Belloc in my mind: he did not really, as a writer, speak to me. That this was partly prejudice I readily admit: I was out of sympathy with his own Catholic *préjugés*. They were more than prejudices, it is true; as an historian he did not much care whether what he said was true or not. A professional historian has a vested interest in truth, and in my eyes Belloc's blithe disregard of it was so obvious that, when I was young and innocent, I once described his variations on the Elizabethan age as 'a farrago of lies'. This, of course, was libellous (G. M. Trevelyan, in conversation, roundly called him a liar). That it was all the same true, I knew from a mutual friend, Douglas Woodruff. Belloc was then having a controversy with that *enragé* Cambridge champion of truth, Dr Coulton; to close it Belloc came out with something devastating. Woodruff asked him, 'But is it true?' Belloc replied blithely, 'Oh, not at all. But won't it annoy Coulton?' I thought, and still think, that rather wicked.

Something of the same sort happened over the Eellowship election at All Souls, about which Belloc – like some other Oxford historians – had a lifelong complex. When he was dined formally before the election, the young man held the floor in the smoking room on the subject of the French military manoeuvres, in which he had done service. He went on to engage in controversy with redoubtable Hensley Henson on the Dreyfus case. Belloc had a ridiculous anti-Jewish line, only partly a pose, and to answer Henson he came out with some outrageous 'fact' unknown to anyone else and inherently improbable. This did not recommend him to the College. I have heard F. E. Smith (Lord Birkenhead) say that he was present on that occasion, and that he asked Belloc as they went away, 'And do you think you have improved your chances in that ancient house of learning?'

Of course he had not. The College, proceeding conscientiously on that basis of the written examination, elected a better historian but duller man: H. W. C. Davis. When Davis' *England under the Normans and Angevins* came out, it was unfairly attacked by Belloc, who always resented his non-election – as Namier and others have done too. But no candidate has a right to expect to be elected: the All Souls examination is an open competition. Perhaps something is to be said against going wholly on the results of an examination, when one reflects that better examinees have excluded men of genius – that All Souls elected a Dougal Malcolm (a good classical scholar) instead of John Buchan, an E. L. Woodward rather than Aldous Huxley, a John Foster instead of a Lord David Cecil – and H. W. C. Davis instead of Belloc. An even more interesting College could have been constructed out of the non-elected (one must not say 'rejected', as Belloc regarded himself) than out of those elected.

So – while I am sure that the College was right as to Belloc's qualifications and eventual showing as an historian, I have never doubted that he was something rarer: a man of genius. Belloc nursed a grievance all his life at what he regarded as his 'exclusion' from Oxford, for no other college would make him a Fellow either – including his own Balliol, which he loved. I cannot help wondering what the effect would have been, on him and on us, if he *had* been a Fellow of All Souls. It would certainly have improved his history, but could it have improved his writing?

I doubt it, for he had such a strong persona as to render him inassimilable in any environment. As it was, though he went on living in Holywell for some years in hopes of a Fellowship after technically 'going down', he had to work so hard for a living that we might have been deprived of some of his books and a lot of fun. Altogether there are some 150 of them, most of them good, so that it is impossible to compass him in an essay – though no-one attempts to today, when much less important writers receive far more attention.

Belloc was a strange phenomenon in English life and letters – much of it accountable by his descent. On one side his ancestors were shipowners at Nantes (were they Bretons?), but his grandfather was an academic painter whose son was tutored by the brilliant (anti-English) historian, Michelet. On the mother's side was an Irish officer who fought in Napoleon's army and, oddest of all, a direct descent from the Utilitarian Radical, Joseph Priestley. There it all is in Belloc's work. I recall T. S. Eliot saying to me once, in that quiet precise voice: 'The longer I live the more I realise that one is just the product of one's ancestors. [I think he was then excogitating *The Family Reunion*.] Half-a-dozen of mine were clerics, another half-dozen schoolmasters'. And certainly Eliot became the great clerical schoomaster of his time.

In Belloc the shipowners reappear in his passion for the sea, about which he wrote one of the best of his books, *The Cruise of the 'Nona'*. Joseph Priestley comes out in the political Radicalism – of his novels and verse, though its chief monument is his *The Servile State*, prophetic and penetrating, though wrong-headed in its hopes. The artistic heritage is obvious in his poetry and prose, in which he was a natural stylist; the French bourgeois in his curious fixation on Money as a subject to write about – in that like Balzac. It was rather un-English, certainly to the Victorians; for example, Mrs (Bishop) Creighton: 'To think of money is un-Christian; to talk of it is middle class'. However, Belloc's apogee was the Edwardian age, when money and vulgar opulence were in the ascendant. The Irishman comes out in the fanatical obstinacy. Altogether, it was a very odd mix-up – I suspect that it was Belloc's Irish-Catholic *dogmatism* (quite unlike the old English Catholics) that put him out of court with the English.

When one looks at his face one sees how un-English he was:

square, stubborn, unsmiling (for all his wit), hacked out of rock, as it might be a French peasant, butcher or bourgeois. He really was a Frenchman writing in English: that was his singularity, what gave him his originality and produced the tension and contradictions. It also gave him his exceeding richness of temperament, the range of his interests and gifts – and gives him his distinctive place in English literature.

He began in the 1890s with verse, as so many did then. He was a distinguished poet, little appreciated today because of the strictness and perfection of his form. This is perhaps to be expected in a literary society that has no standards, and cannot tell the difference between poetry and non-poetry, sense and nonsense. Kingsley Amis quotes a long passage by 'an established poet', pushed by the literary weeklies, and alas 'representative,' and then places it properly: 'this is not verse at all in any sense that makes sense'. Belloc wrote for an educated society – I will not use the catchphrase 'élitist', beloved of those unequal to it, but of a mandarin society in which standards prevailed and ruled. In that society the cultured minority were those who held the power. So today, in a society with no standards, in which everybody is like everybody else, it is natural that the sheer distinction of Belloc's work should go unrecognised.

His poetry is not only formally strict but strongly rhythmical, written with the rhythms of music in mind. For Belloc made up his own tunes and sang his verse, in a clear mellifluous voice (again a surprise, one would expect a booming bass). I am allergic to his and Chesterton's cult of drink (for which both duly paid), but can appreciate the romantic feeling for landscape, the sentiment behind 'Ha'nacker Mill':

> Sally is gone that was so kindly,
> Sally is gone from Ha'nacker Hill,

and the Sussex poems, poems of place, Evenlode, Petworth, the South Downs and the sea:

> The channel is up, the little seas are leaping,
>   The tide is making over Arun Bar;
> And there's my boat, where all the rest are sleeping
>   And my companions are.

He had a great gift for friendship, for one whose public stance was so lonely.

Again and again he identified himself with England – and yet:

> England, to me that never have malingered,
>   Nor spoken falsely, nor your flattery used,
> Nor even in my rightful garden lingered: –
>   What have you not refused?

What did he mean by that? I think I understand. In the end he did not belong.

Anyone, especially the young, ought to be able to respond to the fun and rhetoric of the lines to the remote and ineffectual don who dared to attack Chesterton. Or,

> Do you remember an Inn,
> Miranda?
> Do you remember an Inn?
> And the tedding and the spreading
> Of the straw for a bedding,
> And the fleas that tease in the High Pyrenees? . . .

Unforgettable, with one's youth. Or,

> Heretics all, whoever you be,
> In Tarbes or Nîmes, or over the sea,
> You never shall have good words from me . . .

And, come to think of it, they never did. But also when one thinks of it, isn't there something rather silly about it, even as a pose?

> But Catholic men that live upon wine
> Are deep in the water, and frank, and fine;
> Wherever I travel I find it so.

There the dilemma of Belloc is posed: in England he was somehow a fish out of water.

And he was caught in a mesh of contradictions. A rigid, uncompromising Catholic *à l'Irlandaise* he was yet an enthusiast for the French Revolution. He had his reason: the Revolution had guaranteed the land to the peasants. He believed in peasant proprietorship. One of his most successful early books was his life of *Danton* – rhetorical, like Michelet. Perhaps appropriate enough, for Danton was an orator. Myself, I do not much care for revolutionary rabble-rousers, and Danton incited, if he was not responsible for, the September Massacres. Did Belloc never feel that, with the end of the French monarchy, something irreplaceable went out of Fench life? The fracture remained all through the nineteenth century and up to the dissolution of our time. It was more than a break in the social structure, it went deeper than that; France never recovered its integration. The prophetic Burke intuited what came about, and was borne out in his insight that it would end in a military dictatorship. More than the romantic glamour which Burke saw was lost – the poets, men like Alfred de Vigny saw it. I suppose Belloc did not, because he was so little of an aesthete; to anyone who cares for the mainspring of a culture, the loss was irreparable.

Belloc was then a rhetorician, both in his verse and his prose. And the English do not like rhetoric – one reason why they always detested Louis XIV, for all his creation of Versailles, and do not respond to Corneille, or really to Victor Hugo, or even to Châteaubriand. A natural wit, Belloc is at his most brilliant in his epigrams and light verse. He scores a bull's eye in his Newdigate Poem on the Benefits of the Electric Light:

> Aroint thee, Muse! Inspired the poet sings!
> I cannot help observing future things!
> Life is a vale, its paths are dark and rough
> Only because we do not know enough:
> When Science has discovered something more
> We shall be happier than we were before.

He was not to know, when he wrote that, that the 'something more' would be nuclear fission, a nuclear world which gives such reason for being happier than we were before.

I do not know how many generations of children have been amused by his delightful *Cautionary Tales* and *More Beasts for Worse Children*, etc., or today have the wit to enjoy them, for it is the wit that one enjoys. But my young friends in undergraduate days at Oxford were delighted by the lachrymose Lord Lundy, who so disappointed the Duke his aged grandsire, and could recite with him:

'We had intended you to be
The next Prime Minister but three,
The stocks were sold; the Press was squared;
The Middle Class was quite prepared.
But as it is! . . . My language fails!
Go out and govern New South Wales! . . .'
The Aged Patriot groaned and died:
And gracious! how Lord Lundy cried!

In verse as in prose Belloc depicted Edwardian society, half caricature, half satire. Robert Speaight, in his sympathetic biography, seemed to think that this put the old upper class against Belloc. Not a bit of it: they were his proper audience, they enjoyed him most. A mandarin society has a sense of humour and can laugh at itself and its denizens:

Lord Hippo suffered fearful loss
By putting money on a horse
Which he believed, if it were pressed,
Would run faster than the rest.

Lord Finchley on the other hand – and I have known a peer who was an amateur electrician:

Lord Finchley tried to mend the Electric Light
Himself. It struck him dead: And serve him right!
It is the business of the wealthy man
To give employment to the artisan.

In Belloc's Edwardian days the class-structure was still unimpaired, and well it is rendered, in lighter or darker tones, sometimes with sharper edge to its irony, throughout his work. But we can still recognise as contemporary the figure of the Statesman, though it is doubtful whether its representative characters, Welfare State politicians, appreciate the joke:

Insensible and cretinous,
He was admitted ONE OF US.
They therefore, (meaning Them by 'They')
His colleagues of the N.C.A.
The T.U.C., the I.L.P.
Appointed him triumphantly

To bleed the taxes of a clear
200,000 Francs a year
(Swiss), as the necessary man
For Conferences at Lausanne,
Geneva, Basle, Locarno, Berne:

One sees that Belloc's relevance was not confined to the Edwardian age, though that was his heyday. 1914 was the turning point for him, as it was for Kipling, Elgar and so many others. Much of the *joie de vivre*, so abounding in early Belloc, was lost. Survivors have assured me that we have never known since 'ce que c'était que la douceur de vivre!'.

Irony was a natural tone of voice to Belloc; it runs all through his political novels – especially the early ones, *Emmanuel Burden*, *Mr. Clutterbuck's Election*, and *A Change in the Cabinet* – with such consistency that otherwise one would think them simply *tours de force*. As in a way they are: it is an extraordinary achievement to keep it up, to have irony pervading a story from beginning to end. Irony is essentially aristocratic, a weapon of a mandarin society. Demotic societies do not understand it: one reason why it hardly exists in American literature (if at all), and Americans often fail to recognise it. One more element of sophistication to be counted out in contemporary culture.

Political novels are rare in English literature; we have the classics of Disraeli and Trollope, but I cannot think of a single one worth remembering since Belloc's. Of his, *Emmanuel Burden* is the weightiest. It is inspired by Belloc's hatred of the brash imperialism of the South African war, the days of Chartered companies with the corrupt mixing of money and political influence, the social prominence of diamond and gold millionaires, the vulgarity of Edwardian opulence. There are recognisable references to Rhodes and Mercantile (i.e. Rhodes) Scholarships, and Oxford in-jokes of Belloc's roaring Balliol days. Mr Burden walks with his son Cosmo to Kipling Gardens. Kipling was a Rhodes Trustee; Cosmo Lang was a Balliol contemporary, to the fore at the Oxford Union with Belloc.

The story turns on the fraud that is put across the public with the flotation of the bogus M'Korio Company in Africa. The Press is squared to suggest that gold grows beneath the marshes of the M'Korio delta – the Press has to refer to them as lagoons. When the whole scheme is in danger of being shown up, the Government is induced to buy the Company out at 5⅜. 'Mr. Burden did not live to see that great silent scene when the Government announced their intention of buying out the Company. It would have set his foolish doubts at rest, and would have preserved a life of such value to the Empire, to the City, and to the residential portion of South London.' As for Mr Burden, 'the expansion of the British Raj, his faith in its future, the example of so many nations created out of nothing, above all, the remarkable wealth acquired by those who had risked all upon the destiny of the Empire, led him on to boldness'. Innocent, middle-class Mr Burden 'would have felt a very genuine horror at hearing that a Cabinet minister had held, or had been given, such and such shares in a company connected with our Imperial development'.

It is odd that our Leftists today should not recognise that they were anticipated by Belloc. But, after all, is he so very much out of date? What about the ludicrous Ground Nuts scheme of the post-war Labour Government which lost the country millions in East Africa? Who thought up that piece of economic foolery?

We must confront squarely certain strains in Belloc that are dated and put him out of court in the more sensitive and civilised circumstances of our day. 'Mr. Burden acquired, with little thought of gain, the control of such small trade as could be driven with the naked and debased aborigines of a fœtid African river.' One cannot write like that today, even in irony, now that we know that blacks are better than whites. Mr Burden's evil genius is Mr I. Z. Barnett, of whom it is written that 'his birth was a continual drawback: the change of name necessary to his career in England was another: the slight accent which he retained throughout his career a third. We are a conservative and jealous people, and it is with difficulty that we will admit the genius of an alien, even when that genius flatters or would enrich us'.

In the Edwardian age the South African millionaires, the Solly Joels, Barney Barnatos, Oppenheimers, were much to the fore. In several references to Isaacs Belloc did not hesitate to glance at his Liberal colleague, Rufus Isaacs' dealings in Marconi shares, which much embarrassed Asquith's government. Anti-Semitism is highly distasteful to us, who have witnessed the European tragedy to which it has led. Fortunately, it has not been an English inflexion. When Disraeli was being made leader of the Conservative Party it was not objected against him that he was a Jew, but that he was not a landed gentleman. A sensible old Duke there-

upon proposed that he be made one, and Hughenden was bought
for Disraeli to qualify him. Belloc's strain of anti-Semitism is,
again, French; it is like the appalling Charles Maurras, who led
the disgraceful hue-and-cry against the cultivated and noble Léon
Blum. In Paris in the 'thirties one constantly heard the *canards*
about Blum's collection of *argenterie*. Idiots will believe anything;
it is true that Blum's apartment had a fine collection of books,
music, and a grand piano, as I can witness – perhaps enough to
damn him with Philistines of all kinds.

On the other hand, Belloc was capable of turning the joke (too
much for us to stand) against himself. In *Mr. Clutterbuck's Election*
a leading character

> saw Jews everywhere: he not only saw them everywhere, but he
> saw them all in conspiracy . . . . The disease advanced with his
> advancing age; soon all the great family of Arnold were Jews [I
> have myself encountered that piece of silliness]; half the English
> aristocracy had Jewish blood; for a little he would have accused
> the Pope of Rome or the Royal Family itself. Every widespread
> influence, from Freemasonry to the international finance of
> Europe, was Israelite in his eyes.

The influence of Freemasonry was another bee in Belloc's bonnet
– in that, too, entirely French, just like a lot of French Catholics. It
teamed up with their campaign against the anti-clerical legisla-
tion of Combes and the Third Republic, in itself disagreeable
enough. (I sympathise with Péguy's *La Grande Pitié des Eglises de
France.*)

Mr. Clutterbuck's Election is a more light-hearted affair. Mr
Clutterbuck is the kind of nit-wit to whom success comes willy-
nilly – as it never would to Belloc – and he ends up, because money
just increases in his hands, without his doing anything to earn it
(again unlike Belloc), with a knighthood. The process of cheapen-
ing such things with inflation was just beginning. Anyone who has
been through the dreary chores of being selected as a political
candidate and of electioneering will appreciate the truth of Belloc's descriptions. Mr Clutterbuck, a political mug but welcomed
for his money, is gravely summoned before the divisional Executive. 'Of the various functions filled by an Executive, a Committee, a Body of Workers, a Confederation, and a Deputation to
choose in the organisation of our public life, I will not here treat.

The vast machinery of self-government, passionately interesting as it must be to all free men, would take me too far.' Mr Clutterbuck hás little idea of what he is in for – everything happens passively to him, without asking, but he does learn 'the great truth that practical politics depend on compromise'.

It may be doubted whether Belloc ever did; or, though he knew it intellectually, his temperament was too strong – or possibly intellectual pride – to accept it. He knew about intellectual pride too, the vocational conceit of dons and professors. I have never forgotten a passage asking the rhetorical question why they so often stammer, or jabber at the lips, stumble their words, twist their fingers and other oddities – 'it is all because of the sin of intellectual pride, than which there is no sin more offensive to the angels'.

There followed upon Mr Clutterbuck's selection the horrors of electioneering, where he was equally at sea, and equally success-ful, steered through by an *insouciant* Irishman of family, and hence political, connexions. 'In those days the Irish land upon which Sir Daniel had foreclosed was a very ample provision even for onerous social duties in London.' Charley Fitzgerald has 'just that interest in the acquirement of money [Mr Clutterbuck's] which his Irish character perhaps needed'. Charley is related to the vivacious Mary Smith, a cousin of the Prime Minister – in this world everybody is related to everybody else. Mary is an endear-ing no-nonsense aristocrat, who, having married American money and disposed of her husband, is free to pull political strings and steer the enriched and bewildered Clutterbuck into this new world – every member of which 'seemed free to pursue his own appetite or inclination without restraint or form, and yet the whole was bound by just that invisible limit which is the framework of good breeding'. Mary Smith is a good sort, and the Clutterbucks could have no better guide, for 'she knew every face in London, to the number of two hundred or more'.

Such a guide was indispensable to these upward-rising new-rich, for 'the varying strata of society are the cause of endless misunderstandings . . . Every rank in our carefully ordered society has its conventions; one, which will doubtless appear ridiculous to many of my readers, is that which forbids, among the middle classes, the extension of a warm invitation to people whom one never happens to have seen.' Now – 'our public men would accept or reject such an invite as convenience dictated, and would hardly remember whether they had the pleasure of an acquaintance or no.'

Belloc relished these nuances, for, a middle-class man himself, the political world was as open to a man of his talents as it was 'ready to admit to the directing society of a nation those whose prudence and success in business have shown them worthy of undertaking the task of government'. One notices how he addresses his readers; his prose style is a speaking style, rotund and oracular, the oratory of the Oxford Union, where he was the most scintillating of all the stars, and far more successful than in that more artful assembly, the Edwardian House of Commons. It was probably a mistake that he ever went there – there was no Cabinet office for him, as there was for that well-connected noodle, George Mulross Demaine, of *A Change in the Cabinet*, who could hardly put a question in the House, let alone answer one.

However, Belloc as a writer had ways of getting his own back and being remembered when these fixtures on the public scene would be forgotten within months, or weeks, of their removal.

> There exists a sound rule of public administration in this country which forbids a Cabinet Minister to hold any public directorship at the same time as his official post. Indeed it is this rule which renders it usual for a couple of men upon opposite sides of the House to come to an arrangement whereby the one shall be Director while his colleague is in office, lest important commercial affairs should be neglected through the too rigid application of what is in principle so excellent a rule.

(Today, in default of such arrangements they can make hundreds of thousands from their Memoirs, the newspapers, or TV appearances. In the Welfare State, money still talks – especially among its directors and spiritual leaders.)

A difference is that, though Belloc's colleagues would never make him a Cabinet Minister – he would have been wasted as such – *they* could appreciate the irony, the jokes at their expense. Perhaps even at the expense of the English: 'We are not a logical people; we refuse to be bound by the logical syllogisms so popular with the lower races of Europe, and especially among the dying Latin nations.' Belloc's House of Commons contained his fellows in wit and gifts – members of the Souls like Balfour, George Wyndham, and Curzon, F. E. Smith and the young Winston Churchill, Asquith and Augustine Birrell, the Cecils, Lord Robert and Lord Hugh. How many of such people are there today?

The cardinal statement of Belloc's position in regard to modern society is *The Servile State* (1912), which retains some relevance today in its diagnosis, if not in the programme it puts forward. Belloc saw as clearly as any Marxist that the tide in industrial society was set towards collectivism. He thought, like Marx, that there was an inherent instability in Capitalism, and he compared it, to its disadvantage, with the Middle Ages and the 'free' peasantry. He and Chesterton nursed a highly romantic view of the Middle Ages, Merrie England and all that. In fact, the peasantry were tied to the land, to the servitude of rendering services to their lords; poverty and recurrent famine were rife, plague, disease, insanitary conditions – life was brutish and short. One has some idea of what it was like from conditions in Russia before the emancipation of the serfs; one glimpses it in the novels of Dostoievsky.

Belloc thought that modern industrial society was heading for the servile state under the direction of the capitalist; the capitalist was the enemy. He posed a dilemma –

> if you were to approach those millions of families now living at a wage, with the proposal for a contract of service for life, guaranteeing them employment at his usual full wage, how many would refuse? Such a contract would, of course, involve a loss of freedom ... If we ask ourselves how many men would prefer freedom to such a life-contract, no-one can deny that the answer is: 'Very few would refuse it'. That is the key to the whole matter.

Here we see the clue to Belloc's idealist Radicalism. 'Within the memory of people still living a sufficient number of Englishmen were owning (as small freeholders, small masters, etc.) to give to the institution of property coupled with freedom a very vivid effect upon the popular mind . . . I have myself spoken, when I was a boy, to old labourers in the neighbourhood of Oxford who had risked their skins in armed protest against the enclosure of certain commons' – this would be the pitiful rising against enclosures on Otmoor. And Belloc appealed to the memories of small-loom weavers in their Lancashire cottages – with no realisation of the below-subsistence conditions they endured. Belloc's ideal of freedom in the past was much of a mirage.

What of the future? Communist countries know the fatal truth that the masses don't care about freedom (they leave that to unpopular minority-minded dissidents); all the masses care about is wage-increases, i.e. material objects, gadgets, radio and TV sets, time off work for mass-leisure, Bingo-mania, etc. Communist Russia deliberately allows them unlimited drink; in Britain we might say TV is the opium of the people, it is certainly their religion.

Belloc's ideal of small proprietorship in land and small individual ownership in industry reflects again his French and Irish background. Redistribution of property to that end – the 'distributist' state, with its apparatus of gilds – was certainly fanciful in English conditions, or those of any other industrial society. The set of the tide was all the other way, whether desirable or not. He thought that the English still had a choice, though they would not listen to him. A more sceptical mind would see that men have little in the way of choice. The tides move with the moon – all that men can do is to adapt them a little here and there. Profound social movements are ineluctable, if not inevitable; there is little we can do about them.

The collectivist tide has set even more strongly than Belloc could have foreseen in his own time, when he pursued the faint hope that it could be reversed. Things have gone in quite the other direction. He saw then that 'to increase the weekly stipend of the wage-earner is an object which they vividly appreciate and pursue. To make him cease to be a wage-earner is an object that would seem to them entirely outside the realities of life.' It certainly was, and is. The Trade Union objective may be described as an eleemosynary one, the end the Welfare State in which everybody expects to be supported by it. And what, Belloc asks, 'of the gambling chance which the Capitalist system, with its necessary condition of freedom, permits to the proletarian of escaping from his proletariat conditions?' In the nineteenth century there was always the chance of emigrating to better oneself. The consequence of the Welfare State has been the reverse – the flooding in of aliens who have never had it so good, with the dilution of the national strain and vigour.

Belloc was anti-capitalist. He did not apparently reflect on the *cultural* consequences of taxing the old governing classes out of existence, with the felling of hundreds of country mansions and town houses, the dispersal of art objects, pictures, books, silver, china, manuscripts – a denuded England, impoverished of what was distinguished in its cultural heritage. The capitalist today makes his millions by catering for the demand of the masses in a consumptionist society, multiple stores, supermarkets, by property deals, TV, juke-box, or Bingo-hall ownership. Any improvement?

Belloc returned to the charge in a later book, *The Crisis of our Civilisation*, in which he tried to bolster his case with a good deal of dubious history, regarding civilisation as having taken a wrong turning, of course, with the Reformation. In truth, the Reformation led to an immense expansion of economic energies, particularly noticeable in England and Holland. It is difficult to have much patience with Belloc as an historian, or to render him justice. I suppose we should allow him credit for his contradiction of the nineteenth-century Teutonists who saw the very diverse origins of Britain simply in the Germanic *Ur-wald* – Freeman and Stubbs and Green – and for seeing our history more in the perspective of Rome and the Mediterranean, and all that we owed to them for civilisation and culture. But Belloc laid it down as dogma, without going into the evidences or balancing his conclusions. The impact of his historical writing can hardly, on balance, be considered a good one. Its snap judgements about the Reformation and its personalities – Elizabeth I, for example – had the deleterious effect of encouraging writers in the lower *échelons* of the Catholic press to still more biased views. A type like Hugh Ross Williamson built up a façade which was totally at variance with the truth; it had its influence on better writers, Evelyn Waugh, for example, who began to have his doubts by the end.

It may be doubted whether Belloc ever doubted, or did his homework; he certainly never did enough reading for an historian. He was too ready with summary, ill-considered judgements, such as – 'Trevelyan, a typical product of the highly anti-Catholic English universities and governing class'. Actually, as I know, Trevelyan was very pleased to have a good Catholic historian, a monk to boot – Dom David Knowles – to succeed him as Regius Professor at Cambridge. 'As for Trevelyan, he is, of course, nothing more than the echo of his great-uncle Macaulay.' There was a great deal more to G. M. Trevelyan than that – and, *per contra*, Dom David Knowles wrote one of the most perceptive and sympathetic portraits of Macaulay. This example is only one of many of the way in which Belloc would throw away the respect of his fellow writers for the man of genius and original achievement that he was. I used to think that he threw away more genius in his work than most writers have as their original endowment. A Frenchman summed up Belloc's singular perversity of mind: 'J'avais l'impression d'un prophète qui se trompe toujours'.

Perhaps this is taking it too far. But to his Roman dogmatism, we all prefer his *Path to Rome*, to his absurd Ultramontanism, his topographical books that took him across and over the mountains. *The Path to Rome* was an early success, and many think it his best for it has all the gusto, the sheer joy in living his young manhood calls up in so many fields, tramping, riding, sailing, arguing, politicising, drinking, praying. I like its brisk Preface, dismissing the silly habit of writers introducing in prefaces 'a mass of nincompoops of whom no one ever heard, and saying "my thanks are due to such and such" all in a litany, as though anyone cared a farthing for the rats'. American academics should note this, with their habit of wasting pages of good paper on citing everybody down to their typist, the taximan who took them to the Public Record Office (if they did not go by bus), and their wives who put up with them. *Verb. sap.*, if they know what that means.

Belloc wrote several admirable travel-books, *The Pyrenees, Paris, The Old Road, Stane Street*. The most moving, I think, is *The Four Men* (1912): a record of those last days when it was possible to walk the length of Sussex, along downs and lanes, through woods and shaws, calling at rustic inns, singing as he went with those shadows, his companions, before the world was polluted by petrol. Those were his days and ways, that was his *floruit*. It is really a strange, autumnal book, touched by melancholy and poetry, the inner Belloc, quiet and questing, which he exposed too rarely.

Renée Haynes, daughter of one of his many friends, properly praises his essays on the French Renaissance, and regrets that he did not write more literary criticism.[1] I do not: far too much 'criticism' in the world today: Belloc was a creator, not a critic. When one considers the mass of 'criticism' devoted to less important writers! – to Forster, for instance, who had much less significant things to say (except on one subject, where Belloc was conventional and prudish, an Irish Puritan). Belloc was a man of much more powerful and diverse genius, while the literary world gives more attention to altogether less significant spirits. The booksellers are better indicators: Belloc has a faithful following, and his best books are 'collected'. A rarity, *The Highway and its Vehicles*, was offered at Oxford recently for £77.

Paradoxically, Forster speaks more to me than Belloc does; mere justice of mind compels me to recognise which was the more important writer.

NOTE

1.   Renée Haynes, *Hilaire Belloc* (*Writers and their Work*, No. 35).

THE POETRY OF JOHN BETJEMAN

The other day I came across a snooty dismissal of Betjeman's poetry by an unmemorable critic, as just 'social verse'. Anyone can appreciate the element of social verse in Betjeman, what used to be described, in more cultivated days, as *vers de société*, the wit and humour, the fun and frolics, the gentle satire. Sometimes the poem is specifically put forth as such – as with, 'How to Get On in Society':

'Phone for the fish-knives, Norman. . . .

But I hope to show that there is more, far more, in Betjeman than meets the eye.

Even the intellectual admirers of his poetry, those who have written about it – the late Lord Birkenhead and John Sparrow, Raymond Mortimer and Mr A. P. Jones – miss some of the wider and deeper aspects of his poetry, those that have made him something of a cult-hero in our time, with an appeal to the heart of a whole people, here and beyond. That takes some explaining, and it seems to me that they do not explain it.

The essential point they miss is that Betjeman is a complete poet – *the whole of life is in his poetry*. There is not only what appeals to intellectuals, the wit and sophistication, the irony and private jokes, the sheer cleverness and virtuosity; besides the sophistication is simplicity, along with irony is sentiment and even sentimentality (why not?). In his poetry he is not afraid to express *every*thing – failure of nerve before an operation ('A Real Fright'), religious belief alongside of doubt; remorse and repentance;

sympathy for all sorts and conditions of people – an elderly woman dying in hospital, an upper-class gent, of Devonshire Street W1, condemned to death by his surgeon:

> No hope. And the X-ray photographs under his arm
>   Confirm the message.

From early on there is the compassion that swells to indignation, as in the incident in the life of Ebenezer Jones, the young poet, when a brute of a schoolmaster flung a perishing lurcher dog out of his school:

> Look on and jeer! Not Satan's thunder-quake
> Can cause the mighty walls of Heaven to shake
> As now they do, to hear a boy's heart break.

The ubiquitous interest in churches, architectural and ritualistic, High and Low (even Nonconformist chapels get a sympathetic tribute), in all the trappings, incense and gaslight, the musty smell of hassocks and cassocks, leads on to something deeper and more philosophic, though Betjeman would eschew the word.

Years ago I remember his telling me that he could remember visually a dozen or fifteen churches in a day (I doubt if I could remember half a dozen distinctly); and I recall the play-acting in a church porch, that was not in fact all play-acting, the excitement, hand on the door: 'What will it be like inside? What shall we find?'

In the poems this deepens into the mixture of religious belief and doubt, a faltering hope that is perhaps all that a modern mind can command (like doubting Thomas: 'Lord, strengthen Thou my unbelief') – in 'Christmas', for example:

> And is it true? And is it true,
> This most tremendous tale of all,
> Seen in a stained-glass window's hue,
> A Baby in an ox's stall?
> The Maker of the stars and sea
> Become a Child on earth for me?

That is about all that anyone could say today, as far as anyone could go – perhaps rather farther.

Anyhow, here the poet has reaped his reward – as Eliot did – in the whole-hearted support of the C. of E. in return. It is something to have a Church behind one as a writer (something that this 'flying buttress' of the Church, as G. M. Trevelyan used to describe himself, could never hope for): another element well deserved in the nation-wide appeal of the poet.

On the technical side there is the astonishing virtuosity of the metres, the variety and originality of the rhymes. I admire almost equally Betjeman's command of blank verse; that moving verse-autobiography, *Summoned by Bells*, is almost wholly in blank verse, with rhymed pieces interspersed. But – something that too many contemporary poets overlook – unrhymed and unmetrical verse is much less memorable, that is, it is much less easy to remember, does not naturally wind its way into one's memory as regular, rhymed verse does. This is apart from the consideration that most of these 'contemporary' poets can't write in regular metre and rhyme anyway. (I similarly respect much less 'abstract' artists who cannot draw, or 'contemporary' composers who have no melody in their souls.)

Betjeman can do both, an expert, natural metrist who has a recognisable command of blank verse and *vers libre* when he chooses (infrequently enough). A consideration of wider import: he can write both poetry *and* verse (an indispensable qualification for a Poet Laureate, by the way). These are by no means the same thing. A well-known, and candid, versifier confessed to me that, though he had written thousands of lines of verse, he had not been able to write one line of poetry. They arise from two quite different processes: verse from the intellectual, even ratiocinative, faculty; poetry from deeper levels of the consciousness, and the subconscious, from the whole man, heart and mind.

Even in these technical matters, Betjeman again is not afraid – as I should be – to use cockney rhymes; a cockney himself, they are true to him, authentic with him. Many rare words occur up and down his poetry – some of them architectural, that bespeak his lucky apprenticeship on an architectural review. And he is not afraid to invent a word when he needs one – 'coniferously', for example, appropriately for a Surrey garden. Or there is 'obsequations' in the poem in memory of an old Pembroke don at Oxford – a masterpiece of technical virtuosity:

> They remember, as the coffin to its final obsequations
> Leaves the gates,

Buzz of bees in window boxes on their summer ministrations,
Kitchen din,
Cups and plates,
And the getting of bump-suppers for the long-dead generations
Coming in
From Eights.

The word 'obsequations' doesn't exist as a word in my *Shorter Oxford English Dictionary* (in two fat volumes); I do not possess the longer in twenty volumes, marooned as I am on my Cornish headland.

What immense variety in place, subject and atmosphere his poetry offers, what a span it covers! First and foremost London in every mood and aspect, churches, railways and railway stations, clubs and offices and occupations. I love his poem on being sacked from his job as literary editor of *Time and Tide*:

And though I admire
Your work for me, John, yet the need to increase circulation
Means you must retire:
An outlook more global than yours is the qualification
I really require.

I reveal no close secret when I say that that is the late Lady Rhondda speaking – and how it hits off that impossible, rather absurd woman to a 't'.

If London, where he was born and bred, and has spent most of his life, comes first, certainly Cornwall comes second. London, Cornwall and Oxford occupy almost the whole of *Summoned by Bells*; but the Cornish poems – and there are many of them – are among his most moving. So many of them are about childhood; to retain the inspiration of childhood and to be able to express it in later life is a poet's gift. Third come the Oxford poems, more varied and mixed, facetious and comic turns along with the serious ones. Next comes Berkshire – the church bells of Wantage and Uffington, the horses and horse-riding of Upper Lambourne. All the counties around London get their poems: coniferous Surrey, afternoon tennis and evenings at the golf club, driving

Into nine-o'clock Camberley, heavy with bells
And mushroomy, pine-woody, evergreen smells.

So too Hertfordshire and Middlesex, Essex, Suffolk, Kent – if only Margate; then farther afield to Lincolnshire:

> Kirkby with Muckby-cum-Sparrowby-cum-Spinx
> Is down a long lane in the county of Lincs.

And so around to Staffordshire and Worcestershire, Devon ('Exeter'), Somerset and back to Hampshire; shooting up to Norfolk and even to Yorkshire, with 'The Licorice Fields at Pontefract' (who had ever heard of them, until put into poetry?). Even Cambridge gets a mention, with 'Sunday Morning, King's Cambridge'.

There are a few poems about Wales, and quite a number devoted to Ireland. The Irish poems are among the oddest and, in a way, most idiosyncratic: Betjeman caricaturing himself, seeing himself in that cracked mirror; though the seedy side of Irish life, the remnants of the broken-down Anglo-Irish Ascendancy, speaks authentically enough to the sense (and smell) of romantic decay. These are not my favourites among the topographical poems; the Cornish ones are, for they are among the best poems about Cornwall ever written (and by a non-Cornishman).

As a preface to *Old Lights for New Chancels*, Betjeman makes a statement about topographical verse, one of the best pieces of criticism I know. (He does not waste time 'criticising' poetry, any more than Philip Larkin does: he writes it). As a topographical poet myself – but even more lest anyone thinks that my love for Betjeman leaves me incapable of criticising – I am going to take issue with him here. 'I find,' he says, 'with this absurd topographical predilection, hardly any pleasure in the Elizabethans.' Really, Sir John – and Michael Drayton one of the greatest of topographical poets! Have you never read his *Polyolbion*?

He puts forward an excuse – 'the excessive reverence' for that age 'from unsympathetic "tutors"'. That means C. S. Lewis. But Betjeman gets his own back in his 'May-Day Song for North Oxford':

> Oh! earnest ethical search
> For the wide high-table *logos* of St C. S. Lewis's Church;

and

> Objectively, our Common Room
> Is like a small Athenian State –

> Except for Lewis: he's all right,
> But do you think he's *quite* first rate?

– still more when the Poet Laureate received an honorary docto-
rate from his old university – which had sent him down – and he
saw the painted clouds of the Sheldonian sky open to reveal the
surprise on the face of his former tutor.

All the same he cannot be excused (by this Oxford don) for
failing to appreciate Shakespeare as a topographical poet: the
citations of the Warwickshire countryside in *The Taming of the
Shrew*; the Forest of Arden itself in *As You Like It*; the marvellous
scenes with Justice Shallow in his Cotswold garden. Or what
about Shakespeare's London scenes – the wonderful transcripts of
Elizabethan life, at the Boar's Head in East Cheap? Or, for that
matter, Ben Jonson's London, in *The Alchemist* and *Bartholomew
Fair*; or both London ('Sweet Thames, run softly till I end my
song') and Ireland in Spenser?

C. S. Lewis may have much to answer for, and Betjeman's was
always a gentle spirit; but the Poet Laureate should have got over
that bullying Ulster dogmatist by this time.

Since admiration has not mesmerised me into critical imbecili-
ty, perhaps I may dare to return to appreciation. Betjeman is not
afraid to express some of the deepest, most intimate and distress-
ing of human feelings. In the poem 'Remorse', he writes:

> She whom I loved and left is no longer there . . .

> But my neglect and unkindness – to lose the sight of them
> I would listen even again to that labouring breath.

Or, walking the Norfolk lanes, remembering his father:

> Time, bring back
> The rapturous ignorance of long ago,
> The peace, before the dreadful daylight starts,
> Of unkept promises and broken hearts.

And there is the touching poem on his own child when ill:

> So looked my father at the last
> Right in my soul, before he died. . . .

My father looked at me and died
Before my soul made full reply.
Lord, leave this other Light alight –
Oh, little body, do not die.

Some of us who write can hardly summon up the courage to express these innermost things. A lesser poet (though an admirable writer), my old friend Q, was too shy to do so; a greater poet, Kipling, could and did.

The width and depth of Betjeman's sympathies impress a solitary writer most. Perhaps, in the end, each and every soul is solitary, face to face with the mystery of life. But Betjeman is a family man, with normal human affections for children and friends – to a degree not given to many poets. I have always found most poignant the nostalgia for childhood and innocence of 'Trebetherick':

Then roller into roller curled
And thundered down the rocky bay,
And we were in a water-world
Of rain and blizzard, sea and spray,
And one against the other hurled
We struggled round to Greenaway.
Blesséd be St Enodoc, blesséd be the wave,
Blesséd be the springy turf, we pray, pray to thee,
Ask for our children all the happy days you gave
To Ralph, Vasey, Alastair, Biddy, John and me.

And there are just the friends, or old acquaintances:

Where is Anne Channel who loved this place the best,
With her tense blue eyes and her shopping-bag falling apart,
And her racy gossip and nineteen-twenty zest,
And that warmth of heart?

Where's Roland, easing his most unwieldy car
With its load of golf-clubs, backwards into the lane?

This should give him a fellow-feeling for Shakespeare, who has given us *his* verse-autobiography in the Sonnets:

When to the sessions of sweet silent thought
I summon up remembrance of things past . . .
Then can I drown an eye, unus'd to flow,
For precious friends hid in death's dateless night,
And weep afresh love's long since cancell'd woe,
And moan the expense of many a vanish'd sight

There you have the two poets, the Elizabethan not so far from us, or from his present-day fellow: both family men, children, with normal social affections and ties – and this is why they have the common appeal to the great heart of the people.

There is besides an extraordinary width of human interests. Betjeman began by presenting himself as an eccentric, with his passion for churches, Anglo-Catholic congresses, gaslight and steam-trains. But what more normal for thousands of boys than a passion for railways, or, for a great many public school boys – like the 'rather dirty Wykehamist' who 'settles down to Norman fonts' – for architecture? (John *was* a bit eccentric in his devotion to Archibald, the teddy-bear, which he carried into matrimony – but doesn't that make him all the more lovable?) And the games! – the tennis in a Surrey garden, with 'Pam, you great big mountainous sports girl'; golf at St Enodoc; sailing with Father on the Norfolk Broads; church-crawling on a bicycle down hundreds of lanes; motor-cars – I have never known one more dilapidated, or more full of character, than that in which John took me across Shakespeare's Cotswolds to introduce me to Cheltenham. (There follows a poem about Cheltenham, to tease Maurice Bowra, who would prefer to have been an Etonian, or at least a Wykehamist – as Sparrowby in Lincolnshire is a tease for John Sparrow. The poems are full of private games.) We even hear of billiards and other deleterious sports.

For all is not so simple as meets the eye. As early as 'The Arrest of Oscar Wilde at the Cadogan Hotel' sympathy declared itself for that Other Side to life, unmentionable for Lord Tennyson, despite the intensity of his feelings for Arthur Hallam. And so compelling is the poet's angle of vision, so compulsive his expression of it, that I never pass the Cadogan Hotel without remembering. Or there is the recent poem, 'Shattered Image' in *A Nip in the Air*, a marvellous conjuring-up of an all too frequent human situation – the cruelty and anxiety, the failure of friends, the indifference to a life wrecked. Whatever his beliefs – and, unlike his Oxford tutor,

Betjeman is no dogmatist – the poet's is a Christian soul. On a lighter plane we have the unpublished epitaph on Tom Driberg, always solemnly thanked in prefaces as Thomas Edward Neil Driberg (for his grammar!):

> The first and last Lord Bradwell was to me
> A paragon of Socialist integrity. . . .

There they all are, those amusing, carefree Oxford friends, the nostalgia for those good old days, a freer, more enjoyable society. For the poet's attitude towards the 'modern' society of which he is the Laureate is no less disgustful than mine, though more kindly expressed – except in 'Slough'. (Where he writes of 'brick-built breeding boxes' in a far overcrowded island, I am apt to think (and sometimes speak) of 'the f.h's of the I.P.').

The point is that in our Poet Laureate all is not so simple as people think. To anyone who catches all the private jokes and arcane hints – no one can know them all – a new dimension again is opened up. Even I, who have lived much of my life on the margin of John's acquaintance, though with an eye open, find the poetry further enriched, the fun enhanced.

Here then is the clue to the paradox – that the poet who began as an esoteric taste of the few should end up as the Poet of the People, read and heard and appreciated by hundreds of thousands, when the intellectual establishment of the day has all but killed the response to poetry in the general public. It is not only that television has made the Laureate a cult-figure – though here too he is a born actor, of a sophisticated simplicity, of a carefully considered and deliberate naturalness, an aesthete, with that irresistibly plummy voice of an archdeacon or canon-in-residence. It is that, underneath all this, underneath the fun and the jokes, public and private, the sophistication and wit – which is what the intellectuals appreciate, though it takes a practising poet to appreciate the metrical and verbal dexterity – there is the whole of life; and hence no more *complete* poet than our Poet Laureate.

FLANNERY O'CONNOR – A GENIUS OF THE SOUTH

The best new literary experience that I have had in years of going to America has been the work of Flannery O'Connor. She is already recognised as a classic over there, though not wholly understood. Outside she is as yet hardly known. But she should be. I regard Flannery O'Connor as comparable with Emily Brontë. Pure genius which, in a short life, achieved absolute expression in art; an unflinching view of life which revealed alike its tragedy and its poetry, penetrated by the sense of the mystery behind it all; disciplined by an uncompromising stoicism. Emily Brontë may have had more poetry; Flannery O'Connor had much more humour.

The Americans think of her as a humorous writer; in fact she was a tragic ironist – and that they rarely understand. Then, too, she was a Catholic, but lived in the Bible Belt of the Protestant South: it gave her her difference, her identity, besides the extraordinary, outrageous subjects that astonish because they are authentic. She realised that character reveals itself in extreme situations: it is the strange encounters that appeal to the deeper levels of imagination of the real writer, 'for whom the ordinary aspects of daily life prove to be no great fictional interest'.

She was probably the greatest short-story writer of our time. The fact that her genius was for the *short* story does not deny her greatness, any more than it does with Chekhov or Maupassant. Her volume of Collected Stories – which contain some of the most remarkable ever written – should be published in Britain. She is already recognised as a classic. This volume of her non-fiction[1] is a good introduction to her mind – it contains characteristic things – but is subsidiary to her main work.

The book begins with her famous account of 'The King of the Birds', the peacocks she bred in Georgia; it ends with a 'Memoir of Mary Ann', the happy record of a child born with a facial cancer, never daunted by life. The range is from the peacock in his pride, with 'the unfurled map of the universe floating by', to the Communion of Saints.

In between are her comments on the life and literature of our time, fearless and ruthless, deadly on the target.

There are, first, the values that the United States stands for, the archetype of a modern country in the modern world. 'The writer who emphasises spiritual values,' she says, 'is very likely to take the darkest view of what he sees in this country today. For him, the fact that we are the most powerful and the wealthiest nation in the world doesn't mean a thing in any positive sense.' That was written during the self-satisfied euphoria of the post-war period. Things have since caught up with what she so harshly diagnosed. When driven to answer the question put by a *Life* editorial, 'Who speaks for America today?', her answer was: the Advertising Agencies.

As against such authorities she has other standards: 'in the long run, a people is known, not by its statements or its statistics, but by the stories it tells.'

As for American writing in general, the popular clichés that do duty for 'criticism', the beloved sentimentalities that set up schools for 'creative writing' in the universities, the writers that a public conditioned by advertising buy in millions – they are all shot down without pity in the briefest space.

'Everywhere I go I'm asked if I think the universities stifle writers. My opinion is that they don't stifle enough of them. It is a fact that if, either by nature or training, these people can learn to write badly enough, they can make a great deal of money.'

Asked to examine the products of such a school of 'creative writing' at one college, she reports that the stories 'might all have originated in some synthetic place that could have been anywhere or nowhere. These stories hadn't been influenced by the outside world at all, only by the television.' And the language? 'The characters spoke as if they had never heard any kind of language except what came out of a television set.'

Her characters speak with authenticity and power, because they speak from a real place – the South. She admits that to belong to a region is 'to declare a limitation, but one which, like all limitations, is a gateway to reality.' For all the extremism of her imagination, the strange forms of experience she observed, her emphasis is on reality and the concrete. Not for her the vapid theorising of critics: 'if there is any value in hearing writers talk, it will be in hearing what they can witness to and not what they can theorise about.' A literary mandarin like Van Wyck Brooks gets his comeuppance just as much as the million-salesmen like James Jones or Thomes Wolfe, or the San Francisco school from Henry Miller downwards. From these 'you may have got the impression that the first thing you must do in order to be an artist is to loose yourself from the bonds of reason, and thereafter anything that rolls off the top of your head will be of great value.'

A salutary corrective. For her writing involved as much discipline, not without an element of asceticism, as living itself. 'To know oneself is to know one's region. It is also to know the world; and it is also, paradoxically, a form of exile from that world.' It is very much what Eliot thought, and it might be Eliot himself writing when she sums up: 'The writer operates at a peculiar cross-roads where time and place and eternity somehow meet. His problem is to find that location.'

Flannery O'Connor's own work is inspired by the sense of the mystery of the human condition, of our place in the universe, the tragedy of our state without some redeeming power. She herself was so profoundly a Catholic that she did not obtrude it and so diminish the artistic effect, as with Graham Greene and Evelyn Waugh. (She was aware of this defect.)

But it placed her in profound opposition to the superficial rationalism of contemporary society and the humbug it talks to paper over the cracks and crevices. Since the eighteenth century, i.e. since the American Revolution with its democratic optimism, 'the popular spirit of each succeeding age has tended more and more to the view that the ills and mysteries of life will eventually fall before the scientific advances of man: a belief that is still going strong, even though this is the first generation to face total extinction because of these advances.'

There is the real difference between this and all preceding ages: for the first time, an end may be put to the human experiment. She herself realised, like the reflective Christian she was, that the human experiment is a fairly recent development in the history of the world.

As for the ills of life – she never once mentions that she herself was dying from incurable lupus; she was dead before forty. There was no room for self-pity in that courageous spirit: she too could have written,

No coward soul is mine.

As for the contemporary middle-class humbug about 'compassion' – 'Compassion is a word that sounds good in anybody's mouth and which no book-jacket can do without . . . Usually I think what is meant by it is that the writer excuses all human weakness because human weakness is human.'

No weakness anywhere in her, purified and tried in the fire of an anguished body – never a word of complaint. 'Of course, the ability to create life with words is essentially a gift. If you have it in the first place, you can develop it; if you don't have it, you might as well forget it.' – A useful piece of advice to a Writers' Conference, or a PEN discussion. She herself admits to a very high opinion of the art of writing, but 'a very low opinion of what is called the "average" reader'.

The real writer 'knows that the survival of his work depends upon an integrity that eliminates fashion from his considerations'. The historian can corroborate that nothing dates so quickly as the contemporary. And of course she is right that it is never the business of the first-rate to satisfy the requirements of the third-rate. In consequence she has been attacked by the third-rate for not adhering to *their* commonplace view of life, the inveterate American democratic optimism in its uncomprehending and callow superficiality – and amid all the horrors of the twentieth century! Henry Adams was far nearer the truth, and a more penetrating prophet, than Thomas Jefferson.

The novelist, she says, 'must speak as he writes – with the whole personality.' Is this not equally true for the historian? 'Great fiction involves the whole range of human judgement.' Is this not equally true of great history? It is certainly true of the great historians – evidently not of the little.

Though penetrated by the sense of the mystery of life, Flannery O'Connor was not a mystic, but a poetic realist. For her the mystery of human personality expressed itself in the concrete, the character in the action and the words.

From the moment I first read a page of her work I realised, as a fellow-craftsman, here was a master.

I do not often confess to being humble, but the combination of her genius and her spirit has ground me to humility. There are places in her work – glimpses of them in this book – into which I dare not venture.

NOTE

1.   Flannery O'Connor, *Mystery and Manners: Occasional Prose* (Faber).

II

BRITANNICA OR AMERICANA?

With a flourish of trumpets and an American-style promotion-campaign, years of advance publicity – with the adventitious feature of a breach with Sir William Haley who went to Chicago to help to direct the venture, but eventually left it and whose name does not appear – the new edition of the *Encyclopaedia Britannica* has at last made its appearance in thirty volumes.[1] Unlike Aldous Huxley, who usually travelled with a volume of an encyclopaedia for company, I am not encyclopaedia-minded. My attitude is strictly utilitarian; I keep an encyclopaedia just to look things up in – I do not require it for my spiritual or moral, or even intellectual, welfare. I do not need to be told what I am to think about this or that; no doubt some people do, and here they will find it.

For, what is new about this Encyclopaedia and no doubt what the dispute was about, is that it begins with an introductory volume, called *Propaedia,* which purports to sum up the whole of modern knowledge, under one scheme, for your benefit. It is, in fact, a very American idea, and the whole emphasis of the work is American and rather Jewish. It is none the worse for that – we must take the whole outfit on its merits – but it does give it its recognisable character.

Since I am appreciative of the work, rather than critical, I must declare my own bias: I am pro-American by sentiment, and pro-Jewish by conviction. But, while they were about it, why didn't the fabricators call it the 'American Encyclopaedia'? This ranks as the fifteenth edition of the old *Britannica.* We are told that it represents 'a revolution in encyclopaedia making. This work combines the reference and education functions'. This is just promotion language for its marking a new departure in the character of the *Britannica.* What I want from an encyclopaedia is information; it is very useful, and even interesting, to have all this modern knowledge. Let us give the debatable *Propaedia* the benefit of the doubt and discuss it. It gives us the 'Circle of Modern Knowledge' in ten sections. These are: 1, Matter and Energy. 2, The Earth. 3, Life on Earth. 4, Human Life. 5, Human Society. 6, Art. 7, Technology. 8, Religion. 9, The History of Mankind. 10, The Branches of Knowledge.

A little thought serves to show that this is not a very logical or well thought out scheme. (The editors use the word schema, for English scheme – unnecessarily: they would.) The first five sections are in good logical sequence; but after 5, Human Society, there should naturally follow as 6, The History of Mankind. Then should come, as 7, The Branches of Knowledge; the next should be Technology, as a particular application. Then should follow Religion, and finally Art, since these enter into the realm of values, the summit of man's achievement, and his redemption from the mud, the struggle for survival.

Americans, bogged down in the realm of materialism while nattering about ethics, are deeply wanting about real values – as Henry Adams, Henry James, Edith Wharton and Santayana, or Whistler, Sargent and Berenson, Eliot, Frost and Pound all felt, and left the country for long periods, some of them altogether. And it is well known that American academics cannot write the language very well – as one sees from the statement of editorial policy, after announcing that the first principle should be readability and intelligibility. This follows: 'Articles should therefore be positioned [sc. placed] at a level of generality above that of purely specialised detail and should be characterised by an appropriately reduced density of detail [!] rather than by an apparent determination to pack everything known about a subject into an allotted space.'

This, translated into English, might read: 'Articles should be general, with relevant detail, and not too specialised'. Americans, with over two thousand articles, have contributed twice the number of articles by the British (some one thousand), most of the editors enjoying foreign, many of them Jewish, names. Considering this, it is surprising that the new *Britannica* is as readable as it is. I do not think that that will be much appreciated in France, where intellectual standards prevail, or used to prevail – one can imagine how contemptuous De Gaulle would have been: he thought Americans rather callow.

The American inflexion and options are everywhere evident. There is no objection to that in itself; after all, America is immeasurably more important than Britain in the world today: the question is simply one of intellectual standards. A good, concise article on a man of genius, Cardinal Newman, is followed by one occupying more space on the subject of 'New Thought', of which the proponent was one Phineas P. Quimby. Have you ever heard of this great man, or the electrifying movement of thought to which he gave rise? It is thus characterised: 'though it is very difficult to generalise about the social and ethical consequences of New Thought, there is evidence, as suggested by its popular literature, that New Thought has been individualistic in its ethical concerns. It has attempted to promote a positive personal attitude towards life and to encourage a success mentality in an industrialised America.' In other words, it is a characteristic expression of American humbug, of no intellectual importance or value whatever – and one can think of similar expressions on a vastly wider scale, spreading round the world along with America's power in it, invented by females of low-grade intellectual standards, or none, but with great promotional ability, who would be held in contempt by women of such real standards as Edith Wharton, Willa Cather or Flannery O'Connor.

These women, because their work has first-class quality, are written down and receive short shrift. (The editors can look up the meaning of the word 'shrift' in a good English dictionary.) The fact is that the standards of these encyclopaedists are second rate. They are American academic popularisers – in the good sense of the word as well as the less good. They are middle-of-the-road men, of no real distinction or original achievement in themselves, who naturally opt at every point for people whom the mass-media feature, or some up to date *claque* would be back. But – encyclopaedists beware – nothing dates so quickly as up-to-date popular choices.

Take the fatuous over-estimation of the muddled Sartre, largely because he is so much to the fore in the newspapers and literary journalism. He appears twice over, under Literature and Thought. We are solemnly told that 'he, more than any other philosopher, has drawn attention to individual freedom and creativity.' What rubbish! – and this of a man who wrote that Soviet Russia was the realisation of human freedom on earth. When disillusioned of what a grain of commonsense should have told him was nonsense, he could then write another book taking the opposite line. 'With the entry of the Soviet tanks into Budapest in 1956, however, Sartre's hopes in Communism were sadly crushed.' Any person of sense could have told this clever ass what to expect. We learn, however, that 'he still believed that Marxism is the only philosophy for the current times'. In other words, he is not to be taken seriously. A truly great Frenchman, De Gaulle, showed how little real importance intellectuals have, even in France.

But this is not my point. The point is that Montherlant was a far better writer than Sartre, a better novelist and a better dramatist: he was, in the years before his death, probably the greatest European writer alive. The encyclopaedists of Chicago, with their derivative second-rate standards simply would not know. Montherlant gets little attention in these thirty volumes. So, for that matter, does the greatest contemporary American historian, Samuel Eliot Morison. That raises a general point of importance: these academics with their journalistic standards are unaware of the significance of history, even as a part of literature, and have no idea of the real importance of historians. The two Trevelyans are given tiny postage-stamp entries in the *Micropaedia*; no entry at all in the *Macropaedia* where the fuller entries appear, with the caption 'Knowledge in Depth.'

All sorts of defects come from these false standards. Though the great historian Morison has no place, Stanley Morison the printer is given an entry, because of his connection with *The Times* newspaper, I suppose. Anne Ridler receives notice as a poet (why?), but not a much more powerful poet, Roy Campbell – I know why: he didn't have the Leftist literary *claque* with him. Bishop Colenso appears for his Biblical criticism; nothing is said of his championship of the blacks in South Africa, which was not less important and occupied at least half of his life's work. Nothing about his cousin, William Colenso; the first naturalist of New Zealand, friend of the Maoris. Pelagius is described as English when the whole point of his name and work was that he was British – the name itself is a Latin transcript of Welsh Morgan. I suppose that from the perspective of Chicago they cannot see that Welsh and English are two separate peoples. Even the history of Ireland is somewhat disappointingly treated together with Britain as one.

F. W. Taylor, 'Father of Scientific Management', an American of course, gets full treatment: I could dispense with him, as with their New Thought (really Old Humbug). There is the usual boring American fixation on mere size and quantity – as if that impresses a civilised person. The greatest contributions to civilisation have come from the smallest units, Athens, Rome, Florence, Venice, Paris or a tiny country like Holland, not the immense land-masses. We are supposed to be impressed by the fact that electrical 'waves and electrons [discovered and forecast by two men of genius, Faraday and Clerk Maxwell] enable lesser men to preen themselves on television screens in 260,000,000 homes'. This does not impress me.

Nor am I moved when told that the annual budgets of New York City hover close to $8,000,000,000; that annual welfare costs are $1,200,000,000, not including over $160,000,000 on staff and $410,000,000 on Medicaid. In education at a cost of $1,500,000,000 the system included almost 1,150,000 pupils, from pre-kindergarten through high school, some 70,000 teachers and 41,000 administrative personnel . . . more than 400,000 lunches are served daily to the students. Americans are impressed by this sort of thing; not so cultivated Europeans – one reason why the highly intelligent French regard Americans as somehow unfinished and, if not half-baked, not fully baked. No indication is given among all these unbearably boring figures – silly to cite them, for real values are changing with inflation every year – that the system of high-school education in New York has in fact been seriously damaged by the racial conflict between black students and Jewish teachers.

Since these encyclopaedists are so much more concerned with current trends than real values, there are two very full sections on the 'Teacher Profession' and, believe it or not, on 'Teacher Education', as if the education of teachers was different from education. Perhaps it is over there. Anyway, I found Tea Production more interesting – though why Ceylon should be described unrecognisably as Sri Lanka beats me.

Then what did I find that was good and/or interesting in this new Encyclopaedia so anxious not only to provide information but to educate one? (An intelligent Frenchman would be affronted by the presumption of the latter – and from Chicago!) I found everything on Jewish subjects fascinating, and there was a great deal of it, much to the fore everywhere: the Bible, Biblical Literature, the history of the Jews, the archaeology of Jerusalem, etc. Never before have I been so much up in those blistering bores, the Old Testament Prophets, Isaiah, Amos, Hosea, the jeremiads of Jeremiah – no wonder people put him into an empty cistern from which he could not get out, to shut him up. Even this didn't do it. As for the prophet Habakkuk, Voltaire told us – 'il est capable de tout'. I much sympathise with the eighteenth-century lady on first reading the Major Prophets: 'Mais quel ton! Quel mauvais ton!'.

The general approach is middle-of-the-road; and this has its advantage in dealing with controversial topics, like Moses and Jesus Christ. My own sympathies are conservative and traditionalist, and the article on Moses sensibly accepts the historical existence of such a person – none of the mad fantasying of Freud's last book, *Moses and Monotheism.* (Freud gets very respectful, but not uncritical, treatment.) The awkward topic of Jesus of Nazareth, which has for nearly two thousand years been overlaid by Christian doctrine and rendered impossible to treat sensibly, affords one of the most valuable and illuminating articles in the book, treating his life and career more than sympathetically while making rational sense of it. So, too, with an awkward and less pleasing subject, St Paul. Their remote follower, Luther, is too generously estimated – tributes to his 'profundities' (there was nothing profound in his thought) and the 'lovely' classics that he wrote – Ugh!

Middle-of-the-road is not so rewarding when it comes to Shakespeare: the article is not bad, just irredeemably second-rate. And imagine the silliness, and waste of space, in devoting a whole paragraph to Baconian, Oxfordian, Marlovian lunacies, which should not be noticed, and then omitting the definitive and unanswerable findings of the leading historian of Shakespeare's age! No real conception of the actual circumstances and back-ground of the time in which he wrote. As to the Sonnets, just waffle: 'How long before 1609 the sonnets were written is un-known . . . some of them may belong to any year of Shakespeare's life as a poet before 1609 . . . Shakespeare's sonnets, however, do not give the impression of an ordered sequence as it exists in Sidney, Spenser and others'. In fact, they give the impression of a sequence rather more than Sidney's and much more than Spenser's. To such second-rate perceptions the suggestions of crackpots in this field are to be mentioned on a par with the conclusions of first-rate historians of the age!

Fields where this Encyclopaedia will be found more valuable are the up-to-date results of archaeology, up-to-date reports of recent history. Here one has the advantage, as against the disad-vantages, of the American perspective. Americans are rather more objective and impartial, less nationalistic, in the treatment of different countries' histories – that of Italy, for example (one couldn't bear to read about Germany's record), even the treat-ment of De Gaulle, such a *bête-noire* to Americans, struck me as just. And, of course, there is the equalising effect of the journalistic perspective which hardly distinguishes between more valuable countries and less valuable, culturally speaking. The perspective is un-European, so it is shocking to read that there was no medieval French literature – when there were all the romances of the Roman de la Rose, of Tristan and Arthur. Scholars know that the medieval French romances virtually created modern literature – see that great literary scholar, W. P. Ker.

However, if you want to read about Camus, Le Corbusier and Nervi, Brasilia and Otto Niemeyer, Brazil (too much about ethnics), Werner von Braun's rocketry and his characteristically named 'Vengeance' weapon; Proboscidea or Cephalopods, Spectrometry or Geraniales; Meat and Meat-packing; or Mass Society – here is your book. I suppose it is very well suited, in its way, to mass-society. The spirit that presides over it is that of Benjamin Franklin rather than Leonardo da Vinci.

When A. P. Herbert put up for the University seat at Oxford, his campaign leaflet contained the sentence: '*Agriculture.* I know nothing about agriculture.' Hundreds of people voted for him on the strength of that piece of candour. I must similarly plead: 'Science? I know nothing about science', where I must assume that this Encyclopaedia is at its best. However, a passage about Atomic Weight attracted my attention. It said: 'the concept of atomic weight is basic to chemistry, because most chemical reactions take place in accordance with simple numerical relationships among atoms. Since it is almost always impossible to count the atoms directly, chemists measure reactants and products by weighing and reach their conclusions through calculations involving atomic weights.' How like this is to the processes of history, involving countless unpredictable individuals and masses that can yet be estimated, and the way of arriving at historical judgements. It gives one a comforting feeling of the possible unity of human knowledge. Then comes the cold douche: 'even the most precise methods of measurement presently available introduce uncertainties that limit knowledge'. We are up against the unknowable, with Schrödinger, who, for all his scientific discoveries and achievements, ended with 'a scepticism toward the relevance of science as a unique tool with which to unravel the ultimate mysteries of human existence'.

We are thrown back on the realm of Values – on which this book, like the civilisation it expresses, is short. My own ultimate values are those of knowledge – to which this Encyclopaedia contributes in its own popular, utilitarian way (I would not take *my* education from it); but, even more, they are aesthetic, those of art and music, for they are what chiefly redeem man from the slime.

NOTE

1.   *Encyclopaedia Britannica*, 30 vols, 33,000 pp, 26,000 illus (Encyclopaedia Britannica International)

BIBLIOGRAPHY IN EXCELSIS – THE NEW STC

I suppose that to literary persons and the reading public the initials STC stand for Samuel Taylor Coleridge; but in the indurated world of research they have a more sacred connotation. They stand for the Short-Title Catalogue of English books printed before 1640[1] – that tool (a word beloved of researchers) so indispensable to those in the trade. A generation ago, in present-ing the original edition, its editors, A. W. Pollard and G. R. Redgrave, were able to promise that, when completed with a supplementary volume containing an Index of publishers and printers, 'it will have put England a long way ahead of any other country in Europe in its record of its early printed literature'. That was written in the glad promise of 1926, after the First German War, though not even yet has the happy consummation of that Index arrived – it is now promised as a third volume to this revised and enormously expanded edition of the original STC. Are we yet ahead of other countries with this much larger tool, the second of two vast volumes, covering our earlier printed literature? I do not know; it is obvious that this edition is still more indispensable – if there are degrees of indispensability, as there are of dispensability – than even its predecessor.

Meanwhile I wonder whether STCs of French, Italian and German printed works would not be even vaster and more complicated undertakings, since there was so much more (and better) printing in each of those countries. We were beginners in the sixteenth century, young and ardent and anxious to catch up; we were backward then . . . And now where are we?

The inspirer of this great undertaking, this revision – a kind of Revised Version of the Bible to us researchers – was significantly, an American: the finest, as well as the most humane, bibliographer of his time, Bill Jackson. He was a slave-driver, to himself as well as everybody else. I suppose he killed himself by overwork (very unlike the English of today). I remember Bill telling me how, on one of his visits to an old cathedral library, he could not get through the collection by the time he was due to leave for the USA; so he had himself locked in the library all night to finish the task he had allotted himself. Shades of ancient monastic or capitular ghosts! – it is like a *mise-en-scène* by M. R. James or Meade Falkner, those ghostly book-worms. Myself, I should have been picked up dead from terror in the morning.

My earliest meeting with Bill was characteristic in every way. On my first visit to the Huntington Library, innocently enough I decided to present them with the best book I possessed. This happened to be an exceedingly rare black-letter tract of the reign of Henry VIII, Christopher St German's *An Answer to a Letter*, dealing with the question of the Royal Supremacy. I knew that there was one copy in England, in the splendid library of Queen's College, Oxford; and I thought that, according to my usual principle, if there were a first copy in Britain, the second ought to be in the United States. In my innocence I fancied the book might be worth $150 – an appropriate present. When I got to Harvard, and to the Houghton Library where Bill benevolently presided, he was able to tell me at once about my rare book. He said: 'there are three examples of your book in existence: one in the British Museum, one at Queen's College, Oxford; the third is in the Folger, and now the fourth in the Huntington. I would have given you $750 for it'. I was a little crestfallen at this: I had intended to give of my best, but – with $750 I could have spent a couple of months more in the United States. I suppose that book today might fetch $1750.

Incidentally my story may be checked, while the fact itself provides an example of the new knowledge regaled, in the revised STC. In the original STC the tract appears as anonymous, only one copy given, in the British Museum. In the new STC the tractate appears under St German's name, the four examples as Bill Jackson stated them to me.

I think now what a fool I have been in parting with rare books. When Exeter University gave me an honorary degree I presented the Library with a first edition of Newton's *Optics* – worth now £1500 – besides others rarities I could do with. (I don't suppose that the other honorands, including then the portentous Lord Robbins, signalised the occasion so superfluously.) I once parted with Lyly's *Sixe Court Comedies* of 1632 for £18 – now, I suppose, worth several hundred. The incredibly rare little chapbook of Wystan Auden's first poems, amateurishly printed by Stephen Spender – a copy recently fetched £1750 – I lent to a not particularly appreciative young friend who disappeared during the Second German War. But his name is engraved on my heart, like Calais on Mary Tudor's.

The proper principle is that of a bibliographical friend of mine at Oxford (he appears in this book; no wonder he has such a fine library): 'Never give away a book, and never sell one'. To which I should add, now that I have learned my lesson 'Never lend one'. This was the advice of an old collector to a young tyro, showing him the contents of his shelves: 'Never lend a book'; then, with a sweep of the hand, 'All these books were borrowed once'!

To the matter in hand – I do not want to make it too excruciatingly bibliographical, even if I were capable of it. The original STC contained twenty-six thousand entries; 'to this the new edition will add about ten thousand new entries'. And this is in addition to giving us a great deal of new information about many entries, and about the location of these early books. We are presented now with the second volume first, containing L to Z, since

the earlier completion of volume 2 is the result of Miss Pantzer's taking over the work of final revision on the death of William A. Jackson in 1964 at the letter R. The later letters of the alphabet represented a later stage in Jackson's own revision, and Miss Pantzer has felt that this, and the fact that she has personally overseen all these parts of the work, [I detect a superfluous comma here, faulting the grammar] enable [sic] her and the Society to lay this volume before the public as having reached as definitive a stage as is possible in a work of this nature.

Miss Pantzer, one assumes, is also an American. From Pollard and Redgrave to Jackson and Pantzer: one sees the Americans taking over the inheritance, the literature as well as the economy, and shortly, no doubt, the whole country. A work of reference is all the better for American thoroughness – Bill Jackson was a perfectionist at his trade – but there is a law of diminishing returns in bibliography as in other carnal pleasures. I notice this in regard to the school text-books of the age – somewhat ungratefully, for it is here that I have most to learn. My old acquaintance, T. W. Baldwin, author of *Small Latin and Less Greek*, vast tomes on Shakespeare's education, had the finest collection of sixteenth-century school text-books outside the British Museum and Bodleian. (He would have had much influence in the field of Shakespearean scholarship if only someone had taught him how to write – but they just don't do that in America.)

The largest number of entries here go to an early Tudor schoolmaster, John Stanbridge, whose grammars went into many editions. 'Because of the difficulty of dealing with the complexity of texts, quantity of editions, and imperfections of copies, the title and colophon transcriptions are here given in more detail than elsewhere in STC.' Columns and columns of it indeed – one can really have too much of a good thing. Stanbridge was a complete Wykehamist – Winchester and New College – and then went on to Magdalen to become the second Headmaster of the pretty little grammar School one sees in the front quadrangle. His pupil, Robert Whittinton, was hardly less successful with his school-books; to his grammars he added translations of Cicero and Seneca. From the number of entries one sees that they, and still more Ovid – Marlowe and Shakespeare's favourite – were the most popular classical authors; while Whittinton comes second only to Stanbridge in the number and complexity of his editions.

Far more interesting is William Lily, whose brief Latin grammar was remodelled and adapted to become the one national grammar in use over the whole country in the Elizabethan Age. This was the grammar Shakespeare was brought up on in Stratford, and from which he quotes Latin tags. Lily's career and family were alike interesting. Another Magdalen man, he made the pilgrimage to Jerusalem in the 1490s and spent some time in Rhodes with the Knights of St John. Thus he became proficient in Greek, a rarer accomplishment, as well as in Latin; a friend of Sir Thomas More, he collaborated with him in turning epigrams from the Greek Anthology into Latin. He died young, from an operation for a boil, which the eminent physician and Grecian,

Linacre of All Souls, advised him against. Lily was fortunately a family man. His son George was a Catholic, who lived in Italy as chaplain to Cardinal Pole and wrote about English people and places. A grandson was John Lyly the dramatist, the popularity of whose productions is attested by the number of entries here, especially of *Euphues* with fourteen editions in the thirty years between 1579 and 1609, after which time its vogue faded.

Few are the jokes lying beneath this mountain of information about books. John Field was the highly competent organiser and director of nasty Puritan propaganda against the Elizabethan Church; but his handsome son Nathaniel (better known as Nathan) Field, was a leading, much admired actor in Shakespeare's company at Blackfriars, author of naughty plays like *Amends for Ladies* and *The Merry Pranks of Moll Cut-Purse.* He has not yet received revision. But we have Nicholas Udall, the brilliant Headmaster of Eton, who was sacked for misconduct with his boys, and promptly made Headmaster of Westminster. (No reflection on Westminster intended.) His neighbour in this chaste publication is John Udall, the godly Puritan, author of sermons on *Amendment of Life.*

The Puritans are indeed too much in evidence in the publishers' world, as they were in the pulpits of the time, prolific, prurient and propagandist. The number of their publications is witness to the taste of the time: this was the kind of nonsense that appealed, the mania of the age for sermons, divinity, theological disputation, controversy, conflicts over non-sense doctrines – inflammable material that led to the combustion of the Civil War. Here they all are: John Preston, William Whitaker, the loud-mouthed Perkins, who all had such a deleterious influence in making Puritans of students at Cambridge; 'silver-tongued Smith' and Weemes, of whom STC says, with perhaps superfluous conscientiousness: 'the attempt at a systematic listing of Weemes's works has been foiled by the insuperable complications surviving copies present'. I think we can survive that. Here is Sibbes, with his *'Bowels Opened,* or a discovery of the love, union and communion betwixt Christ and the Church'; and his *The Bride's Longing for her Bridegroomes Second Comming.* Here are all the Rogerses, ten of them, of whom four were Johns – think of the difficulties for the bibliographer! One of them concentrated his venom against the harmless, and rather distinguished, Family of Love – a kind of pre-Quakers, distinguished by their minimising of nonsense doctrines. John Rogers wrote, '*The displaying of an horrible secte of grosse and wicked heretiques, naming themselves the Familie of Love*', and other libels display the sweetness of his own Christian spirit.

Sensible Anglicans like Richard Hooker, John Whitgift, Richard Bancroft, the brilliant and sceptical Chillingworth, are less in evidence; John Hales, who had so much to offer to an age ulcerated by doctrinal disputes, did not publish at all; Archbishop Laud was detested as much for his freedom from Calvinist superstition as for upholding an Anglican middle way.

Such was the age before the Civil War. We are apt to think of it in terms of Shakespeare and Ben Jonson: for one who read them there must have been a hundred who read Biblical folklore and theological nonsense. It would have done them more good to read Shakespeare. Of foreigners who made popular reading here it would seem that Calvin came first, followed by Luther, Beza, Erasmus, Philippe de Mornay and Fra Paolo Sarpi. It all goes to show how dominantly Protestant the country, or at least the reading public, was.

My awed congratulations on such pieces of technical virtuosity as that on Liturgies, the pre-Reformation provincial uses of Sarum, York, Hereford, etc – though when one contemplates such pages of esoteric symbols, like algebra, on pages 87–90, one wonders whether the journey was really necessary.

I fear that my interest in the work is rather Philistine from the bibliographer's point of view, grateful as I am for the tool he presents me: as a simple historian I am interested in the *content* of the work, what it has to say, rather than how it looks, feels, smells, etc. My Oxford bibliographical friend is more cultivated: holding out the rarity, 'Smell it', he says – 'Vellum' – sniff, sniff – 'First Edition, or, rather, second issue of the first edition', as the case may be. But I rather doubt whether he *reads* the books.

NOTE

1. A. W. Pollard and G. R. Redgrave, *A Short Title Catalogue of Books Printed in England, Scotland and Ireland, and of English Books Printed Abroad 1475-1640.* Vol 2 L-Z (Second edition, revised and enlarged by W. A. Jackson, F. S. Ferguson and Katherine F. Pantzer) (Oxford University Press/The Bibliographical Society).

ATTITUDES TO HISTORY

'Those who can do; those who can't, teach.' There is something in the popular saying, especially where historians are concerned. Really distinguished historians do not waste time discussing how to write history, or giving away the secrets of their art or craft: they get on with the job. They leave it to the not so good at it to discuss how it should be done.

How lucky the leading nineteenth-century historians were! They had the field so much to themselves, so few competitors; above all, none of the hundreds of people of all sorts today churning out history-books for the publishers, though few of them have any claim to write history, or even to write at all. They should be cultivating their garden, growing food; with society the way it is we shall shortly be coming to that.

Burckhardt had the luck to muscle in on the Renaissance when it was new territory. Now traipsed over by people who can't tell a Renaissance building if they see one, particularly if they are Americans who have no visual education and do not use their eyes – as I have had occasion to notice again and again with American academics. Perhaps it is a general demotic failing, for the people see and hear and savour nothing. This merely corroborates the point about the hundreds of superfluous history-books a year churned out.

Ranke had the advantage of pioneering in archives, with all those really significant documents to uncover. Today academics scrape the bottom of the barrel – to what point? Macaulay was able to make English history as fresh and exciting as a novel – and reaped the reward: he beat most novelists in circulation. Gibbon had an even greater advantage in eighteenth-century circumstances, with only himself, Hume and Robertson in the field.

Professor Gay[1] has essays on Gibbon, Ranke, Macaulay and Burckhardt. With a German-oriented author what he has to say about Ranke and Burckhardt is of more value to an English reader. (All the same it was a mistake to duplicate quotations: one does not need them in English, then repeated in German – without, the price of the book could have been reduced.) Ranke had the further advantage of living to be over ninety, still active, writing all the time, so that he loomed like a German Colossus over nineteenth-century historiography.

There were good things about him. He is much preferable to the power-prostitutes – like the odious Treitschke, Droysen and Sybel – who sucked up to Bismarck's successful course of achieving German ascendancy by Blood and Iron. (It is true that Louis XIV's France behaved badly to Germany, and so did Napoleon: I excuse no power-mad militarists in history.)

On the other hand, Ranke was deeply conformist: Luther was his hero, he never questioned the Lutheranism he was brought up in, God was in his heaven, all was going well for Germany, so it was all right to break treaties or pounce on other people's countries. (Compare Frederick the Great and Silesia, or Belgium and France in 1914, Hitler's Germany and Poland, Denmark, Norway, Russia, etc.) Ranke, typically German, was sucking up to success in admiring the awful Luther, who succeeded in dividing Europe from top to bottom. How much happier Europe would have been if, *per impossibile*, it could have gone the way of the defeated Erasmus, hoping for reason and sense, moderation and toleration. I say '*per impossibile*' because humans are too hopeless to be able to follow a sane course in history for long.

Today we admire the Swiss Burckhardt much more: disillusioned aesthete, cultivated, sceptical, who realised that it is works of arts and intellect that redeem the follies of the human record. Burckhardt, living his reflective life to himself, watching from the side-lines, observed with horror the movement to mass-society, though even he – in the civilised nineteenth century – cannot have intuited how murderous and ghastly it would be, when the people came into their own. How right he was for a historian, too, in his attitude and opinions! In repudiating the megalomaniac pretensions of Hegel, for example, in eschewing generalisations, and emphasising direct perception (few are capable of it).

Burckhardt, for all his scepticism, was criticised as opinionated. I have been criticised as opinionated myself – by a common literary journalist. Of course Burckhardt was right to have opinions about the Renaissance – no-one more so – as I am about the Age of Shakespeare. I am not opinionated about mechanics or biology, mathematics, law or love, botany, entomology, engineering, or practically anything. But if my opinion on the Elizabethan Age or Shakespeare was not of more value than that of any literary journalist – after a lifetime of research in it – I should not be worth my keep. The trouble in a demotic society is that every ass thinks his opinion as being as good as anyone's about anything – rubbish of course. (I wouldn't dream of setting up my opinion, on a matter of art, against Douglas Cooper's, or Kenneth Clark's, whom I read with positive reverence.)

What historical writing is going to become like in a mass-society we can see from the official *Short History of the World* issued from Moscow by Progress Publishers.[2] To begin with – unreadable, because inhuman, as we should expect. To go on with – no sense of truth, as we should expect from Russians (Custine saw that as a leading characteristic long ago). And what is the point of *history* without a sense of truth? It stands or falls, as history, by whether it is true or not; without, it is just propaganda. As such it has a point, for ordinary people can hardly ever tell about the truth of a matter or not – Stalin understood that quite as well as Hitler.

Let us apply the fundamental test of historic truth to this book for the instruction of the faithful. 'On 17 September 1939 Soviet Army units crossed the frontier of Poland, which had virtually ceased to exist as a state, and began a mission of liberation . . .'. Not a word about the Molotov-Ribbentrop Pact which had divided Poland between the two predators, Nazi Germany and Soviet Russia, and enabled Hitler to unleash his war. Without that Pact between Communists and Nazis it is doubtful if Hitler could have started his war. Then, suddenly in June 1941, when Hitler attacked Soviet Russia, the war which till then had been merely an 'imperialist' war suddenly became a war of liberation for holy Russia. I well remember the embarrassment it caused the Stalinist leaders of the Communist Party of Great Britain, when the direct face-about was ordered by their Mecca, Moscow.

And why did Soviet Russia – a dozen times the size and resources of Nazi Germany – make such a bad show at resisting Hitler's attack? The faithful are informed that 'the war had begun under auspices favourable to Germany'. They are not informed that Stalin's purges, from the able Tukhachevsky downwards, had pulverised the Russian army and enormously reduced its fighting efficiency, in spite of vast superiority in numbers. Nor did Stalin and his clique expect the attack, in spite of the warnings they had received from Churchill and Stafford Cripps. This is admitted, disingenuously: 'miscalculations as to the possible date of the German attack on the Soviet Union also played their role'. They did, indeed! When the attack came, Molotov said, 'Did we deserve this?'. I suppose the explanation is that one set of thugs would prefer the word of another set of thugs to that of honest men – at least they would understand each other better.

However much Britain's role in the Second German War is here belittled, the horrid fact is that Hitler's Germany would have beaten Soviet Russia alone, if Britain had not hung on in the West, in the air, and at sea.

Sometimes a word of truth spoken. 'The Second World War was unleashed by militarist Germany, just as the First had been'. The truth in history is often simple; only third-rate perceptions have a way of obfuscating themselves until they can see no difference between black and white. Here is another comparable case. This book has no difficulty in seeing that the Japanese attack on Pearl Harbor, under the cover of diplomatic negotiations, was 'outright perfidy'. This is the truth, plain and simple. But if you take the American pro-German historian, Charles Beard (German wife and all), you would think that at Pearl Harbor the Americans attacked the Japanese! Charles Beard, like Harry Elmer Barnes, was no historian, just a liar – as G. M. Trevelyan used to call Belloc: people who do not care whether what they say is true or not. For the real historian this is the ultimate sin.

Plenty of examples of it in this book. The only reference to Trotsky is to 'the pernicious policy of developing large-scale industry at the expense of the peasantry (Trotsky, Zinoviev, for instance)'. No reference to their having been murdered by Stalin, along with the majority of Lenin's Politburo. And apparently in the October Revolution – in which Trotsky bore a part second only to Lenin – Trotsky didn't exist; at any rate his existence is not mentioned.

The revolution liberated the masses from 'the heavy Tsarist yoke, which tolerated no manifestation of a longing for freedom'. How many manifestations are permitted and how much freedom is there today? The Revolution 'was destined to achieve a noble historic aim ... a new society in which there would be no oppressors and no oppressed'. Mr Brezhnev has boasted recently that in this new society every Russian has three pairs of shoes; the *Guardian* pointed out that each Russian also has the equivalent of forty tons of high explosives. 'As Lenin pointed out in 1917, humanity's only salvation lay in socialism.'

Enough: too sickening.

Another style of historical writing is exemplified by Mr Cobban's book on the Medieval Universities,[3] that of the English academic, blameless, learned, unexciting, truthful. Mr Cobban knows the truth about 'student-power' – silly cliché for a silly thing – though he wraps it up a bit. When we were undergraduates at the university we were there to learn what the university had to teach. From evidences all round today it is obvious that the young are not as well educated as we were. I do not repine at this so much as might be expected, since – unlike Lord Robbins – I do not regard most people as educable in any significant sense of the word, e.g. up to a proper university standard (quite a proportion of those there today, for example, are not).

Kingsley Amis, having a touch of genius and therefore independent-minded, intuited this perfectly when he saw that More Means Worse, as it certainly does. The public humbugs who have succeeded in lowering university standards in Britain can hardly be expected to agree, since this result is more in keeping with their own genius.

Mr Cobban sums up cautiously, but convincingly:

> the unsettling nature of student power, with its weapons of the boycott and the migration, posed too great a threat to the more ordered character that the universities were acquiring in the 14th and 15th centuries. Society expected an adequate return for the investments sunk in the universities. [It is certainly not getting that today from the mushroom universities.] That return was deemed to be put in jeopardy by the machinations of student politics. The indifferent student record in university administration ... provided the establishment with a more immediate reason for the phasing out of student participation as a vital force in West European universities.

Well, well. The professor goes boldly forward to suggest,

> the lessons of medieval student power are not necessarily of direct relevance to the 20th century. But those who are concerned with university management could do worse than look over their shoulders at the aspirations and actions of students in the medieval past.

He goes so far as to tell us that 'it is difficult to discover what students themselves thought about the purpose of education at the medieval universities', and that our picture of the medieval student is not an individualised one, but one of the mass.

But, of course. What this means in plain English is – as if it mattered what a mob of adolescent youths thought about the purpose of university education, or anything else for that matter! They were there to learn, or – if not – get rid of them. Naturally an individual picture of the average student isn't recorded, for it is not worth recording; as H. A. L. Fisher, that enlightened Liberal Minister of Education, said even of Oxford undergraduates: 'They recur'. Only the elect leave some memorial of themselves.

The later medievals, concerned at the waste of society's limited resources, managed to get obstreperous youths under better discipline. In England the Tudors completed the process by penning them into colleges, where they could be properly supervised. They were only boys after all – and discipline is the absolute condition of learning anything.

Mr Cobban concludes his academic study academically.

Much research still needs to be done in the socio-economic area of medieval university history: matters such as the maintenance and expenditure rates of different categories of university personnel, the size of private incomes, salary scales, methods of external support, the numbers frequenting universities, the degree of stratification within the academic community, the fabric of hall and collegiate life, these and other topics relating to university sociology are being vigorously pursued on the monographic scale.

Oh dear! I do hope not. There will shortly be nobody left to do any real work or grow any food – all employed into researching into others doing nothing much either. I am in favour of history being written by men of genius with a call to write, like Gibbon and Macaulay, Ranke and Burckhardt. As for ordinary professors, they should *teach*, and their students *learn*.

A fourth example of historical writing is that by a young lady, Miss Josephine Ross.[4] I hate being discouraging to the young, and Miss Ross is promising. She should therefore have taken for her first book a less trampled theme than the suitors for the hand of Elizabeth I: we have had it all too often. Something about the Empress Josephine, or even the Rosses, would have been better.

We can do better on the subject of Queen Elizabeth's rejected lovers with Sir John Neale, who was a real historian, or with Lytton Strachey and Elizabeth Jenkins, who are real writers.

NOTE

1. Peter Gay, *Style in History*. Illus (Jonathan Cape).
2. A. Z. Mander (ed), *A Short History of the World*. Vol 2. Illus (Progress Publishers).
3. A. B. Cobban, *The Medieval Universities* (Methuen).
4. Josephine Ross, *Suitors to the Queen*. Illus (Weidenfeld & Nicolson).

WORLD HISTORICAL EVENTS

Grateful as I am for such riveting information as that 'Smim Htaw, brother of Takayutpi, king of Hanthawaddy: defeated by Bayinnaung of Toungoo; Tabinshwehti assassinated; empire collapses', I suggest that no one human being can properly compass an encyclopedia of world history. It needs a committee, or at least two or three gathered together. I am astonished at how much the editor has managed to compass, what useful information we can pick up from this compilation, along with much that may be discarded in a second edition.[1]

Hopelessly Occidental as I am myself, rooted in what was the end of the Western World – and beyond, nothing but the great sundering Flood, wrote a medieval bishop of Exeter – I fear that the editor here is too Britain-centred. After all, France was the dominant country in European civilisation for so many centuries, medieval and modern. One notes many British references that could be spared for more important French ones. The greatest of French architects, for example: Mansard, who built the Invalides (Wren was much influenced by its dome for St Paul's) – has the editor never heard of a Mansard-roof? Mme de Maintenon appears as 'letter-writer' – she was far more important politically as Louis XIV's morganatic wife; her grandfather, Agrippa d'Aubigné, the most important French poet of the later sixteenth century is not here. An even more influential Huguenot leader – influential intellectually in England and the Netherlands too – was Duplessis-Mornay: missing.

Wishing to be helpful, I suggest that the invaluable *Larousse* gives a better indication of who is important, who not; and the test must be who is historically influential, whether one approves or no. For example, though I detest the Puritans, they are seriously under-represented.

To notice only the M's for a moment, Michelet was about the most influential French historian of the nineteenth century: missing. Charles Maurras was a malign man, though a gifted writer; but he was historically important as the inspirer of the monarchist *Action française* and in undermining the Third Republic. The editor is right to include the silly Sartre, for the influence he has exerted, but Montherlant, a far better writer, is missing.

In the realm of architecture the Roman writer, Vitruvius, exerted a vast influence, not only in antiquity but throughout the Renaissance. He should be here, and so should the greatest of Austrian architects, Fischer von Erlach, to whom we owe such superlative buildings and churches in Vienna, the magnificent monastery of Melk, etc. I am not sure that our Pevsner should not be included, for the nation-wide influence he has exerted; certainly Betjeman should for the historic influence he has had on taste, opening our eyes to what was best in Victorianism.

Under Religion and Culture we are given recent archbishops of Canterbury – reasonably enough. But, with Fisher, there is omitted the one historic event of his primacy: his official reception by Pope John XXIII in Rome, the first visit by an archbishop of Canterbury since the Reformation. The diplomats had a joke on the occasion; the Pope, whose English was not good, was supposed to have said, 'Long time no see'.

Influence, effect on others, is what counts in history – so we must replace names for which we may have more affection by those for which we may well have less, but recognise to have made an impact. Fond of my old friends as I am, we must recognise that Charles Morgan and Lord David Cecil have had much less influence than Leavis and C. S. Lewis, both missing. I suppose that Lewis had far greater impact than anyone at Oxford in my time, especially in the field of religion. One may regard Leavis's influence as, on balance, deleterious; but it has been prodigious, in universities both in England and USA, and in schools among innocent schoolmistresses, and in the *Times Literary Supplement* during a deplorable period. I am not sure that Grigson might not be promoted, not for his verse, but for founding *New Verse* and propagating Auden and the poets of the 1930s like mad. And perhaps Connolly, again not for his own work, but for his creation of *Horizon*, which made a mark in literary history. These are hardly of European, let alone world, importance, but if we are to be Britain-centred they have more than provincal interest. Far more important, the *Nouvelle Revue française* is not here: it was the organ for much of the best of modern French literature as *Die Neue Rundschau* was of German.

To come to history. I fancy the best way to judge such a work is to take a field in which one has some knowledge. I give the editor a good mark for noting that African slaves were first imported into the West Indies in 1501 – English sentimentalists like to blame it on Hawkins, who only entered an established trade half-a-century later. Another good mark goes to the editor for describing Drake's activities as 'privateering' – the uninstructed like to describe them as 'piracy'.

The decisive subject of the English colonisation of North America is inadequately dealt with. Gilbert did not 'establish' a colony in Newfoundland in 1583, but simply took empty formal possession. The crucial first Roanoke Colony of 1585–6, from which all the rest flowed, the gathering of experience, the collating and writing it up, all that upon which the ultimate founding of Jamestown was based in 1607, is missing – only the second (lost) colony of 1587 is present.

There is no notice of Sir Ferdinando Gorges, who devoted his life's work and fortune to propagating the colonisation of New England, and is regarded as the founder of Maine; nor of Captain Mason, founder of New Hampshire; nor of Edward Billing, Quaker founder of New Jersey. But really shocking is the omission of John Winthrop, the creator of Massachusetts, and indeed of the Winthrop dynasty. I suspect that the editor has not consulted my book, *The Elizabethans and America*.

A propos of the Puritans, we may not love the unlovable Cartwright, but again he is important as laying down the model for Presbyterianism in England, which held the field for decades right up to the Westminster Assembly of Divines. This was again influential throughout the English-speaking world for its Directory of Public Worship, etc (missing). I cannot bear such loud-mouthed sermonisers as the ineffable Perkins, or William Ames, or the Mathers of New England, *et hoc genus omne,* but there is – alas! – no doubt of their influence under the heading of Religion, if not of culture. I find this section perhaps the least satisfactory.

Take Oxford, for example. In this century a man of genius there, Sir John Beazley, initiated the study of Greek vases. With an incomparable combination of scholarship and aesthetic sensibility, he covered the whole field in his life's work – one might almost say, began and ended it: no-one comparable to him in this century. He is not here.

Nor, among the W's, do we find Wolfenden – surely he has made his historic mark: does it come under Religion or Culture? – as morals, I suppose it comes under Religion, but the subject has its cultural aspects too. And fancy omitting Wittgenstein (while including a Whitelaw!) – the most important philosophic influence of our time in the English-speaking world. Or what about Agatha Christie, the world-mistress in a whole *genre* of modern literature, detective fiction?

I hope that some of these suggestions may come of use for a second edition. But the editor will need to employ an elderly assistant, the older the more likely to have a wider range of knowledge. However, knowing my limitations, I am not applying for the job.

NOTE

1. G. S. P. Freeman-Grenville (ed), *Chronology of World History from 3000 BC to AD 1973* (Rex Collings).

SOCIOLOGICAL VERSUS REAL HISTORY

Why do I not subscribe to the exaggerated esteem for sociological history which is fashionable among academics today?

One must give reasons for one's opinions – they are not just prejudices. My reason is that history is a portrait of life as it is lived, in all its subtlety, its fluidity and variableness, and this cannot be caught and rendered in sociological generalisations. They are too rigid, and apt to deform what is true about the past. The life of history is in the detail, the unexpected, the unpredictable, what escapes generalisation. That is not to say that one cannot draw conclusions, even morals – as in life itself (history is the life of the past, all of it). And since this weighty and important book merits proper critical treatment, I should say that some of its less general, more modest generalisations are unexceptionable.[1]

The rigidifying of life into abstract concepts yields dubious results. Does one really learn anything by proceeding from the Open Lineage Family 1450–1630 to the Restricted Patriarchal Nuclear Family 1550–1700, thence to the Closed Domesticated Nuclear Family 1640–1800? The truth about life, about human nature and human beings, their relationships, emotions, affections, convictions, escapes when strait-jacketed in this way. We are invited to consider this work as an example of 'the new trends in historical writing, in its interweaving of theory and example'. But history is not a theoretical subject – one cannot *theorise* about life, the natural history of man, though one may draw conclusions from experience, even offer some modest generalisations. If one wants to theorise, take to sociology proper.

Professor Stone, an historian, places himself under the wing of one Professor Geertz – I suppose a sociologist – from whom he quotes as motto the kind of pronouncement that impresses American academics. 'The problems, being existential, are universal; their solution, being human, are diverse. The road to the grand abstractions of science winds through a thicket of singular facts.'

What does this man mean by 'existential'? – no more than 'they exist', I suspect. In history it is the detail, the actual facts, the reality of life in its myriad variations that is important. To begin with 'universal' problems is to invert historical method; in history, as in life, what generalisations are possible arise from the facts, not the other way round. One does not pose universal problems and expect the facts to answer – with statistics, graphs etc. If one does the answers are rigid and unsatisfactory, really – unreliable. Professor Stone is at times aware of the dusty answers one thus gets – more than in his earlier work; even so they are apt to be too crude, as I propose to show.

Not so crude, however, as the sociologist *pur sang*, Lévi-Strauss, who writes patronisingly, 'biographical and anecdotal history is low-powered history, which is not intelligible in itself'. Isn't it? It is just as intelligible, as life itself. This sociologist goes on, with obvious self-approbation, it 'only becomes so, when it is transferred *en bloc* to a form of history of higher power than itself', i.e. to a form of sociology. It is like saying that people in life are only intelligible when generalised about in the mass – when we all know that we learn about them pragmatically from experience and observation, and make our deductions from that.

That said, we may cite more modest generalisations which are acceptable.

> The four key features of the modern family – intensified effective bonding of the nuclear core at the expense of neighbours and kin; a strong sense of individual autonomy and the right to personal freedom in the pursuit of happiness; a weakening of the association of sexual pleasure with sin and guilt; and a growing desire for physical privacy – were all well established by 1750 in the key middle and upper sectors of English society.

And there are good observations. In the eighteenth century

> the fact that the children of the poor were freer to make their own choice than the children of the rich did not mean, however, that effective considerations weighed more than the same prudential ones that would govern if made for them by their parents.

Or,

> under conditions in which everyone knows and accepts his place, the deferential system provides a comfortable framework for all social relationships, at least as comfortable as the egalitarian norms of American society today.

That is well observed by the Professor for himself.

He is right, too, to cite a sharp contemporary observer in Francis Place as to the *benefits* of the Industrial Revolution improving the condition of the poor, as against the populist sentimentalism of J. L. and Barbara Hammond in their day. (They have had their day.)

On the other hand, there is the crudity of insisting that, earlier, the aim of parents was to 'crush' the will of the child – 'mould' would be a better word; 'this passion for crushing the will of the child' – the aim was not to crush but to control. 'Immature children were regarded as mere animals lacking the capacity to reason, and therefore to be broken in just as one would break in a puppy, a foal, or a hawk.' Not *'mere'* animals, professor; and not 'just as'. Of course young animals are wilful and their wilfulness needs to be curbed; this was what parents favoured in the earlier period, not crushing the will of the child 'just as' with an animal, nor were they engaged in 'breaking in' their children like animals.

There were always some parents who were stern and unloving, and others who were indulgent and affectionate. In schools there were always some masters who were beaters and others who were not. To speak of 'the extension of the use of physical punishment throughout the whole educational system at home and in school' is a crude exaggeration, as anyone who knows the facts of social history knows better than a sociological theorist. The fact that so many people in the sixteenth century protested against the beating they received shows that they were aware that not all masters were similarly addicted – the excessive beaters were regarded as exceptional and complained about as such.

Take the evidence of the best-known Elizabethan book on education, Roger Ascham's classic *The Schoolmaster.* It starts off with the subject of beating in schools being discussed by the leading figures of the Privy Council at Windsor, the top men in Elizabethan government. Now the significant thing is that of these men, Sir William Cecil, the most powerful man in the country, was against beating; so were Sir Richard Sackville, of the Exchequer, and Dr Wotton, diplomat; only Sir William Petre, 'as one somewhat severe of nature', was in favour of the rod; Sir John Mason, of the Privy Council, merely laughed and was merry.

Ascham himself was all for gentleness and against beating; the argument of his book 'is to observe nature and disposition', the psychological make-up of the boy – what could be more modern? He thought that boys from seven to seventeen were well enough brought up, but that young gentlemen were allowed too much liberty. From my knowledge of Elizabethan social life I think that was true, and that young aristocrats were apt to be spoiled and kick over the traces. Of course, they needed stronger regulation and control than today, for they were more uncontrolled, primitive and passionate.

Now there is no discussion of the views of this most important Elizabethan educationist in the book; he merely gets a passing mention. 'From Guarino to Vives to Erasmus, and from Elyot to Ascham to Mulcaster, they were to a man opposed to the indiscriminate use of severe physical punishment.' That is a welcome and candid admission – and it indicates that the situation was more varied and more flexible than these sociological generalisations allow. The well-known passage about Lady Jane Grey's parents, and the harshness with which she was treated, would seem to suggest that it was exceptional – that was why she resented it so much. There is no indication that her cousins, Henry VIII's children, were treated like that; as for his spouses, Anne Boleyn and Catherine Howard, there is every indication that they would have been the better for more discipline in their bringing up.

In quoting Lady Jane Grey, the Professor sums up,

> one recognises in this bitter description the paradigm [fashionable cliché of this school] of the perfectionist parents, who were to dominate middle and upperclass English upbringing for the next hundred years.

I do not: there were unkind parents, and kind ones, as always. The permanent facts of human nature are more reliable and revealing than the sociologist's stratified abstractions from them. Again:

> the stress on domestic discipline and the utter [?] subordination of the child found expression in extraordinary outward marks of deference which English children were expected to pay to their parents in the 16th and early 17th centuries.

This seems to me rather a clumsy way of failing to notice that the formality in upper class life was the obverse of the indiscipline and horseplay only too ready to break out. Again,

> one of the most effective methods used to socialise children in the 17th century was to teach them, at a very early age, to be afraid of death and of the possibility of eternal damnation.

This is described, in sociological terms, as 'a common psychological control device'. Well, really – the plain fact is that this is what the parents believed. As for excluding emotional attachments of parents for their children – described as the 'effective' side of family life – all the literary evidence on the illnesses and deaths of children, the artistic evidence from portraits, sculpture on tombs, the expressions of grief in letters, the evidence from Shakespeare and Ben Jonson, go against the abstractions and the graphs, which are indeed hardly in keeping with common sense. The Verney letters are quoted for the formal deference with which the children addressed their parents; but the contents of the letters, to anyone who has read them all through, show a remarkable warmth of affection among that widespread family.

We are assured that as we move into the eighteenth century the home

> became more closed off from the kin. After marriage, social ties with relatives were now increasingly confined to parents, uncles and aunts. Contacts with cousins diminished.

I just don't believe it. Anyone who knows one county intimately will know how frequent it was to marry cousins. Carew in 1600 had already said, what everybody knew, that almost all the Cornish gentry were of a cousinage. I am now studying the interweaving of two families, the Byrons with the Trevanions: within less than a century there were five or six marriages between cousins, besides extra-marital relationships. There was, indeed, a great deal to be said for marrying cousins – one at least knew whom one was marrying; and there were good economic reasons, as well as the social and personal, for it too. And everyone knows the close interbreeding there was in remote and static country districts – though notorious in Cornwall, the county was not exceptional in this respect. Look at Hardy's Dorset, or for that matter, the Hardy family story itself.

From the historical point of view the detail, the actual facts, are far more valuable and interesting than the sociological theorising, and one must be grateful for the immense amount of research that Professor Stone – more industrious and productive than his mentors – has put into it. One learns new facts.

> Calvin had decreed the death penalty as the punishment for disobedience to parents, and in the 1640s both Connecticut and Massachusetts turned the precept into legislation, although so far as is known only a handful of children were executed for this crime.

If this is true, it justifies Maurice Bowra's description of Calvin *tout court* as the 'enemy of the human race', and is not one's detestation of the Puritans perfectly reasonable?

The chief gap I notice in the wide field Professor Stone draws upon is that of local history: in parish histories there is an immense amount of material that would enrich, and correct, his generalisations about kin, the marriage of cousins, etc. That would make a fruitful field of future research for his well publicised seminar at Princeton. I find all his chapters about sex-life entertaining (the illustrations too!) and amusing, though that was hardly his intention: all sex is rather comic, and makes fools of us all. (No indication of a sense of humour among solemn sociologists.) I notice hardly a mistake with this conscientious researcher, though John Marston, the Elizabethan poet, was not a homosexual: like the American preacher on the subject of Sin, he was 'agin it'. I am glad that Professor Stone has found my researches into Simon Forman so useful, though I doubt whether the sex-life he reveals was that of a minority – he drew from such a wide spectrum of Elizabethan life.

Altogether, it will be seen why I prefer the descriptive findings, based upon thorough research, of a sceptical and subtle historical mind, to the paradigms and stratifications that the sociologist seeks to extract from and impose upon the infinite variableness and uncertainties of life.

NOTE

1.   L. Stone *The Family, Sex and Marriage in England, 1500-1800*, Illus (Weidenfeld & Nicolson).

UNIVERSITIES AND SOCIETY

These expensively produced volumes are the product of a Princeton seminar, handsomely financed, which brings together a group of scholars on a subject chosen for 'its intrinsic importance, its relative underdevelopment in the historical literature, and its interest to a core of members of the History Department at Princeton'.[1] The result is a couple of volumes of disparate essays on different aspects of the interactions between universities and the societies of which they are part. The essays are of very varying value, and could have done with more conscientious and strenuous editing. There might then have emerged one, not large, volume containing what was of any value.

The first volume is almost wholly devoted to Oxford, heavily overbalanced; Cambridge gets only a look-in – it would have been interesting to learn more about it, and of use for comparative purposes. One learns, indeed, little that is new, and the obvious is supported by an immense, but unimpressive, mass of statistics, graphs, maps – though two maps were mistakenly transposed after proofs had been corrected: a characteristic symptom of demotic education in our time.

What these studies show is that, on the whole, universities reflected the social trends of the time, if with a tendency to lag behind – though no greater than that in the professions of law and medicine. There has been a continuous rise in the age of students, from the sixteenth century when most undergraduates were mere boys. In the late seventeenth century, at Oxford, half of them were poor. Throughout the next two centuries these were more and more squeezed out. The notable reforms of the Victorian age benefited the middle class; this reflects its remarkable expansion, its increasing social and political importance after 1832.

We are told that eastern and northern England were underrepresented at Oxford. Is this an example of sociological myopia? For, of course, Cambridge was the university for eastern England – and that has real significance, for the Reformation, Puritanism, Parliamentarianism, Latitudinarianism, Whiggery, etc: the kind of *real* significance these statistical authors usually miss. In an essay on the German universities in the eighteenth century, for example, we are given no answer to a simple question, such as why Göttingen was the best. By the same token, university figures of cardinal significance, such as Kant or Hegel, are not even mentioned. Or again, in an essay on the mission of New England educators to teach the blacks – the word is 'acculturate' – in the Southern States after the Civil War, there is no mention of the most interesting of them: T. S. Eliot's grandfather founded Washington university at St Louis for this very purpose. Lost in their forest of statistics, most of these seminarists do not know what is historically significant and what is not.

Why did the colleges at Oxford – and at Cambridge – come to dominate the university? The answer is simple and concrete: because they were more efficiently organised, they possessed endowments, could teach students more and more within their walls – one cannot learn without discipline – and they could provide for some of their members by the patronage at their disposal. Heavy weather is made of 'Patronage Patterns' as a sociological subject: what does this mean but that human beings, in the struggle for existence, depend on each other? And not only the weaker on the stronger; the strongest – Kings, Lords, Bishops – need service, i. e. ministers, administrators, clerks, people who could read and write. One new thing I did learn here: apparently the medieval English monarchs did more for scholars than anywhere else in Europe (always excepting the Papacy).

The essay on Cambridge deals with the two-way traffic between the colleges and the countryside where they owned land and whence they drew students, supporting the obvious with a mass of statistics. We learn that East Anglia enjoyed greater educational opportunities – naturally, for it was richer. We are told that after the sixteenth century Bishops were no longer the chief benefactors – naturally, for after the Reformation they were (a) much poorer, and (b) had their own families to provide for.

The second volume offers a diversity of subjects, some of which promise to be interesting; they are mostly ruined by an inability to write plain English and should have been edited into sense. 'The use of the percentage of unhabilitated faculty is a parameter in measuring the "professionalisation" of the professorial career' reads like a translation from German. Of Edinburgh we are informed that by the 1720s it had 'acquired a structured literati' – we learn more about Edinburgh in the Enlightenment from an enjoyable reading of 'Jupiter' Carlyle's Autobiography.

Some of the subjects were not worth investigating, let alone writing so badly about: silly student unrest in the German universities after the Napoleonic wars – there were just too many of them, as in democratic societies today. 'American Student Societies in the Early Nineteenth Century' begins with a remarkably fatuous long exordium about the myth of 'The Choice of Hercules', with yards of useless footnotes.

The writing is comparable – sociological jargon in place of plain sense. No-one can use the simple word 'teaching' – it is always 'propaedutic, pedagogical function '. An essay on the universities of Spain – there were too many of them, most were no more than schools, without the discipline – speaks of the 'fluorescence' of the Renaissance. Sometimes one simply does not know what the man

means – for example: 'consistent adherence in academic appoint-
ments and promotions to disciplinary standards sustains the
modern dualistic professorate' (sc. professoriate). The book is
riddled with the exaggerations of contemporary sociological history: this or that 'crisis', of aristocracy or what not; the 'educational revolution', and now the 'information explosion', simply the
result of improved communications.

The overriding lesson one learns from the book is that American universities do not need to finance more research, but simply
to learn – and then teach – how to write English.

NOTE

1. *The University in Society.* Edited by Lawrence Stone (Princeton University
    Press, 2 vols).

CLASSICS OF COUNTY HISTORY

The delightful study of local history – very rewarding to anyone
who appreciates the landscape around him – has always had its
devotees. Today the pursuit is stronger and more widespread
than ever, partly by reaction to the monotonous and characterless
standardisation of everything. But it has become impossible to
buy the classics of the subject, the splendid folios with their plates
and pedigrees – Dugdale's *Warwickshire*, Nichols' *Leicester*,
Hasted's *Kent*, Surtees' *Durham*; prices have rocketed up, with
competition from all the university libraries of America, Canada
and now Australia.

An enterprising Yorkshire publishing concern, E.P. Publishing
Limited, has come to the rescue. How grateful we have reason to
be for their initiative, imagination and public spirit – they should
all be made peers for their good work: peers have been made for
less. They have called on Professor Jack Simmons of Leicester to
edit the series and Leicester University is the focus to which we all
look for a lead in these studies. Professor Simmons has got a
leading authority on the particular county to write the introduc-

tions to the volumes. Here we are with already a small library produced, folios, big quartos, all with their original complement of plates, in their latest and best editions, printed on good substantial paper, firmly and well bound, at reasonable prices.

Kent has a certain primacy among English counties, from its proximity to the Continent, first to be Christianised, and its possession of the metropolitan see of Canterbury, etc. Certainly Hasted (pronounced Haysted) thought so;[1] in dedicating his last folio volume to the younger Pitt in 1798, then Lord Warden of the Cinque Ports, he referred simply and naturally to the 'county which stands foremost in the rank of all others, so deservedly proud of its pre-eminence in every respect'. Hasted was himself a Kentish man, and local patriotism was not only the inspiration of all these historians but their consuming passion (it often consumed their substance).

Kent has, too, a number of distinctive features. Gavelkind – the custom by which the inheritance is divided among all the sons, not concentrated on the eldest – multiplied the number of Kent gentry: here there were many more than in a comparable county, say Suffolk. Among these there was a cultivated interest in history and antiquities, law and theology, that was 'truly astonishing', as Alan Everitt says, in his Introduction. Kent produced any number of such writers, from Lambarde 'the Perambulator' onwards – witness the Dering Collections and the charming Oxinden Letters in the British Museum.

Hasted brought it all together in the work to which he devoted his life. All of us who have occasion to use his work know that he is indispensable. Indefatigable and tenacious, 'his passion was always for facts rather than interpretation, for historical substance rather than literary form'. What a work he accomplished! Pushing his way on horseback into every parish, penetrating to obscure places in the vastnesses of the Weald, chasing up documents wherever they happened to be. He was helped by other antiquaries, and by the clergy and gentry to whom by birth he advantageously belonged. His book is a rabbit-warren of the proliferating Kent gentry – pedigrees and all, needing time and scholarship to construct – who largely made the history of their county and contributed richly to that of their country.

Hasted added to his difficulties by the odd conduct of his life. Reliable in his facts, he was led astray by his fancies: a married man of fifty-three, with nine children, he absconded with a girl to

France for a bit. Having inherited an estate of £1,000 a year, he plunges deep into debt, borrowing from his lawyer – until this sharper ended up with the whole estate. 'The historian who knew so much about Kentish law . . . was no wiser than a child when in the hands of the law himself.' It was the history, not the practice, of it that enchanted him; and the result was that he spent eight years in the King's Bench prison for debt. Nothing daunted, he pursued his researches wherever he was: early on, 'I write in the midst of pipes, tobacco, on bad paper, worse pens and ink, and every inconvenience of a tavern.' It reminds me of Hazlitt; and though Hasted had not Hazlitt's sensibility, he had his tenacity and enjoyment of life in the midst of squalor.

It was the muse of History, not Mary Jane Town, with whom he 'unfortunately became acquainted' and lived for twelve years, that brought him down: here was the real passion that exhausted his purse, the sheer expense of producing all these volumes. But he is our creditor; we are his debtors.

How valuable it is to have a reliable history of all those parishes – over five hundred of them in that rich and populous county! Then, too, the last two volumes in the present edition contain a history of the city and cathedral of Canterbury. (It is odd, though perhaps in character, that Hasted does not mention Christopher Marlowe; when Dugdale, only a generation later than Shakespeare mentions his birth already to the honour of Stratford-upon-Avon.) In addition, there is the history of another cathedral city in Rochester, and of such castles and towns as Dover, Deal, Sandwich, etc. Each parish and place has a topographical description of much value, for much has changed; there are the monuments and inscriptions, the buildings that have gone, the charities founded in every town, many of which have disappeared. In short, Hasted *is* indispensable.

Though he is out to inform, not to amuse, all kinds of things catch one's eye and give one amusement. Volume III has for frontispiece a plate of Chevening House, as it was before it was spoiled – into which the Prince of Wales is to move, since Lord Stanhope left it for such use. In Queen Anne's time the succession was challenged by the three Dacre co-heiresses, by custom of gavelkind, and there was a law-suit. One sees how inconvenient, however egalitarian, this was – and the Kent gentry from Edward VI's reforming days are engaged in dis-gavelling their lands. At beautiful Boughton Malherbe, high up on its wheat-lands looking out over the Weald – a fragment of the great house left, the little church packed with the monuments of the Wottons – they disgavelled theirs.

Hasted has a tribute to that distinguished family, who contributed so much to the service of the state, in law and diplomacy, scholarship and literature, and to their numerous 'honours, at times when honours were really such'. The Wottons were one of many such families of which Hasted gives us useful accounts: Sidneys, Wyatts, Walsinghams, Cobhams, Sackvilles, Derings, Filmers, Sandyses, Scotts of Scotts-hall. (I have a particular devotion to Reginald Scott, whose book on Witchcraft is one of the most enlightened and humane classics of the Elizabethan age – and least read.)

We hear about the recent beginning of Ramsgate as a sea-bathing resort, since George III had set the fashion, the band playing 'God save the King' as His Majesty submerged. Broadstairs was the centre of the Iceland cod-fishery, and produced cod-liver oil, when places earned their living by producing not just consuming. Lamberhurst produced the splendid iron railings that surrounded Wren's St Paul's. Romantic Scotney had no romance for prosaic Hasted, but already the Husseys, to whom it owes so much, were in possession. At Rochester there was the oyster-fishery, with its Free Company of Dredgermen – does it still continue?

Hasted notices everything – botany too, the rare plants that grew about Cobham, as well as the damage wrought by the Puritans in Canterbury Cathedral during the Civil War and their plunder of Sir Robert Filmer's house, the Royalist author of *Patriarcha*. Usefully, he often gives the portraits or pictures in houses; in the east window of Waldershare church he considered 'several female figures seem singularly indecent, at any rate very improper, for the place'. Apart from Mary Jane Town, he was rather conventional; anyhow, in spite of her, he lived to be eighty and finished his book.

Robert Surtees didn't finish his *Durham*;[2] though it was almost done when he died at only fifty-four; but a society was thereupon founded, the famous Surtees Society, to carry on the good work. Though a contrast to Hasted as a man, their careers had much in common. Surtees stuck to his wife and had no Mary Jane, but he too was seduced by his passion for History into incurring a load of debt. At his death his collection of pictures, books, manuscripts, coins were all sold off to pay the debts his big book had landed him in. His passion too went back to his boyhood, when he would exchange his pocket-money for Roman coins, and from Christ Church days he intended a History of Durham. He also penetrated into every parish and farm; the driver of his gig said, 'we never could get past an auld beelding'.

The chief contrast with Hasted is that Surtees had a sense of humour – witness his account of the Lambtons and the folklore about the Lambton Worm, which was apparently of a prodigious size. They were said to fear neither God nor man, they were so profane; so a judgement came upon them. A young man of the family had committed some transgression, or 'the transgression is sometimes attributed to a wicked *quidam*, with many vulgar additions'. Surtees gives us the popular version of the Lambton Worm, with an account of Worm Hill on the estate to corroborate, while, among the pictures in the house, was 'The Woman taken in Adultery'. Some peculiar fate followed the heir of the house in consequence of the tradition. Newspapers don't know what they miss from not being up in county history.

Surtees, at Oxford the friend of the future Bishop Heber, had literary tastes and a gift for ballad-writing in antique vein – some fifty of his poems are scattered anonymously, and beguilingly, through the History. Well read in old plays and romances, he collected Border ballads and traditions. This brought him the friendship of Scott, upon whom Surtees perpetrated one of his jokes: he passed off one of his own ballads as an old one into Scott's collection. The great man, magnanimous in every way, had no small-minded incredulity: he was always readier to accept – as he accepted R. S. Hawker's Trelawny ballad as authentic. The correspondence with Scott is set out in full in Taylor's Memoir of Surtees in volume IV, adding much to the literary value of the work.

As history it is first-class. Durham was distinctive in being not a county but a palatine bishopric – Surtees appreciated the policy of the Normans in having a quasi-royal appointee in so powerful a position on the Border instead of a too powerful hereditary family. Surtees' lives of the Bishops are excellent, with his sense of character and fairness. A Whig himself, with a touch of Gibbon in his writing, he had a properly commonsense view of the Reformation and saw that the clergy were behind the silly Pilgrimage of Grace. Henry VIII, though a Catholic in his own view, was rather anti-clerical. Once, when one of the Durham Cathedral clergy asked Surtees why they no longer possessed a certain property, he replied, 'Don't ask me: ask Henry VIII'.

His book is most illuminating as to the depredations and losses of the Civil War – not only in the destruction wrought in the cathedral but of documents and archives. Surtees notes the families that lost almost all their estates for their royalism, Blakistons, Riddells, Hiltons. He makes the important point historians of the Civil War are beginning to realise – that the greater gentry were dominantly Royalist, the lesser Parliamentarian. Envy? – a much more powerful motive than academics, oddly enough, allow for in history in general. There are full-length portraits of those admirable prelates, Morton and Cosin. Cosin was persecuted by a Puritanical prebendary Smart, simply out of personal revenge, an intolerable type. Sir Arthur Heselrigg, the Cromwellian, got Auckland Castle, and pulled down Anthony Bek's chapel.

Of honest John Lilburne's family, George got the valuable lease of Harraton collieries cheap, when a Catholic recusant was sequestrated; he also managed to cheat the state of some £300. The the 'thieves quarrelled about the division of the plunder', and Heselrigg – who had made not hundreds but thousands – turned out the Lilburnes and put in the regicide Colonel Hacker and his fellow-officers. So much for the purity of Puritans.

Of course the Reformation had been no less destructive: Surtees notes the crosses that were defaced and broken by Elizabethan Puritans, and there are the empty niches on screens and monuments, eloquent in the splendid plates, that testify to the destructive seriousness with which silly people take their beliefs. Cynics, sceptics, compromisers are more reasonable and less destructive: Cromwellian Montagu, as Earl of Sandwich at Charles II's Court, always prefaced any remarks about the recent past with 'When I was a rebel'. Bishop Crewe, who eased into his bishopric with a handsome donation to Nell Gwyn, and made up to both James II and William III, turns out to have been not only a handsome gentleman but a highly benevolent man, leaving legacies and benefactions from which we still profit at Oxford.

The shortest of these classic county histories is devoted to the smallest county, James Wright's *Rutland*,[3] and is given an excellent Introduction by the general editor, Professor Simmons, from which we learn much that is new. Wright is different again from

Hasted and Surtees: he was a lawyer, who lived in London away from his county. He was also much earlier, a seventeenth-century Church-and-King Tory, whose inspiration was again Dugdale. Having written his book, he passed on to write others; subsequent editions added Supplements, and these have been incorporated in what is now the fullest and best edition.

Professor Simmons sums him up well: 'though well read, he was not a trained scholar. He was capable of assembling and ordering his materials competently and of carrying his task through to a conclusion, for he had the constructive sense and the tenacity to make a book. . . . It is appropriate that the book should be reprinted now, complete with all its Supplements, at the very moment when Rutland itself, as an autonomous unit of local government, is to disappear.'

How much we must wish this magnificent – and gallant – enterprise Good Luck! And how much more rewarding it is than sociological theorising!

NOTES

1.   Edward Hasted (intro by Alan Everitt), *The History and Topographical Survey of the County of Kent.*
2.   Robert Surtees (intro by E. Birley), *The History and Antiquities of the County Palatine of Durham.*
3.   James Wright (intro by Jack Simmons), *The History and Antiquities of the County of Rutland.*

VANISHING ENGLISH LANDSCAPES

Several friends of mine, coming at the end of an old country family, have put all the passion of their lives into preserving house, estate, possessions, pictures, books, archives – all the more so because they were at the end of their line – and handing on what they treasured so much: to whom? Usually, the National Trust. And what a good thing – better that it should be pickled and preserved than destroyed and dispersed.

It often seems to me that it is like this with the famed English countryside, never more poignantly appreciated than now when it is threatened and largely doomed, considerable areas of it vanishing before our eyes in the decades since the war. When one thinks of the destruction that has been wrought in only the past twenty years, one can envisage how little of it will be left in the next two hundred, with the mad population explosion of our time, which is at the bottom of all our troubles – and which governments do everything to encourage instead of to discourage. (What price the politics of our demotic age? – Complete and spreading disrespect for them and for politicians, here as elsewhere.)

Paradoxically all these authors make the point of the extraordinary continuity of the English landscape, 'the oldest and richest record we possess: for some four thousand years it has been written upon over and over again in a kind of code.' It is just at this juncture, too, that a school of landscape history has come into being, largely under the inspiration of W. G. Hoskins.¹ His book provides a fascinating introduction to the subject as a whole. There are a hundred landscapes in England, he tells us; and I can well believe it, since there are at least six in the small area of Cornwall alone. Everything is older than you think – that is his theme; invaders come and go, dynasties and political conditions change, but farming, cultivating the soil, must go on. He has a wonderful eye for reading the code lying all round us, where ordinary people see nothing.

Hoskins had a large part in recognising the sites of medieval deserted villages under the grass, well over two thousand of them. Years ago he took me to Ingarsby in Leicestershire, on a summer evening when the long shadows revealed the outlines: there were the village streets and lanes, the humps where the cottages had been, the largest where the church was. There it all lay beneath one's eye. Air-photography has added enormously to our knowledge of such sites, ancient field systems, Roman villas, British villages, fortified camps, barrows all but obliterated by the plough – to which in our time we add the more destructive bulldozer.

Anyone who lives on the western side of our island should have no difficulty in recognising the continuity with the prehistoric: villages not far away from an Iron Age one, such as Chysauster (of which there is an illustration, among the many fine ones in this inspired booklet), stone circles, monoliths (an impressive one stood just outside my back garden at Polmear Mine), frowning camps ringed with earthworks in every parish. Hoskins now brings out how much more of even the man-made landscape is prehistoric or Romano-British. 'Though many villages bear today an old English name, they stand upon sites that were first chosen in Roman times, if not earlier. I now suspect indeed that some of our villages stand upon sites first chosen by Bronze Age farmers. There are places where one treads on three thousand years of history. . . . How could one bear to live in a country with only a hundred or two hundred years underfoot?' The answer is that most people don't mind, because they don't notice, let alone know, anything.

Hence the destruction. There are endearing Hoskinian touches – he really is the Cobbett of our time: there are 'the planners with their money-grubbing eyes moving in before the machines arrive for the kill'; the big motorways, compared with a rural lane with all that it speaks to him, are 'boring in the extreme'. 'Now the little country railways decay, and all is Inter-City.' Fast expresses, motor-coaches, motorways take people 'from a dismal illiberal life in Birmingham to a dismal illiberal life in London'. He does not mean 'illiberal', he really means trivial and stupid; and of course he is absolutely right in his dislike and contempt for the destructive contemporary world.

His view, however, is not wholly a consistent one, any more than Cobbett's was. His affection for farmer and peasant and what they did for the landscape – the folk and communal elements – is so great that he has less sympathy for, or understanding of, what the vanishing gentry accomplished: after all, something much more distinguished, country houses of all periods; parks, plantations, woods – theirs was really intelligent planning in their day. There is a grudging tribute to their decaying houses, demolished at the rate of a hundred a year, 'melancholy memorials of a lost civilisation, for such it was at its best'. In fact theirs *was* civilisation – a better balanced one than any other worked out in the world, except possibly mandarin China; it is all the civilisation I care for anyway, and it is mortally wounded.

No doubt there are prefigurations of a new kind of society forming – in the creeping suburbia that is the real landscape of contemporary England, the TV culture that goes with it, the TV masts at every house (TV is the contemporary religion), the high-rise tenements to accommodate a madly inflated population for so small an island, the neuroses that go with over-population, the pushing and shoving, the violence, the drugs, the wish to escape. All I can say is that I agree with Hoskins in detesting everything about contemporary society (except its dentistry).

In his enchanting book I notice one major omission: there should have been a chapter on the effects of climate, for it is known to swing to and fro over historic periods. There are a few Cobbett-like judgements, endearing but wrong-headed. The Normans were not just 'plunderers', they were organisers and builders – look at their castles and cathedrals. Henry VIII was not just a 'plunderer' – too sentimental a view; he also was a great builder, and the Reformation has at least the excuse that it created far more than it destroyed – so did the Tudor squires, here deplored. Nor in fact did the Crown create all those boroughs in Cornwall in order to 'pack Parliament': it was the expansive gentry who increasingly wanted somewhere to sit for. Hoskins has an addiction to the word 'vast', which his disciple Norman Scarfe shares:[2] if they knew the spaces of the Middle West they would know the scale on which it applies. *A propos* of words, I question a little Mr Scarfe's use of 'tool', which has become a favourite *cliché* of research, part of the process of mechanising everything; but it makes me laugh equivocally – what is wrong with the old word 'aid'?

The pupil's book is well worthy of the Master: both Hoskins and Scarfe have imagination and a sense of poetry to light up their pages. I have learned so much from Scarfe's book, and there are so many acute observations his eye has made going about his native county. He brings home to us that Suffolk has never been a unity, West and East being divided up by the clay woodlands down the middle. East Anglia had its prehistoric henges, but in the absence of stone they were of wood. The prehistoric is less in evidence and, since Suffolk was for long one of the most highly populated of counties, more has been obliterated; but there are still the barrows, earthworks, dykes, and such a fabulous find as the burial at Sutton Hoo. Greens are characteristic of East Anglia, while churches provide the bone-structure of the landscape. We learn with surprise that concentrated villages are *not* characteristic; but then the pattern of nucleated and dispersed settlement is more diverse and complex than a previous generation thought.

Mr Scarfe's book is as much history, for the earlier periods, as it is geography; it is surprisingly learned about archaeology. One can sometimes have too much of a good thing: one does not really want to know the precise measurements of a Roman road at different portions of its length – one can't see the road for the measurements: enough to say that it varied from 15 to 32 ft. But he is undoubtedly right to insist that one must go back behind the place names to the archaeology; in this way he reveals how much of earlier Romano-British settlement exists just under the surface. He is candid about the squalor of the way of life of the Germans who broke in, the Roman dykes and drains neglected so that fen and marsh took over. He is strong on the contacts of these barbarians with the Frisia they came over from, and has explored its comparable archaeology.

So well spread before the reader – with compelling illustrations – one can yet not entirely repress a Gibbonian regret for the decline and fall of the Roman Empire. What *would* Britain have been like, with its altogether higher civilisation, the villas with their mosaics and hypocausts, the temples and monuments and walled cities? Bede could not but admire, and one gets some idea of it still from Bath – *there* was civilisation.

Now in turn our civilisation is breaking down under its own weight. Ancient halls and settlements are being submerged to appease 'the water-god of Ipswich'. What wonder when the West Suffolk County Council reveals 'the appalling estimates that, a mere decade from now, three of the best historic towns in England will be virtually doubled: Bury from twenty-three thousand to forty thousand, Hadleigh from four thousand four hundred to eight thousand, Sudbury from seven thousand to sixteen thousand.' They will be ruined, of course, as Ipswich has been irretrievably. Of St Mary's Square at Bury, where Wesley preached and Clarkson lived, what 'slow, slow centuries this beautiful small square still manages to suggest.' Slow? – 'it is traversed now by motor traffic of which we long to see it rid.' Far more likely is what has happened to the almost unique boundary of Hundred Lane, 'south of the one thousand feet mast of the IBA's television transmitter. To the west of the main road, the Hundred Lane has lately lost its ditches, and looks like any farm track'.

Of another unique site, an Elizabethan open-air playing-place only recently discovered, Mr Scarfe writes, 'what is so maddening is that the discovery, after four long centuries, of so rare and remarkable a theatre-in-the-round should coincide exactly with the site's being built on, for the first time ever, and by a large neo-Georgian house covered, so characteristically, in shingle-dash or rough-cast'. But, of course: they wouldn't know or notice.

Why bother any more? – the present is beyond praying for, only the past is worth caring for.

Of Suffolk's greatest inheritance, its five hundred medieval churches 'many of them are now threatened with redundancy, alas, in our over-peopled, financially incompetent society'. It is more usually referred to as the Affluent Society, though it is not merely a dirty word to me but an insult to anyone who cares for our heritage. To philistines no matter: they see nothing and understand nothing. But they are the great majority. Culture has always been the creation of a small minority; but in the past it was that minority that had the power. This is no longer so; and in the laying waste all round we see what the great mass of human beings really are without order, standards, or direction. (They are incapable of operating without direction from above – as the Communists well know, liberals not.)

It is rather surprising, with someone so exquisitely aware of those wonderful Suffolk churches, that he says nothing about the destruction wrought by an earlier generation of philistines, the Puritan fanatics of the Civil War, whose bestial doings in the smashing of hundreds of stained glass windows, brasses, statues, monuments, are faithfully recorded in the Diary of the hateful Dowsing.

In a perceptive sentence Mr Scarfe sums up the theme of all these books: 'England's most original contribution to the whole history of art lies in the landscape, and was an affair of creating harmonious pictures with the land itself.' This is obviously more true of the Suffolk landscape, home of the great landscape painters, than of the Lake District, where nature still dominates: mountains and lakes, not churches and streams. Yet even here man's contribution to the look of things has been decisive. The Cistercians converted the fells to sheep-pasture; in the course of centuries the surface has become heavily over-grazed sheep-walk, the woodlands denuded. 'This down-grading has been accelerated during the last few decades.' It can be arrested only by afforestation, which we must favour because it replaces and builds up soil. Even so, there is unsightly afforestation, and sightly – the latter is to be preferred.

The ghastly population explosion is having its deadly consequences here too. Pollution is 'the cause of the destruction of every reason why man wishes to use lakes for the supply of water or for his enjoyment'. 'The southern basin receives the sewage of

Windermere and Bowness and the outflow of Esthwaite Water. Will Windermere become another lake whose beauty [what does the idiot people care about beauty?] and recreational value is reduced by the development of algal scums and tangles together with the products of their decomposition?' Windermere is already suitably described as 'an urbanised lake'. 'Grasmere [Wordsworth's Grasmere] is threatened by a new sewage scheme due to come into operation shortly.' Esthwaite Water has been protected by the ancient family of Sandys – Hoskins might notice; but for how long? We all know the contemporary amenity the Lake District can boast – the great nuclear power-station of Calder Hall.

Pearsall and Pennington's book[3] is quite as good as the other two – they are all first class – and much fuller on the side of natural history: geology, climate, ecology, flora and fauna. Here too one protests occasionally at excessive knowledge, distracting the reader: does one need all those wild-bird counts, any more than counting the shrubs in ancient hedges, a fad Hoskins and Scarfe have swallowed from a Dr Hooper? In the writing of books one should always have a graduated scale of relevance to the subject.

The Lake District is the scene of the National Trust's most spectacular work in preservation and rehabilitation. Anyone who wants to lend a hand to preserving what is left of the vanishing landscape of a better England should join it -- practically the only institution of contemporary society one can wholeheartedly approve.

NOTES

1.   W. G. Hoskins, *English Landscapes*, (B.B.C. Publications).
2.   Norman Scarfe, *The Suffolk Landscape*, (Hodder & Stoughton).
3.   W. H. Pearsall and Winifred Pennington, *The Lake District. A Landscape History*. (Collins).

DARK AGES

Writing in the security of eighteenth-century rational aristocratic society Gibbon regarded the scuffles of the Dark Ages as the battles of 'kites and crows'. They were not the less destructive. Mr Blair tells us[1] that the first half of the seventh century in England was 'an age characterised by war, murder, treachery, apostacy and infant mortality'; and that 'the normal expectation of a Northumbrian king in the seventh century was to be killed in battle. . . . The history of other Anglo-Saxon kingdoms in this age – Mercia or Wessex – has left much the same sort of record in their annals'. Such were the charming Germans who invaded Britain in the fifth century and largely conquered the best half of it in the sixth century.

More important – since the Britons were just as good, or bad, at fighting and killing – were the losses in civilisation and civilised skills upon the decline and withdrawal of Rome. The Germans emerging from their forests naturally built in wood; they had not much notion of stone building, couldn't mix mortar, let alone make brick or glass. The Roman canals and irrigation system, which had made the area around the Wash a good granary, collapsed into fenland. Anglo-Saxons could neither read nor write; Mr Blair tells us that literacy was destroyed in all the parts of Britain occupied by them. As for Roman hypocausts and central heating, it was not until the twentieth century that anything like them were seen in the unfortunate island again.

A civilised historian cannot help but grieve at the decline and fall of Rome; an imaginative one cannot but wonder what the character and fortunes of the island would have been if the English had not conquered it, or more than half of it. More like France, with its basically Celtic population? More like Ireland? – that would have been no improvement, as we can all see. It is the absence of the Roman element that is so regrettable – though it shortly came back again in the shape of the Church. We can never be sufficiently grateful to the Church for what it did in civilising the barbarians, teaching them two Rs, even if the third was still beyond them.

In a sense the Britons never forgave the Anglo-Saxons for the conquest of their island. Bede disliked the Britons and held it strongly against them that they would do nothing to convert the

English to Christianity. But why should they? The invading
Germans had taken the best part of their land from them, killed its
inhabitants – in some areas exterminated them – enslaved others,
while from the south-west many fled to constitute a lesser Britain
in Brittany. No wonder there has always been a residual hatred of
the English among the Welsh – and, as a pure Cornishman, I am
certainly not starry-eyed about the English or very sympathetic
about the fate they have called down upon themselves today. But
I am not concerned in their fate or fortunes today; I am interested
only in their past, their quite remarkable record – under the lead
of the ablest governing class in Europe – in history. The past of
this country is vastly more interesting than its future is likely to be.

Historians are now coming to realise that the Germans began
infiltrating into Britain before the end of the Roman Empire. Few
in number to begin with, they have left evidences of their early
presence in their pagan cemeteries at Winchester and York, in
Norfolk and the Thames valley. On the withdrawal of Rome the
Britons employed them as mercenaries when the province was
under attack all round by Picts, Scots and Irish. The day came
when the Germans – always good at breeding and fighting,
land-hungry and having spied out the 'capabilities' of the land –
called in their kinsmen from overseas and revolted against their
masters. From the mud-swamps all the way round from Jutland
to Frisia the Germans had an inexhaustible reservoir of man-
power, and woman-power, behind them. The great weakness of
the Celts was their inability to combine, their individualism and a
certain unpracticality: the Irish Celts gave no help, they con-
tinued to attack western Britain; in the north-east the Picts
combined with the invaders against the Britons.

Nevertheless, the struggle was a long one. It was not for a
century and a half that the issue was decided and southern Britain
became finally dominated by the English. Today they are receiving something of their comeuppance; the unity of the island, or
islands, which was the achievement of their governing class, is
caving in with the caving in of that governing class. Ordinary
people, of course, care nothing about such things; they cannot
govern themselves, let alone govern an Empire! (Who can care
tuppence about such a society?)

When the Anglo-Saxons came to be brought by Christianity
within the orbit of civilisation the campaign was led from the
south-east by Rome, with Augustine's mission, and from the
north-west by Irish Celts from Iona – not, be it noticed, from

Wales or the south-west. The original Britons, whose land it had been, preferred withdrawal. Nevertheless, as Mr Harrison tells us,[2] a tremendous barrage of missionary enterprise was directed upon the English all through the seventh century from these two sources. We must not neglect the large part played in it by the northern Celts, though the southern wouldn't play. It seems that their activity still continues. Recently during the Second German War, on the night when Durham was to have been shattered by a Baedeker Raid, St Cuthbert shrouded his city in a dense fog so that the bombers could not get through to wreck his cathedral. On the other hand, the oldest text of Nennius' *Historia Brittonum* was destroyed in the Second German War.

Mr Harrison's book is a work of specialist Anglo-Saxon scholarship, of importance for establishing a firm chronology for the early history of the English. As G. M. Trevelyan – not an English name – says: 'There is no appeal from the verdict of a date'. (Eng. Lit. scholars dealing with Shakespeare should take that to heart: most of them have no idea of the decisive importance of getting the date right, are all over the place with the dating of the Sonnets and are in consequence in needless confusion about their interpretation – witness the nonsense written about them by Dover Wilson and Douglas Bush.)

Mr Harrison is indispensable on his subject, quite convincing, but rather technical. The complicated business of working out a reliable calendar was of crucial importance; for practical secular reasons as well as the religious one of arriving at a uniform date for the observance of Easter. That, too, was a practical matter in a Christian world, where diverse dates for religious festivals were highly inconvenient as well as a matter for scandal. Even centuries later in the thirteenth century R. L. Poole illustrates for us how awkward diverse chronologies could be.

If we suppose a traveller to set out from Venice on March 1, 1245, the first day of the Venetian year, he would find himself in 1244 when he reached Florence; and if after a short stay he went to Pisa, the year 1246 would already have begun there. Continuing his journey westward, he would find himself again in 1245 when he entered Provence, and on arriving in France before Easter (April 16) he would be once more in 1244.

The awkwardness of it all reminds one of our perplexity in the early days of Relativity:

> There was a young lady named Bright,
> Whose speed was far faster than light;
>   She set out one day
>   In a relative way,
> And returned home the previous night.

Working out a firm calendar depended on astronomical observations and correlating lunar with solar months. I never had much head for mathematics and, as a choirboy, I was not amused by the tables for calculating Easter in our Prayer Book, though I am by the name of the worthy to whom we owe them – Dionysius Exiguus. The issue of the calendar and the correct date for Easter was the symbolic issue of the struggle between Rome and the Celts for the souls of the English. The battle was joined at Whitby in 664 and, as everybody knows, Rome won. It is just like the Celts to adhere to an antiquated system years behind the times. Wales would not even catch up with it for yet another century; Iona accepted defeat and recognised common sense in 715, Wales not until 768.

The Anglo-Saxons – besides producing a man of immeasurably more genius in Bede than the Britons did in Gildas – were far more practical. Bede wrote two works on chronology, on top of everything else; his *De Temporum Ratione* 'enjoyed a European fame throughout the Middle ages. Thus England, and England alone, had acquired an era at once stable and Christian'. In addition to being

> the most significant historian of the early Middle Ages, in his hands the Christian era was lifted from a narrow legal background into a larger usefulness where it has remained ever since. Apart from the wealth of information he supplies, the writing of history was thereafter placed on a more secure foundation than almost anyone had known since classical antiquity.

Justice compels me to admit that the Celts never produced anybody like Bede.

Mr Herm, who is a German, has written a book on the Celts which might have been entitled more appropriately, 'Who were the Celts?'.[3] He shows at least how complex the subject is. The first thing to be clear about is that it is not a racial concept; the word is first and foremost a linguistic one and applies to those who speak, or did speak, Celtic languages. Then, it is true, other characteristics come in, especially the sense of affinity, the sense of belonging together: Cornish folk all over the world, for example, have a sense of belonging together (as I know from observing it, and from my fan-mail). It is too subtle a matter to go fully into here.

Mr Herm shows – though with rather too much archaeological hypothesis to please me altogether – that the Celts, when they become recognisable by their art and language, have diverse origins, not so very different from other components of Ur-Europe – the Celtic languages are closest to Italic. When we come to characteristics that stand out we get plenty of information from observers and descriptive writers. They all agreed on Celtic drunkenness – and what about the Bretons and the Irish? One of the things I find most insupportable about the Irish is their failing for drink. Reading a recent biography of T. H. White, there it was – along with several other recognisable traits, the double dose of egoism, the vanity, the generosity, the sheer personalism, the inflated personality. Neither himself not his biographer (awarded a prize for her biography) seemed to be aware of it: the family had been deracinated for a couple of generations, and yet, there he was – the unreconstructed Irishman. Nothing surprises me more than people's imperceptiveness in these matters. Cyril Connolly was another, his characteristics irretrievably Irish, and yet – to judge from his writings – hardly aware of it or what a clue this was to his personality. Or Eugene O'Neill. Or Scott Fitzgerald. As Henry James used to say: 'Nobody ever understands *any*thing'. (Another verbose *deracinated* Irishman, by the way, courtesy and all.)

Mr Herm's subject is the emergence of the Celts, the extraordinary impression they made on Greece and Rome, their brief apogee and sputtering out. For, of course, they achieved no integration. Mr Herm makes the point I have made earlier about the Britons. The Celts seem never to have undertaken 'the hard work of exploiting and organising their resources. They manifestly failed in the attempt – if indeed they ever made it – to set up one or more large states; although on a smaller scale they did here and there create what they never managed on a larger scale'. There we are again. The Irish have always girded against the Elizabethan conquest of Ireland, but the Irish were incapable of achieving any satisfactory integrated state on their own: people like that, in human history, lie open to having one imposed on them.

Greeks like Polybius were struck not only by the vanity and quick-temperedness of the Celts – quarrelling at meals, etc. – but appalled by their habit of head-hunting. I suppose that this is a feature of all human societies at a certain stage of development, compare the American Indians. To this nasty habit the Celts added an unpleasant method of divination.

> They consecrate a human being to death, drive a dagger into his belly and draw conclusions about events to come from the squirming of the victim and the spurting of his blood. They have been practising this custom since time immemorial.

Mr Herm is much interested in this aspect of things. He tells us that before their distinctive emergence the Celts were not far different from Germans, both tall and fair, as against dark and short Romans. Then there was the sacrificial habit of cutting victims' throats into beautifully chased basins. Nice animals, humans!

NOTES

1. P. Hunter Blair, *Northumbria in the Days of Bede*, (Gollancz).
2. Kenneth Harrison, *The Framework of Anglo-Saxon History*, (Cambridge University Press).
3. Gerhard Herm, *The Celts*, (Weidenfeld).

III

GERMAN HALF-COUSINS

How far are the Germans cousins of the British? They are certainly not cousins of mine, for I am one hundred per cent a Cornish Celt. They are only half-cousins, if that, of John Mander[1] for on his mother's side he is Cornish too – he seems to be unaware of that.

This reflection serves to point up a consideration of general significance. Mr Mander proceeds on the old-fashioned Victorian assumption that Britain is peopled exclusively by Anglo-Saxons. In fact, the British are a mixed lot: it would probably be better to describe them as Anglo-Celtic, for at least a third – all down the western half of the island and including pockets, for example, in Yorkshire – are pre-Anglo-Saxon: they descend from the original Britons, Picts and Scots. So, when Mr Mander tells us as an 'evident, embarrassing, incontrovertible fact about the English people, that they were once Germans themselves', he is referring only to one of the elements that make up our people, though the dominant one.

The British, even the English, are a mixed people, like their language: not to appreciate that accounts for much misunderstanding of our history and character, particularly on the part of the Germans. I seem to have written *The Spirit of English History*, on this theme, in vain – evidently not read at Mr Mander's Cambridge (his is a very easterly, Cambridge book). What about the other side to the proposition: are the Germans all that German? Anybody who knows anything about such matters realises that the German people must be – from Saxony eastwards – one-third Slav. So the second leg of the stool on which Mr Mander sets his book is seen to be somewhat rickety too. However, we must not be too severe: Mr Mander is not a scholar but an intelligent journalist. He has made a spirited attempt to tell the curious and eventually tragic story of the relations between Britain and Germany. In the course of it he makes some good points and produces some interesting information, actually better on literature than on politics.

His book could easily have been so much better if he had read more of the first-rate instead of settling for the second-rate. He cites a historian such as Bracher, and does not seem to have read the first German historian of the day, Fritz Fischer. That would have corrected his perspective; for Fischer makes no doubt of the fact that the two German wars of this century were but two crests of the long wave of German expansion, aiming at the domination of Europe and *Weltmacht*.

This would have prevented Mr Mander from repeating the old rubbish about 'the disaster of Versailles'. The 'disaster' for the Germans was simply that they didn't win. The most judicial international lawyer at Oxford, J. L. Brierley – a man of the Left – always held that the territorial settlement at Versailles was *all too just*. (We can see what the Germans would have done, if they had won, from the Treaty of Brest-Litovsk, taking territory right up to St Petersburg.) As for the economic consequences of Versailles, Mr Mander swallows Keynes's view that the Germans were unable to pay the Reparations claimed from them. The point is that they never attempted to; Etienne Mantoux, in *The Carthaginian Peace*, showed that Nazi Germany spent twice as much on Armaments as the Reparations they defaulted on. It is true that the Armaments expenditure was internal, but they took far more in Loans from the U.S.A. – and spent it internally – than they ever paid in Reparations.

Mr Mander realises that Keynes 'had no special knowledge of Germany'; he had not indeed – and a Liberal like Arthur Salter realised that *The Economic Consequences of the Peace* did untold damage.

With regard to the deliberate Naval challenge to Britain – when Britain depended on sea-power for her very existence and Germany already enjoyed safe military superiority – Mr Mander should have read first-rate authorities like E. L. Woodward's *Great Britain and the German Navy*, and Marder's first volume on the British Navy. The American Marder shows that the Germans could have had an understanding with Britain, but they always insisted on the condition of a free hand in Europe, i.e. European domination. Even Tirpitz realised in the end that the Naval Challenge to Britain's existence – it was intended as such – had been a mistake. But the Kaiser, with the General Staff, would not accept this: their aims were completely continuous with Hitler's – the domination of Europe.

Mr Mander sees that the Kaiser's love-hate complex about Britain was quite 'typical of his generation in Germany, and particularly of the industrialists and shipping magnates who backed the Navy League'. But not only of them: it was widespread throughout the German middle-classes, to go no further. It is superficial to describe other peoples' distrust of the Germans as just on account of their 'unpredictability'; they are, of course, a schizophrenic people. Travel anywhere on the borders of Germany, and ask people – especially the Slavs – what they think of them: those people know them from experience and recognise their hysteria and brutality. Even their former friends, the Dutch, know it today.

So there was nothing wrong with Vansittart's diagnosis: it was exactly borne out by their behaviour. German aggression had 'three elements to work on, all of which are well-known to those with any knowledge of German psychology. The three are Envy, Self-Pity, and Cruelty'. Precisely correct in each term. The interesting thing is that it is always the second-rate who are pro-Germans in Britain, the first-rate who recognise what is what about them. Among the pro-Germans, a Kingsley Martin or a Crossman, a Brailsford (who had an aggressively German wife), the Headlam-Morleys (half-Germans), the Astors (who had a German origin), etc. Among those who knew the Germans for what they were – not only Vansittart but Dalton (he described them as 'a race of carnivorous sheep'), Winston Churchill, Eden, the Cecils; among writers, Kipling, Chesterton, Rebbeca West, Waugh.

When it comes to scholarship, the influence of Luther on English Protestantism was very small, largely confined to Henry VIII's reign and Cranmer. English Protestantism had its own origins in Wyclif and the Lollards, long before Luther. After Cranmer, the influence of Calvin was immensely more important. The theology of the Elizabethan Church was largely Calvinist and so were all the Puritans.

In the nineteenth century, where the German influence was beneficial was not in literature but in scholarship: in more exact standards in historical, classical and Biblical studies. There is little about this, or about the influence – much less salutary, possibly on balance deleterious – of German philosophy. On this subject, Mr Mander misses a first-class book, Santayana's *Egotism and German Philosophy*. And there is nothing whatever about the field in which later Germany led Europe: chemistry, physics, metallurgy, dye-stuffs, optics, etc.

Among the interesting points Mr Mander does make is the new one to me, that Engels wrote the pro-German articles in the *Pall*

Mall during the Franco-German war of 1870–1. He would. A Czech once said to me in a bus in Germany: '*Ein Deutscher ist dreimal Deutsch*'. And Mr Mander brings out well that it was Madame de Staël who put the consciousness of Germany into Europe's mind with her book, *De l'Allemagne*; as it was the odious (on the whole) Carlyle who impressed it upon the Victorian middle-classes. I say 'on the whole', odious, because he hated art, the redeeming feature and the redemptive faculty of man. 'It is expected in this Nineteenth Century that a man of culture shall understand and worship Art: among the windy gospels addressed to our poor Century there are few louder than this of Art.' Nothing like the amount of wind he gave vent to – and who wouldn't prefer a pre-Raphaelite picture, or a Millais or a Frith, to any one of his works? There is a funny thing about Carlyle's Teutonism: his name, after all, is Celtic, while his wife was Welsh on both sides. If a Celt – and he came from the Celtic South West of Scotland – he took the wrong turning; as he certainly took the wrong turning when he spent ten years of his life exalting the homosexual unbeliever, Frederick of Prussia, as the virtuous Protestant hero. (Did Carlyle not *know*? He seems to have been singularly unaware of the facts of life, even his own.)

Mr Mander does not seem aware that there was this streak in the Kaiser too. And there is nothing whatever on the music, the field where the Germans were supreme, or on its influence in England. Handel was adopted as an Englishman and, if any German was a cult-hero to the Victorians, it was Mendelssohn, worshipped by them and not even mentioned here.

NOTE

1. John Mander, *Our German Cousins. Anglo-German Relations in the 19th and 20th Centuries* (John Murray).

EUROPE'S HISTORY AND GERMANY'S

These two good books reflect on history, and conclusions we may draw from it, to some purpose: the first,[1] on the patterns of Europe's history, seen by an American who realises how much America belongs to it; the second,[2] by a German whose exile and long residence in America have yielded him revealing insights into his homeland not given to many enclosed in it.

Professor McNeill's is full of fresh suggestive thoughts: American in its fair-minded impartial view of things, in its emphasis on the material forces making for historic change, and in the dispiriting business-American in which it is written, scarred by dreadful words. He starts from the nineteenth-century Western idea of history as the progressive realisation of liberty, particularly associated with Acton and expressed in the first issue of the *Cambridge Modern History*. He notes how superior that was to the recent new *CMH*; but this is not owing to the absence of Acton's liberal organising principle only, but to the fact that the select academic historians of a generation ago were so much better.

What remains of the liberal idea today? Actually, I think more than McNeill allows. In spite of our disappointments, I discern a general march of improvement – in human beings' lot and even in them – as against the horrors and set-backs to be expected. The processes at work are very complex. McNeill holds a just balance between the natural and impersonal forces, the environment, and the active will of man changing it; between societies' resistance to change and the innovations effected by exceptional men; between their unconscious urges and their conscious directives. He is very sympathetic to the anthropological approach – as I am.

The organising principle he would apply to Europe's history is something like this: the interractions of contact between societies produce stimulating results; surpluses above subsistence-level – e.g. the wine and oil of Athens – enable cultural centres to develop. Their cultural achievements – Athens, Rome, Paris, the Italian cities, the Netherlands and progressive North-Western Europe – depend on a surplus for the leisure of *élites*, who create the grand works of civilisation.

There is a good deal in this to account for the changing patterns of Europe's astonishing record of creativeness. And McNeill makes perceptive observations in the course of his brisk *tour d'horizon*: the significance of the Germanic plough that could turn a furrow, the boundary between the long-field cultivation of Northern Europe in consequence and the small-field South; the effects of changing military techniques, of fuel and food shortages, the agricultural and industrial revolutions.

He has a realism worthy of respect – e.g. 'the repeated adjustments of the international balance of power in the seventeenth and eighteenth centuries through war and diplomacy was [*sc* were] a minor triumph for rationality and calculation in human affairs'. This, if bad grammar, is good sense – unlike the usual liberal nonsense about 'playing the game of power politics'. (Do they expect politics to aim at weakness, defeat? *They* manage to.)

McNeill believes – as I do – in the leadership of the Irrational by the Rational, a more profound rationalism which recognises the enormous areas and power exercised by the unconscious and irrational. 'Yet reason has its way of outwitting unreason: the discovery of irrational levels of psychic life was itself a triumph of reasoning.' And he recognises, with the insight of an historian, that the transformation of the whole world today stems from Europe – essentially Western Europe: 'with the spread of industrialism and of modern patterns of economic and political management all the earth has in some measure become the heir of European thought and technology'. He concludes, 'it now seems premature to suppose that the old centres of European civilisation have exhausted their creative power'. Hence the inexhaustible interest of European history – though few see it as a whole.

The central problem of European history is that of Germany and the Germans – about which the English would not take telling, in spite of all the evidence, before 1914 and again would not listen (unforgivably) before 1939. After all, Vansittart was roughly right. The Germans are the largest of European peoples – except for the marginal Russians – occupying the strategic centre of the continent, and should have formed the keystone of the arch. Instead of operating as such, they have done their worst for the past century, like blind Samson, to bring the temple down. Why couldn't they operate responsibly, and unaggressively, as Europe's proper centre-piece?

Kahler has the answers; indeed they have become truisms now – though, for most of my life, one could hardly get a hearing for them.

What makes Germany unique among the European nations is that she did not experience normal growth and never achieved anything like maturity. She never progressed beyond a protracted puberty and endless becoming, and achieved national coherence only in the intellectual realm but never in the political one.

Perhaps it was too big, as it certainly was too difficult – yet bigger areas have achieved it, Russia, China, USA. There is a certain boundlessness in the German mind, an inadequate hold on the external universe – hence the greatest German achievements, their music (where the experience and the form are *innerlich*) and their philosophical idealism, hopelessly subjective as it is. (I agree with Santayana that their philosophy has been, on the whole, a disaster for Europe and themselves, like their politics.)

Kahler, following the analogy of Freud, takes it all back to the childhood of the *Volk* and the failure to be conquered and licked into shape by Rome. Here he has a typically German lack of proportion himself: whole chapters on the early German tribes and hardly anything about the abysmal Bismarck. After all, the nineteenth century is far more important in the story, Bismarck more significant than Ataulf.

In one sense, I am less defeatist and more liberal in my interpretation of German history: there *were* numerous eminent liberals in nineteenth-century Germany, there was even a strong liberal tradition which *might* – conceivably – have moved towards responsible self-government. But Bismarck's triumphant unification of Germany by Blood and Iron aborted all these hopes and seduced Germans along this retrograde path. It has put the clock back for Europe by a century or so.

It can be argued, as A. J. P. Taylor cynically does (his book *The Course of German History* might be entitled *The Curse of German History*), that it couldn't have come about in any other than Bismarck's way, German liberals were always so ineffective. But one must never take an inevitabilist view of history: people can take a right course, as well as a wrong one. Bismarck hated responsible government – he called it the 'revolution' – and destroyed its prospects of effectively rooting itself in Germany. That was the real turning-point for us, not Ataulf or Alaric.

But Kahler is completely right about Luther, the central figure in German history and the most characteristic German of all time. Idiotic that the Victorian English so venerated the brute – a brute of tremendous force and genius, as Hitler was: each driven by the typical German daemon, compounded of resentment, inflamed sense of inferiority, boundless energy and force of will. It is a defect that Kahler never mentions Schopenhauer, with his emphasis on the World as Will and Idea. Germans project their inner, subjective view of the universe upon the external world with such force that they have twice almost succeeded in inflicting their nightmare vision of it upon the world.

Kahler is right enough in carrying all this back to Luther – though naturally Luther was so successful (like Hitler) because he so effectively expressed what was already there. The lust to bring down the walls of Rome and Catholicism, the mixture of brutality and sentimentality, the coarseness and the musicality, the domesticity and bourgeois vulgarity, the daimonic force – 'Why don't we wash our hands in their blood?' The Thirty Years' War, which set Germany back for two centuries, was one result. Then, though his own revolt against authority had helped to precipitate the Peasants' Revolt, there was his appeal to the Princes:

> Dear lords, stab, slay and strangle wherever you can. It is better that all the peasants be killed than that the princes and magistrates perish, because the rebels took the sword without divine authority.

Kahler diagnoses the pernicious influence Luther and Lutheranism have had in the disjunction between spirit and body, the fatal over-emphasis upon faith as against men's works and deeds. We observe subjectivism again, the renunciation of responsible action, submission to authority, supine passivity and lack of moral courage (plenty of physical!), the lust to obey. Kahler points out that the sainted Pastor Niemöller – ex-submarine commander – 'let Nazi atrocities go unchallenged, finally opposing the Nazis only when they attacked the Protestant faith'.

Faith and fanaticism, subjectivism on the scale of a megalomaniac national egoism, inability to see anybody else's point of view or to accept responsibility for what they do (everybody else is always to blame) – these have been the undoing of the greatest people in Europe, with immeasurable resources of genius, energy and ability. It has been a great tragedy, for themselves as well as others, and it does at least go back to Luther, in whom the German *Volk* found its historic expression.

The issue is expressed dramatically in the confrontation between those two Teutons of genius: Luther, from the inner depths of the Teutonic forest, Erasmus from the Dutch frontiers in touch with European civilisation, a cardinal and symbolic figure. The argument was over the Will. When Erasmus put forward the rational case for Free Will, Luther retorted with devastating effect, 'The Holy Ghost is not a sceptic'. There you are – nonsense is more powerful than sense, thinking with the bowels more effective than with the head. Erasmus's manifesto was *De Libero Arbitrio*, Luther's *De Servo Arbitrio*, of course: Luther won, not the argument, but the German people, with the consequences Kahler well describes. (The dangerous thing is that there is so much to be said for the regressive German point of view.)

Today – after two appalling blood-baths in the upshot – the argument is resumed, with somewhat better prospects, I hope, within and for Germany. Perhaps she is coming, at last, to take something like her proper place in Europe.

NOTES

1.   W. H. McNeill, *The Shape of European History* (Oxford University Press).
2.   Erich Kahler, *The Germans* (ed by R. and R. Kimber) (Princeton University Press).

BISMARCK'S RESPONSIBILITY

Of the various biographies of Bismarck in English Alan Palmer's *Bismarck* is the best that I have read.[1] It is also the most sympathetic and the most understanding of the man and even, to a considerable extent, of the politician. Mr Palmer prides himself on keeping a cool head, 'without succumbing to the deep passions which have induced so many historians to feel strongly committed "for" or "against" the Iron Chancellor'.

This is a good line for a biographer to take: he should not be unsympathetic to his subject, and Mr Palmer is a sensitive biographer. We learn at once something significant psychologically. The Bismarcks had been Prussion Junkers (landed gentry) for 500 years. But this one turned after his ambitious mother, a Mencken, of Saxon stock serving in the Prussian administration.

This is where he got his brains: he had 'the mind of a Mencken in the frame of a Bismarck'. His mother saw to it that he had the best possible education and diplomatic training, learned languages, and soon he spoke English perfectly and had an early fancy for an English girl. With travel, and posts in various parts of Europe, his horizons opened out.

We must not deny that Bismarck had genius. He had all the attributes: the tensions and contradictions within, which go with it and from which it springs.

This genius enabled him to see clearly into the essence of a situation and take advantage of it, for he was above all a ruthless realist, who believed only in the facts of power. He hated illusions, and the people who held them; he thought that hate was as much of a motive for action as ever love was.

Of course, he was on an escalator moving upwards. Germany could not have been unified from the south under the leadership of Austria; unification was bound to come from the north, and under Prussia's leadership. But the disastrous thing was that this man of genius was determined that Prussia should retain her autocracy, based on the Army; and that Germany should be unified on that basis.

Again and again he wrecked the chances of representative, Parliamentary government within Prussia, and then within his Bismarckian Germany. He called Parliamentarianism 'the Revolution'. Several times over old William I might have abdicated in favour of the liberal, constitutionally-minded Crown Prince Frederick, if Bismarck hadn't saved the old autocrat.

This was why Bismarck hated Frederick and his wife Vicky, Queen Victoria's daughter: he checkmated them at every turn, and aborted their hopes of a responsible, constitutionally-governed Germany. Vicky wrote that the principles of constitutional government 'are the only ones which can alone be the saving – not only of Prussia's position in Europe and in Germany – but of the Prussian monarchy'.

Wasn't she right, and in the not so very long run? The collapse of 1918 showed that Germany had been fatally led to take the wrong turning by Bismarck.

Mr Palmer's coolness gives him a turn for meiosis. This is all very well for a biographer; but an historian has to consider consequences. 'Within Germany Bismarck failed in one important respect; he never attempted to build up a secure form of government in the Reich,' he writes.

So far from *failing*, Bismarck was all too successful in ruining the chances of one. Even Mr Palmer sees that the result was that Imperial Germany was dominated by the Army and the militarists: hence the aggression that ruined Europe.

Gladstone represented the alternative: 'the bringing about the common accord of Europe, embodying in one organ the voice of civilised Europe'. Bismarck managed to ruin any chance of that, with his alliance of the three reactionary empires, Germany, Russia, Austria-Hungary. Mr Palmer says coolly: 'There was no other statesman whom Bismarck so completely failed to understand.'

Meiosis again. Bismarck understood Gladstone all right (as Hitler understood Chamberlain). Bismarck detested 'Herr-Professor Gladstone' for his civilised liberal hopes of mankind. The results are what we see, for Germany herself, no less than for Europe. And no one bears a greater historical responsibility for it than Bismarck.

NOTE

1.   Alan Palmer, *Bismarck* (Weidenfeld).

THE APPALLING TWENTIETH CENTURY

The first thing to be said about this book is that it achieves its purpose: it gives one a pretty fair portrait of the age we live in, both in its text and its rich gallery of illustrations, quite representative and revealing in all their proliferating and ghastly horror.[1] The editor apologises for omitting accounts of the rise of the mass media, of mass entertainment and sport; but he need not have done so, for the book already provides us with a sufficient diet of the delights of mass civilisation.

Prominently displayed as a kind of text is the editor's declaration, 'It has been an alarming period in which to live; but as a man who has lived through nearly sixty years of the 20th century, I record my conviction that I would not have wished to be born at any other time.' That is neither here nor there, merely one man's personal sentiment.

What the historian has to do is to put a few questions as to the record in general.

What are we to think of a century which – in the centre of the most advanced and civilised Continent – in the shape of the Germans, at its heart and strategic centre, put to death six million Jews, in gas-chambers, etc?

What are we to think of a century which is rapidly polluting the whole planet, oceans, skies, land alike?

The fundamental fact about the twentieth century is that everything has got out of proportion with the human scale – not only the technology, the mechanisms, nuclear fission (which for the first time in history can put an end to it all – *that* is the really new distinctive thing about it), but the human race itself. Uncontrolled proliferation is such, scientists tell us, that in no long time we shall be consuming each other.

Written all over this book, in its appallingly expressive pictures (what a contrast with previous periods, Renaissance, or eighteenth century, with their achieved cult of beauty) and the separate articles, is the fact that this is a *mass* civilisation. This is a contradiction in terms, for a civilisation of any standard is always the achievement of an elect minority.

One of the tutelary deities of the epoch, Corbusier, gives the game away with his dictum: 'A house is a machine for living in'. It is not: it should be a *home*. But a machine it has become for the mass of humanity. No wonder the twentieth century bears everywhere stamped on its hideous face the signs of Neurosis.

There is a sense in which the United States is the type-country of the twentieth century, and all other countries aspire to be like it. (Understandable why de Gaulle hated it.) Can we say that today the United States is so happy and optimistic in itself?

The truth is that the United States is going through an acute crisis of conscience. Growing up to the realities of human nature in history, it is discovering that the callow and superficial rationalism upon which it was founded simply does not apply. This volume quotes the Declaration of the Rights of Man of 1776 as if it were gospel truth. Carl Becker, a genuine historian, showed in his analysis of it that one half was propaganda and the rest lies.

A superficial Leftist rationalism in politics, with its fatuous optimism, is contradicted by the whole findings of modern psychology. As the best chapter in the book, Quinton's 'Ideas and Beliefs of the 20th Century', very well shows.

But every chapter brings this home and exposes the nakedness and horror.

India. Is India any better off than it was when united and at peace under British rule?

Is all so very well in the Middle East?

Or in Africa? The African chapter is the least satisfactory, riddled with sentimentalism, with little sense of realities. The troubles of Africa are all imputed to 'the dangerous legacy of imperialism'. No idea that they were eating each other before imperialism came, and resumed it afterwards, both in Kenya and Nigeria. Is it to be supposed that Nigeria, where hundreds of thousands have been killed, is better off than it was under the beneficent trusteeship of Lugard? The Leftist author gives the game away with his account of the Biafrans' 'atavistic rejection of penetration by educated, thrusting, increasingly successful and wealthy individualists from the south'.

Exactly: in Africa black capitalism, or black imperialism, takes the place of white; as in India native capitalism takes the place of British, with its sense of justice and incorruptibility. Any improvement?

As for Soviet Russia, that blueprint for the future, here the plausible author cannot disguise the cultural deformation since 1932, the killing of men of genius in the theatre, films, literature, the lowering of standards to the common measure. But these authors do not draw the obvious conclusion, dot the i's or cross the t's: *this is what the people really like*: Mass Taste, Mass Culture.

An old-time Marxist myself, I observe that the characteristic movements of the century, nationalist or revolutionary – whether India, China, or wherever – are lower Middle Class, not proletarian or working class.

Naturally the sympathies of the academic authors of this book are middle-class, with their Left-Liberal bias. This gives the book its character, and its unity. It is a one-sided picture, in which the journalist-writers of the age loom larger than the artists of real genius. We are given a portrait of André Gide, a writer of no real creative power; no portrait of Proust, who wrote the Paradiso, Purgatorio, and Inferno, of the twentieth century.

All the sacred cows of Left journalism appear – a Leavis and a Spender, not a single reference to Kipling. We have six references to Bertrand Russell, only one to Sherrington, the greatest physiologist of the age, to whom we owe the exploration of the whole nervous system and of whom all contemporary physiologists are the disciples. Six references to Sartre, who thought Soviet Russia the embodiment of human freedom, and similar nonsense; only a casual mention of Montherlant, a greater contemporary writer.

No mention of distinguished historians like G. M. Trevelyan and Samuel Eliot Morison; though, paradoxically, the chapter on Science points out the new emphasis on the historical:

> As men have moved progressively into the new scientific world during the last seventy years, the social and historical dimensions missing from the original vision of science have re-entered the perspective; and with them also the shadows. . . . As a result, the unmixed optimism of earlier times is no longer an appropriate attitude for natural scientists, and a necessary sense of moral tragedy has re-entered their professional lives.'

Still less is a superficial optimism the appropriate attitude in contemplating the political scene anywhere in the world, or in literature and the arts. This is where the historians and real writers come in, as against the illusory hopes and shallow clichés of journalist-writers in a world of mass media given over to them.

NOTE

1.   Alan Bullock (Ed), *The Twentieth Century* (Thames & Hudson).

THE GREAT WAR IN BRITISH MEMORY

This American author has written a distinguished book on an original theme; already well received, it has not yet had the serious criticism its interest and merit deserve.[1] Its subject is the impact the war of 1914–1918 made in our literature, as a mirror – not a complete one, it should be remembered – of the mark fixed in the mind of the nation. The prime quality of the book is literary, the moving and perceptive depiction of that war in writing of all kinds, especially poetry; its prime defect is historical, the too short perspective in which the subject is seen.

The author occasionally glimpses the truth of history, if unintentionally. 'The way the data and usages of the Second War behave as if thinking in terms of the First is enough almost to make one believe in a single continuing Great War running through the whole middle of the twentieth century. Churchill and the Nazi Alfred Rosenberg both found it easy to conceive of the events running through 1914 to 1945 ... as virtually a single historical episode.' This unwelcome thought is roughly the truth: the two wars were crests in the aggressive determination of the German ruling classes to achieve *Welt Macht* before it was too late.

The overriding necessity for Britain, as for others, was to resist; and if one wills the end, one has to will the means to it. Only this – the necessity to resist, hold out, defeat – justifies the agony, suffering, bloodshed, losses of every kind endured. These were almost unendurable – my memory goes back to them; but they were *not* purposeless. The sensitive reaction of poets and writers, of which this book gives valuable evidence, are often without political and historical judgement. In Sassoon's *Memoirs of an Infantry Officer*, 'George learns the truth about the war: that it is ruining England and has no good reason for continuing'. It was ruining England all right, but it had to continue if the Germans – who believed in it and tried it all over again in 1939–1945 – were to be held in check and defeated. The point can be proved from what Sassoon did, not what he wrote: after being invalided out, he deliberately and courageously went back to the Front to go on with the job.

The unspeakable courage of these men, the fortitude, valour, endurance, irony all appear in the book, but not the sense of purpose that made them endure, suffer and die – what it was that made sense of the experience of 1914–1918. What was it that made it so horrible?

Here, too, Mr Fussell, wanting in historical perspective, does not perceive the conclusions to be drawn from his sensitive perceptions. The war of 1914–1918 was not more barbarous than other wars: he should read something about the appalling consequences for Germany of the Thirty Years' War. Since he is a literary man, he might read Grimmelshausen's *Simplicissimus,* or look at Goya's ghastly scenes of the War in the Peninsula. (It is said that the 'Spanish flu' epidemic just after the Great War killed more people across Europe than the war itself.)

What made the Great War so dreadful to the British mind was that it was fought against the background of liberal illusions that the world was getting better and better in every way, and that all was set towards social progress, improvement, enlightenment, etc. Germans did not have to endure this agony of mind, for (a) they were not indoctrinated with liberal illusions, (b) they were prepared for war, materially and psychologically. It was Hitler's historic achievement to refurbish that all over again.

So great was the hold of nineteenth-century liberal ideals and illusions upon the English mind that it survived the hideous experience of 1914–1918. This took the form of *Never Again.* That thought dominated the mind of Britain at all levels between the wars. This – historically the most important effect of the Great War upon people's minds – is missed in this book. Ironically, it had the dire effect of utterly confusing the British as to the post-war situation, what to expect from Germany and how to deal with her – and directly helped forward the second wave in the historic attempt. As a most thoughtful of Conservative leaders, L. S. Amery, no Appeaser, summed up: 'Germany so nearly brought it off the first time, that it was only to be expected that she would have a second try.'

In other respects also this account exemplifies the too short perspective of the literary man. He objects to David Jones's treatment of the war – who fought in it – in *In Parenthesis* that 'the reader comes away from this persuaded that the state of the soldier is universal throughout history'. Well, so it is: the literary Professor might read Falstaff's cynical account of soldiering and losing one's limbs in battle, or observe the looting behaviour of Pistol, Nym and Bardolph, or types like Parolles. 'The problem is, if soldiering is universal, what's wrong with it?', asks the Professor

– a very naif question; for it seems to be a necessity, rooted in the nature of human nature, which is aggressive, not in accord with liberal illusions.

By the same token, the Professor cannot do justice to the other side of the medal, as David Jones does: the heroic side, the chivalrous, the comradeship, the love of man for man in danger and suffering. He might remember a reflection to the point in the tradition of his own country: Lee before a battle in the Civil War (terrible as that was), sunrise over the camp, troops bivouacking, smoke rising from their breakfasts, the General looking over the scene and remarking to his companion, 'if ours wasn't such a terrible trade, one could glory in such a moment, such a scene'.

Many individual points may be questioned. There is the American cliché-view about the British class-system: *was* Britain actually more 'class-ridden' than Germany, or Russia? I doubt it. Or there is the stupidity of the British officer-class; no doubt they were stupid enough, but *all* human beings are stupid at all times and in all places, almost without exception – see Swift or Shakespeare about that. And it is not immediately apparent that the British Tommy carried over an anti-officer reaction into the inter-war years, when one reflects that the people at large gave the Tories undeserved majorities in the elections of 1924, 1931, and 1935.

There are also good insights: the squalor, dirt and squelchiness of the British trenches, by contrast with the German, some of their dug-outs 'thirty feet deep, with as many as sixteen bunk-beds, as well as door bells, water tanks with taps, and cupboards and mirrors'. As Birkenhead said, 'they are a nation that think of everything'. They prepared for it. Professor Fussell: 'The English were amateur, vague, *ad hoc*, and temporary. The German were efficient, clean, pedantic, and permanent. Their occupants proposed to stay where they were.' Exactly. QED.

There are occasional glimpses of deeper historic truths – that the Great War was the end of the comparatively peaceful liberal civilisation of the nineteenth century (guaranteed, in fact, by British naval supremacy and exemplified by the Empire, however much liberals dislike to own it). The Professor quotes Norman Mailer as asking, 'What is the purpose of technological society?', and comments, 'the only answer that modern history has offered is the one Alfred Kazin proposes: "War may be the ultimate purpose of technological society".' Well, that puts things into perspective; we have the Germans to thank for setting the process going in 1914.

NOTE

1.   Paul Fussell, *The Great War and Modern Memory* (Oxford University Press).

WEIMAR AND WHEELER-BENNETT

Though I suppose I should place the second book first, as more general, Wheeler-Bennett's book[1] makes a better introduction to the subject for English and American readers. It is utterly riveting, at any rate all the German half of it. He had a front-seat view of what was going on under the Weimar Republic and in the first years of Hitler – an entirely private individual, yet with extraordinary sources of information through his German contacts with key-figures. Needless to say, neither his views on the folly of Appeasement, nor his exceptionally accurate information, were taken any notice of by Chamberlain, Halifax and the gang who, in the event, ruined their country.

They were told often enough as to the right course to pursue – a Grand Alliance against the aggressors would have held the balance of power against them, and, when the break came it would have come *inside* Germany. Wheeler-Bennett tells us that Chamberlain could have had that as late as April 1939, when 'the Soviet Government proposed a triple pact of mutual assistance between France, Great Britain and Russia, a military convention reinforcing such a pact, and a triple guarantee of all the border states from the Baltic to the Black Sea'. It should have been seized with both hands: it was our last chance of containing Hitler's Germany and maintaining peace. It was thrown away: 'they missed the essential point, which was that if we did *not* improve our relations with Russia she might herself make a complete *volte-face* in policy and make a deal with Germany.' She did – and Hitler was free to have his war.

'It has always seemed to me that the most remarkable thing

about the Weimar Republic is not that it existed for only fifteen years but that it ever survived the circumstances of its nativity.' The German Left – like the Labour Party in the 1930s – had no sense of power and were divided between Socialists and Communists. Wheeler-Bennett thinks that the Socialists would have preferred a monarchy, with a regency and a Socialist Chancellor. It is possible that that might have worked better – if only there had been a candidate with the liberal views of the Kaiser's despised father, the Emperor Frederick.

For the Republic was sabotaged from the first by the Right, backed by most of the upper classes, and by lying propaganda about the 'stab in the back' and the injustice of the Versailles peace. As to the first, as Brüning told Schleicher, 'at the end of the war it was GHQ [i.e. Ludendorff and Hindenburg], not the army, that lost its head in a panic. *We* could have fought on, it was *you* who threw up your hands'. As for Versailles, it was chicken-feed compared with what the Germans would have meted out to Europe if they had won in the first war, let alone the second.

We have evidence of what they would have done from the Treaty of Brest-Litovsk, imposed on Russia in 1917. This has been forgotten by sentimentalists; Wheeler-Bennett reminds us in a chapter, 'The Forgotten Peace', where he sets out the evidence of the German Foreign Secretary, von Kühlmann, whom he knew. The German General Staff was determined to take all Russian territory up to the threshold of St Petersburg, all the Ukraine, as well as the Baltic States and Poland. *Ost-Europa* – it was precisely continuous with Hitler. Kühlmann was appalled when he realised the damage this would do in the world – ensure American support for the Allies, save the Bolshevik Revolution by identifying it with Russian patriotism, etc. When Kühlmann asked Ludendorff why did he need to annex all those territories, the answer was: 'I need them for the manoeuvring of my left wing in the Next War'. There spoke the real Germany, the dominant Germany; nor do we forget that Hitler began as Ludendorff's *protégé*. The line of continuity is perfectly clear.

These were the people who ultimately sabotaged the Weimar Republic, and in the end gave Hitler power. 'To Hitler's banner rallied the upper classes of the Protestant North, the German Crown Prince, the great industrialists of the Ruhr and the Rhineland and the powerful agrarian interests of the *Landbund*' (Prussian Junkers). Wheeler-Bennett is quite clear that 'the Army

could have disposed of Hitler and the whole Nazi gang at any time
during the next four years, if they had had the leadership and the
intestinal fortitude [*sc.* guts] to do so'. Why didn't they do it? The
answer is given by General Reichenau: 'We shall tolerate this
régime just as long as it suits our interests to do so'.

They tolerated it to the very end; they stayed with Hitler to his
death. Nor should we forget that the Catholic Centre Party gave
Hitler his two-thirds majority for legally suspending the Constitu-
tion, *enabling* him to do all he did. Nor that the upper classes in
Britain and elsewhere gave Hitler the successes, and the covert
support, which riveted him upon Germans. The Germans –
disastrous people – were willing enough: 'there is no doubt that for
twelve years Hitler held the souls of the majority of the German
people under an evil and shameful spell'.

With all the fascinating inside information Wheeler-Bennett
was relaying back to Britain, no wonder the Nazis had him on
their murder-list for 30 June, 1934: that event should have been
eye-opener enough for pious people like Halifax – as it was for
Stalin. Wheeler-Bennett's information was taken no more notice
of in Britain by Chamberlain and Company than that of other
people who told them the truth – their military attaché in Berlin,
Mason Macfarlane, for one. When the rake's progress – or, rather,
prigs' – led them to Munich, Chamberlain specifically told
Masaryk: 'My dear Jan, some people trust Dr Benesh [Czecho-
Slovakia's President]; I prefer to trust Herr Hitler'.

The fact is, they didn't want to know the truth; there comes a
point when obstinate foolery becomes positively wicked.

There is much perception in the character-sketches of these
people. Wheeler-Bennett confesses to experiencing the sinister,
seductive charm of Goebbels, 'plausible, fluent, educated and
amusing', and he lets off Goering too lightly. I notice that people
are engaged in white-washing that thug today; it is true that he
could make rings round the Chief American Prosecutor, Judge
Jackson, at Nuremberg: Wheeler-Bennett watched Goering 'first
confound and then rout' that naif ass. It took Maxwell Fyffe to put
it right. I suspect that Wheeler-Bennett does not fully appreciate
Hitler's genius – for such it was, though a genius for evil. It is
staggering what he achieved, in building up the Nazi movement,
in preparing Germany to try it all over again, achieving the most
propitious conditions for her second bid to dominate Europe –
aided and abetted as he was by the upper classes elsewhere. If

their social order is ruined, they have only themselves to thank.

Wheeler-Bennett had some interesting sessions with a leading relic of the first attempt, the Kaiser in exile at Doorn. Like his cousin, the Herzog von Windsor, obsessed by grievances, and still hating Uncle Bertie, he had constructed a make-believe defence for himself. 'He would never have gone to war if he had known England was coming in.' He had been warned often enough, and again would take no telling from his own ambassador here, Lichnowsky. 'He had only wanted to beat the Russians, who had started it all; but he brushed aside a question from me concerning the blank cheque he had given to Austria-Hungary in July.' The one revealing thing the Kaiser said, on the eve of the second war, was: 'the machine is running away with *him* [Hitler] as it ran away with *me*'.

All this justifies Wheeler-Bennett's title, and more: *Knaves, Fools and Heroes*. His hero appears to be Brüning, whom I think he over-estimates. No doubt he was a man of principle, and of moral courage – unlike most Germans – as well as physical. 'His vital weakness was that he trusted blindly and without question those who had pledged their word to him and then had forsworn it.' To be naif in politics is to put oneself in the class of Fool. Hitler knew how to deal with that sort of thing and, to his finger-tips, what ordinary humans are. I myself put the question to Brüning, in the common-room at All Souls – hadn't he known the extent to which the armaments-magnates had their money on Hitler? No, he confessed he hadn't. As Chancellor, he ought to have done.

Laqueur's[2] is a useful and informative survey of Weimar's cultural history, for which it has received a good deal more credit than it deserved. He emphasises that the real cultural break came in the decade before the first war, the new movements in art, theatre, literature, architecture, largely by way of opposition to the Byzantine sterility of Wilhelmian Germany, the vulgarity, the emptiness. Weimar, however, gave the new movements their head, and some of the results were remarkable. Most people would put the achievements and influence of Gropius and the Bauhaus first; repressed by the Nazis, it carried its inspiration to the United States where some of its best work was done. Laqueur rates the theatre of the period highly, with Brecht as its star; I prefer the theatre of Montherlant.

Laqueur has a less high opinion of the literature of the time, proliferating as it was and popular outside Germany. He is properly critical of its leading figure, Thomas Mann, much over-estimated in my view. Mann had preached the justness of the 1914 war, as a crusade for German *Kultur* as against 'Western civilisation'. 'We knew it, this world of peace,' he wrote, 'it stank of the ferments of decomposition. The artist was so sick of this world that he praised God for this purge and this tremendous hope.' (Himself being the artist *par excellence*, of course.) With Germany's defeat he saw the error of his ways; whereupon he was discountenanced by the Right – *they* never accepted the verdict of 1918.

Laqueur completely corroborates Wheeler-Bennett's picture of opposition and sabotage from the Right – Laqueur names some of the long list of distinguished figures murdered by them, by no means all Leftists like Liebknecht and Rosa Luxemburg; there were Catholics like Erzberger, head of the Catholic Centre Party, Rathenau, the great industrial magnate who enabled Germany to subsist in the first war by the re-organisation of her economy. The universities were strongholds of Rightists, especially the history, law and literature faculties – the humanities – where the historians mostly couldn't see anything wrong with the course Bismarck had directed the country along. The Rector of Berlin University was the author of the leading annexationist manifesto in 1915; for the war-memorial to the students killed he provided the inscription, *Invictis victi victuri*, promising the unconquered-defeated victory in the next attempt. Reinhold Seeberg was the name of this brute. But, indeed, Laqueur points out that the Nazis were the strongest party in the universities well before they were in the country at large. So much for the intelligence of (German) universities!

What is so characteristic of the period is the way the extremists of Right and Left played ball with each other to ruin the prospects of any sensible middle course. On the eve of the Nazi take-over the Communists joined hands with the Nazis to defeat the Socialists over the Berlin tram-strike. Could anything be more insane? But the same lunatic game was played culturally. The Futurist manifesto advocated the destruction of museums and libraries – well, some years later the Nazis partially carried it out. The nonsense of the lunatic Left played straight into the hands of the criminal Right. And how well we recognise the inversion of sense so rife on the Left today in Franz Werfel's idiotic, 'Not the murderer, the victim is guilty'.

Laqueur observes that, for all their cult of going to the people, the gap between the avant-garde and the public grew immeasurably during the decade before 1914. Of course, the great heart of the people wanted none of their cultural experimentation; having no taste whatsoever, they are more faithfully represented by the appalling art and architecture of Soviet Russia, or for that matter by the lower levels of the TV culture that speaks to and for them. German Expressionism, as Laqueur points out, was a middleclass phenomenon. Like the bright sparks of my generation who took to it and went whoring – if that is the right word for it – after Berlin. I always thought it would have been so much better for them, if Auden, Isherwood, Spender and Company had concentrated on Paris, instead of Berlin. It was just what they needed – a more classic sense of form, style, the plastic sense of the Latins, discipline instead of still more *Expressionismus.*

Laqueur confesses to difficulty in defining Expressionism; but surely it implies the limitless indulgence in inner experience to the sacrifice of external form. He is right to see it as the last decadent phase of Romanticism. But, then, I am rather allergic to expressions of the German genius – apart from music, their greatest achievement in art, precisely because it is *innerlich*. (Thomas Mann has an essay on this; but the point is obvious enough without him.)

I don't really like their Expressionism in painting from Grünewald to today, or the inherent madness in so much of their literature from *Simplicissimus* to Hölderlin, from Nietzsche to Kafka. Nor do I like the characteristic figures of German history from Luther to Frederick of Prussia and Blücher ('*Was für Plunder!*', on riding through the City of London); from Bismarck, the Kaiser and Krupp on to Hitler and Göring and Himmler.

NOTES

1. John Wheeler-Bennett, *Knaves, Fools and Heroes in Europe Between the Wars* (Macmillan).
2. Walter Laqueur, *Weimar. A Cultural History 1918–1933* (Weidenfeld & Nicolson).

GERMAN RESPONSIBILITY FOR THE
WAR OF 1914–1918

Fritz Fischer is the most important German historian today, famous – or, rather, with Germans notorious – for telling them the truth that Germany was responsible up to the hilt for the war of 1914–1918 and proving it from all the evidence.[1] If he had dared to say all this just after that war, he would have been assassinated by the reactionary Frei Korps, as so many were – including the Catholic Centre Party leader, Erzberger, for signing the Treaty of Versailles, though this book shows what a deep-dyed nationalist and annexationist he was. Perhaps that taught him, or he had learned something from the war, like Stresemann, who was another.

The point of the book is this. Germans have been ready to heap the blame for the Second War on Hitler – and absolve themselves from any responsibility for the First. Fischer proves – what anyone with knowledge of the facts, and the judgement to appraise them, has known all along – that there was absolute continuity: Hitler carried on the programme, and took over the ideas, of the German governing class right from the Bismarck period. Indeed, one effect of reading this thoroughly documented book is to rob Hitler of some of his originality. For the programme is all there well before 1914: *Lebensraum* in Eastern Europe, i.e. pushing Russia right back to St Petersburg – this objective was carried out in 1917, with the Treaty of Brest-Litovsk; the aim was subjugation, or extermination, of Slavs (as with Jews later) for the settlement of Germans. The reduction of France to a second-rate power, dependent on Germany, seducing the propertied classes by appealing to their class-interest – carried out by Hitler with Pétain. The end of Britain as a world-power and as a sea-power, in the way of Germany's colonial expansion in the outside world. The use of anti-Semitism to bemuse the German masses; control of the press; lies as an instrument of policy, e.g. that Britain, not Germany, began the war; that France had begun by bombing German towns; that in 1918 Germany was not defeated but betrayed by a stab-in-the-back, etc. It is all there.

What Hitler did for the dominant classes in Germany, the reactionaries of heavy industry and the land, was the psychological preparation, mass-propaganda, mass-subjugation, the destruction of all opposition, so that they could carry forward their long-term objectives in the more favourable circumstances of the 1930s. What he accomplished for them was wonderful in its way – no wonder he was mad at the Generals' conspiracy in 1944, after all he had done for them.

It is a terrible indictment. But Fischer puts it forward with objectivity, moderation and complete conviction. It is impossible to deny it or even to fault it – though German historians denied it all along, until now the facts and the documents force them to face the truth. Fischer reveals the steps that were taken by German governments after 1918 to conceal the truth, while German historians helped them to do so. Here is Erzberger on the German Chancellor, Bethmann-Hollweg's, statement of Germany's case in 1914 – this man has always been given an undeserved favourable press in England as a kind of German Asquith: 'it gave historic proof that this is England's war and that England wanted the war. This is what Germany believes today.'

Of course it was untrue: a war was the last thing Britain wanted, and this book shows the exhaustive efforts Sir Edward Grey made to keep the peace. Fischer proves that Germany, so far from restraining Austria-Hungary over Sarajevo, pushed her into making war against Serbia, despite all the latter's concessions. A month before Grey's efforts at mediation 'the plan had been decided on by Germany to use the favourable opportunity of the murder at Sarajevo, for the start of the Continental war which Germany regarded as necessary'.

Once more the truth was put by Erzberger in his programme: 'the bloody struggle makes it imperative that victory is used to give Germany military supremacy on the Continent for all time. The second aim is the termination of England's tutelage on questions of world policy, which is intolerable for Germany. The third the breaking up of the Russian colossus.' Erzberger again: 'An understanding with England would be regarded as a cruel disappointment by the German people ... and the military conflict with England must take place thoroughly and ruthlessly, free from all rules of so-called international law. Germany can only obtain the hoped-for goal, lasting peace in Europe [i.e. under German domination] after this terrible blood bath, if it does not come to terms with England but defeats it.'

Fischer puts it mildly when he describes 'the consensus which existed within the educated and propertied German middle class'.

In other words, these were the objectives of the whole of the German *bourgeoisie*. The Social Democrats were merely their stooges: the war was represented to them as a defensive war against Tsarist Russia. They fell for it (to Lenin's disgust). Admiral von Müller, in the privacy of his diary, gives away the game in August 1914: 'The mood is brilliant. The government has managed brilliantly to make us appear the attacked'. Bethmann-Hollweg was able to answer opponents who thought he was not aggressive enough by pointing out he had managed so well that the Social Democrats had always voted the Armaments budget. In 1914 he was able to assure his Prussian colleagues that 'there was nothing much to be feared from Social Democracy ... a general strike or sabotage was out of the question'. Only one, Liebknecht, voted against the credits for war in 1914; in 1919, after the defeat, he was assassinated.

The German military leadership never believed that they would be defeated: they thought that the Schlieffen Plan, i.e. a blitzkrieg on France through neutral Belgium (as in 1940 again) would infallibly bring victory. When it did not, and the Germans were held up by their defeats on the Marne and at Ypres, they were deliberately concealed from the German people. Moltke, who had egged on war all along, whined: 'the whole world has conspired against us; it looks as if the task of all the other nations was to destroy Germany for ever. The few neutral states are not friendly to us. Germany has not a friend in the world'.

What else could be expected from Germany's whole course and conduct from Bismarck on?

Fischer's moderately phrased conclusion is unassailable. 'As far as Germany was concerned it [the war] was because of the determination with which the politically and economically leading classes clung to their vision of Germany's future position in the world and to their conviction that only a victorious war could guarantee their social and political pre-eminence in the Empire.' This points to a secondary theme of the book: in Marxist terms, the German ruling classes sought to deflect the rise of the masses into the path of imperialist conquest, European domination and *Weltmacht*.

The truth of the matter has always been clear; but the real triumph of the Germans was to cover it up, suppress the truth, organise sympathy in the outside world, and undermine the Treaty of Versailles to resume the attempt. Here is the propaganda programme, in a memorandum to the German Foreign Office: 'it is essential today to draw the attention of the German people with ever new publications firmly and aggressively to the fact that Britain, Russia and France definitely wanted the war and consciously prepared for it. The hour demands that straightforward material is collected which can be understood by the masses, and that this is widely circulated and at every opportunity.' Lies, of course.

Fischer informs us that both the Chancellor, Bethmann-Hollweg, and his Foreign Office officials 'agreed among themselves on how best to play down the most incriminating facts or omissions of the crisis [in 1914] if they were called upon to give evidence before a court or parliament'.

What then are we to think of those fools who allowed themselves, in Britain and America, to be taken in? I do not refer to crackpots like Harry Elmer Barnes and like-minded American Revisionists but reputable liberal historians who had the most deplorable effect in confusing the minds of a whole generation and making them suppose that the Treaty of Versailles was responsible for the trouble in post-war Europe. This played straight into the hands of the German reactionaries – the dominant classes in Germany: what they resented was not so much Versailles as that they had lost the war, and were determined to reverse the result.

What are we to think of liberal and Leftist irresponsibles here – like Keynes, Russell etc. – who played the game of the German Right by attacking Versailles, and ignorantly exonerating Germany from guilt? When I say Germany I mean, of course, the German ruling classes – the Social Democrats were not to blame, except for their ineffectiveness: they were victims. Even as to Reparations: the Germans borrowed from Wall Street and the City as much as they ever handed over in Reparations. And Etienne Mantoux showed that in the 1930s they spent twice as much on Re-arming.

One sees how disastrous the influence of these liberal-minded stool-pigeons was: it enabled the malign forces inside Germany to renew the effort in more favourable circumstances in 1939.

Before 1914 British policy was far more intelligently conducted. We have reason to be grateful that the views of Eyre Crowe and Nicolson in the Foreign Office prevailed. The consistent aim of Germany before 1914 was to secure Britain's neutrality; i.e. keep Britain out of Europe to give Germany a free hand to knock out

France and Russia, and achieve the domination of Europe. What sort of a future would there have been for this country *then*?

Nicolson summed up: if we had let down France, she would have to make terms with Germany, and the whole Triple Entente, sheet-anchor of our security, would be broken up. 'This would mean that we should have a triumphant Germany, an unfriendly France and Russia: our policy of preserving the equilibrium and consequently the peace in Europe would be wrecked.' Before 1914 we were not such fools.

Nor was the Foreign Office wrong in the 1930s, when Germany resumed the aggression with the demand for a free hand in Europe. The ignorant Chamberlain gave it to them over annexing Austria and then Czecho-Slovakia. Vansittart was perfectly right about Germany all along – as Douglas-Home admitted to me the other day, and that he himself had been wrong over Appeasing Germany. To think that commonsense about Germany should have been framed by these ignorant stooges of the Left as 'Vansittartism'! Their stupidity passes belief – if one did not know that Swift was roughly right about human beings, especially in politics.

No doubt whatever about the guilt of Germany's ruling classes, the secondary theme of Fischer's book is subtler and more original, though not clearly expressed, in the German manner. This is the dichotomy between the internal pressures within Germany and the policy of external aggression – expansion, *Lebensraum*, more space, *Weltmacht*. The internal aim was to stave off the rise of Social democracy (which makes the sympathies of Leftist Revisionists all the more ludicrous).

As both a historian, and an oldtime Labour man, I have no sympathy with the European governing classes committing suicide – as they look round at the ruin of their social order, their civilisation going down the drain, they have only themselves to blame. I hope they like what they have to contemplate; I did not much enjoy going through the 1930s when they helped their *confrères* in Germany to bring it all down on us again.[2]

When the end of the Second German War came in 1945, and Europe lay in ruins, a representative collection of German academics was brought to my rooms at All Souls. They were among the first out of the mad-house: a dozen grey-faced, impoverished, pathetic professors. They were quite unable to see the point that this was the result of Germany's whole course from Bismarck onwards: the unification by Blood and Iron, by inflicting three wars (on Denmark, Austria-Hungary, France), a policy of aggression which naturally united other peoples in self-defence.

Only one tough old barbarian answered back: the head of the Technische Hochschule in Munich. Since everything was all right for Germany under Bismarck he thought that everything Bismarck did was all right! I tried to point out the fatal effect of Bismarck's ruining the chances of responsible, representative government in Germany – for one thing, no check on the aggressive militarist leadership. Only one of the group even saw the point: a younger man from bombed Hamburg, on the fringes of inspissated *Deutschtum*, in touch with civilisation. And he, lingering behind the others, dared only to whisper to me that he agreed with the points I had made.

This was the course the German ruling classes were set on all the way from Bismarck. Bismarck's course in itself was, in the long run, disastrous. The Revision so necessary for Germany was not a revision of the Treaty of Versailles but a revision of their whole way of looking at their past, and the conduct of the nation, i.e. their ruling classes, from Bismarck on. It would have been possible for Europe to live with a Federal Germany, under responsible, representative government; it was not possible for Europe to live with a Germany united under militarist leadership and irresponsible, autocratic government, Bismarck or the Kaiser or Hitler.

Fritz Fischer has set going this exceedingly important task of getting Germans to set the record right, understanding their own past and what they have been responsible for. It is much to be hoped that they will take it to heart and get on with it, taking the record back to Bismarck.

NOTES

1. Fritz Fischer, *War of Illusions. German Policies from 1911 to 1914* (Chatto and Windus).
2. Cf. my *All Souls and Appeasement*.

REVISIONIST HISTORY, 1914–1939

This book has already been sharply criticised as a quite inadequate account of the revolution that has overtaken Britain since 1914, as not going beyond the surface events of politics into the deeper levels and the forces beneath, to which politicians were mainly reacting.[1] Not that Mr James has many illusions about run-of-the-mill politicians when he can speak of 'the vapid temporisings which are the stock-in-trade of most politicians, which were particularly evident in the inter-war Parliaments'. There is justice in the criticism; for example, as against much trivial detail about by-elections and quite insignificant members of Parliament, there is hardly anything about the really significant figure of Ernest Bevin, engaged in building up the formidable power of the Trade Unions and much that was constructive in the Labour movement. He was a real historical portent.

As a young man Mr James was for nine years a Clerk of the House of Commons, and this dominates his perspective. This is not a sufficient viewpoint from which to describe a revolution. He is glamourised by that assembly, of which he has now become an enlightened Member. His book ends with a peroration, which is rather a paean of praise to that questionable assembly. He even has a tribute to that body in 1939 which had sat there since 1931, selling the interests of its country at every pass in its own class-interest, conniving at Hitler's Germany resuming its pre-1918 course of aggression, until the imminent danger in 1939 forced them to turn right round and reverse the unforgivable course they had followed with Hitler since 1933. Mr James comments, from his perspective, that Hitler 'had reckoned without the House of Commons. But, so had Chamberlain'. One is reminded of the famous phrase of the Duc d'Aumale after Bazaine's betrayal of Metz: *Mais, il y avait la France!* It would be truer to say, from a deeper perspective, that Hitler had reckoned without the British people and the inspired leadership they found in Churchill.

Mr James's book has many good qualities. It is cool and reasonable, has a number of fresh observations, some of them original, and the book is fluent and readable, if rather bland (a favourite and revealing word), if anything too facile, a surface-book. The author is commendably candid; a liberal-minded Conservative MP, he makes it clear that the Tory Party pursued its own class-interest in domestic politics throughout the whole period – in its return to the Gold Standard, its treatment of the miners, the Trade Unions, the cuts in education, social services, deflation, etc. It is candid of him to admit that Baldwin's Abyssinian policy was 'a fraud'; the election of 1935 tricked the Labour Party – as Amery admitted – and henceforward it would trust neither Baldwin nor Chamberlain.

There could hardly be more summary condemnation of the government of the 1930s than that 'the Prime Minister was incompetent and vacillating, the Foreign Secretary was blandly untroubled by the European situation and instinctively hostile to rearmament, the Chancellor of the Exchequer was obsessed by the economic problems and profoundly reluctant to allocate expenditure for rearmament, and the Service Ministers – two of whom were in the Lords – were politically weak and technically limited.' *Verb. sap.;* an unforgetting opponent could hardly say more.

Mr James is mesmerised by the obvious, if facile, melodrama of the House of Commons and, after this record, can describe it as 'the most brilliant and passionate Parliament of the century. A strong and glorious lustre shines upon all who served in it'. Really! Another historian has described it as 'that unspeakable assembly'. Those who observed the progressive ruin of their country from the margin of events have a contribution to make, undazzled by 'the flaring gas-jets above the great glass-ceiling of the House of Commons'.

This viewpoint has provided the historian with some advantages in observing personalities. The judgements are not always fair, however. Herbert Morrison is described as 'bitter' and 'vicious'; there was nothing 'vicious' about him, and very little, for a politician, that was bitter. His organisation of the London County Council is described as 'ruthless'; it was merely efficient. Attlee 'sounded mean, like an embittered tax-inspector': he was not a mean man, nor was he like a tax-inspector.

Mr James's hero is Baldwin. We are told that 'Hitler and Baldwin were the two best politicians in Europe' – a curious statement of their respective cases. One sees why Baldwin appeals so strongly to Mr James that his book reads like an advocate's case for the politician who dominated the scene throughout this period, from 1922 to 1937 – and the upshot: an ill-prepared Britain facing alone a Germany with Europe under its heel! The preference is in accordance with the perspective: Baldwin was the best House of Commons man – of no constructive genius whatever, unlike Lloyd George or Churchill, or even Ramsay MacDonald and Ernest Bevin.

By the same token – and this is the glaring fault of the book – every opportunity is taken to depreciate Churchill and to reduce those who thought like him in those disastrous years. Churchill made many mistakes – everyone knows that – but on the issues that concerned the safety and very survival of his country he was fundamentally right. Pages and paragraphs are wasted in high-lighting questionable quotations of little real importance. Kitchener's historic tribute to Churchill in the first German War is not quoted: 'One thing they cannot take from you: *The Fleet was ready*'. It is highly probable that, if Churchill had not been at the Admiralty before 1914, it would not have been – and Britain's survival depended upon that.

Similarly with the renewal of German aggression and Churchill's realisation of the growing danger to Britain and his campaign for more effective rearmament. Mr James admits that 'Churchill could point to the fact that this was not nearly enough *relative* to Germany, and this was the vital point'. Germany indeed was what mattered above all. Mr James is too intelligent not to see that deliberately to neglect our allies, to refuse the policy of a Grand Alliance and the containment of Germany, was disastrous, playing straight into Hitler's hands, building him up into an almighty danger. Chamberlain, he sums up, was 'in complete command, and marched forward without fear or doubt into the eager arms of his enemies. They, too, believed that a deal could be made. But it was to be on their terms.' Anyone can see that that would mean Hitler's Germany in control of Europe and Britain, without friend or ally, at his mercy.

This was the whole aim clearly announced in *Mein Kampf:* a free hand in Eastern Europe, *Lebensraum* and eventual domination of Europe, was the aim of Hitler's Germany continuously with the Kaiser's. So that it is superfluous of Mr James to ally himself with A. J. P. Taylor's notoriously erratic judgement on the issue: 'Hitler had no precise plans of aggression' – ludicrous statement. Of course, Hitler was an opportunist in tactics, but the strategic aim was obvious all the way along. No one should have been taken in: there is certainly no need to be taken in posthumously.

It is unreasonable – and self-contradictory – therefore for Mr James to declare that 'this judgement has been borne out by subsequent scholarship': it is, for one thing, completely contradicted by the whole work of the leading German historian of the day, Fritz Fischer.

NOTE

1. Robert Rhodes James, *The British Revolution. British Politics, 1880–1939.* Volume 2. *From Asquith to Chamberlain, 1914–1939.* (Hamish Hamilton).

HITLER AND BRITISH POLITICS

This odd, somewhat eccentric book, covers the well-trampled ground of British politics in the 1930s, upon which there is already an *embarras*, if not of *richesses*, at any rate of information.[1] It is not the less interesting for that, though Mr Cowling did not have the advantage of the active experience of that deplorable decade, which might have provided a corrective to his views. As it is, his book is useful for the information it conveys regarding the politicians chiefly engaged. There are one or two surprises: Austen Chamberlain, with his experience of foreign affairs, comes well out of the sorry story. He was practically right on all the main issues – a pity he had no influence on his half-brother, as ignorant as he was obstinate about foreign affairs, who comes no better out of it than before.

In some ways worse, since the chief value of Mr Cowling's book lies in his numerous quotations from the actors. A leading motive with Neville Chamberlain was vindictiveness against Lloyd George. In 1935, Chamberlain confides to his sister, 'I have thought of such a lot of really nasty things to say about him that I am almost sorry I have no more speeches to make'. In 1939, in the mortal danger from Hitler's Germany, it is still: 'as I looked down at his red face and white hair, all my bitterness passed away, for I despised him and felt myself the better man'. This, from the man who could not run a National Service scheme in the first German war on the man who chiefly led Britain to win it! At the end of the disastrous decade of National Government, in which Chamberlain had been a key-figure, he wrote, 'like Chatham I know that I can save this country and I do not believe that anyone else can'. Of the man who did, Mr Cowling tells us that Chamberlain 'regarded Churchill as an adult child, who neither "knew his motives nor where his actions were carrying him".'

Mr Cowling also tells us: 'a striking feature of Chamberlain's first twenty months as Prime Minister was his feeling that he need have so little fear of opposition that he could do more or less as he liked'. So there is no doubt where the responsibility lay. Nor as between parties: we are told, 'the Baldwin/Chamberlain management of the Conservative Party had been highly successful'. Quite so. The result was that 'the Labour Opposition to Chamberlain was bitter, but its power to change policy was small'. Correct: once more there was no doubt where responsibility lay.

Mr Cowling affects an attitude of impersonal objectivity which works out oddly. Of Churchill, 'it is not clear when he saw that foreign policy might restore him to the centre of the scene. . . . It was not until "destiny" began to come through, alcoholically, at the same time as Chamberlain experienced the feeling without alcohol'. A superficial cynicism is taken a long way in this book; no serious person supposes that Churchill was not convinced of the mortal danger the country stood in from Hitler's Germany. Churchill's visit to Paris to stiffen French resistance to Hitler in 1938 is described as to 'repeat incitements'. His opposition to the disastrous course is described as by 'methods of stealth'; it was indeed open for all alive at the time to see and subscribe to (I did myself, though a Labour candidate). Macmillan's opposition to it is described as 'hysterical dislike of Baldwin and Chamberlain'; it was, in fact, only too well justified opposition by a young man who had fought in the First German war to the course pursued by two old men leading only too clearly to a Second. Nor was the opposition of the Cecils 'on grounds of Church persecution' -- a ludicrous suggestion: it came from their hereditary sense of the safety of the state, and when it was being endangered.

For all the complexities and contortions well revealed in this book, the dominant issue was plain and simple. As a far better historian, Fritz Fischer, has documented for us, the threat posed by Hitler's Germany was but the renewal of her bid for *Welt-macht* merely checked by the Treaty of Versailles. The only way to contain it, in the absence of the United States, was a European Alliance, and that meant coming to terms with Soviet Russia – the only hope there was of maintaining peace. But, 'if Chamberlain had had his way, there would have been no Russian negotiations after the beginning of May. . . . By mid-1939 his fear of war *against*

Germany in alliance with Russia was so much greater than before that he was actively hoping that the Anglo-Russian negotiations would break down'. But then he never believed that Hitler would make war, or that he would make a pact with Soviet Russia either; all that Hitler wanted, this businessman believed, was oil and minerals!

An impersonal Marxist interpretation of political parties in the inter-war years would yield a truer and more revealing picture. Political parties are determined by their class and social make-up. Thus the collapse of the Liberal Party is not to be accounted for in personal or even political terms; all the manoeuvrings and posturings, the programmes and bids for votes are of little historical significance, compared with the collapse of the economic and class foundations for any Liberal Party. There never has been the possibility of its revival, or of any real existence for it since 1931. Thus a great deal of the personal gossip on a journalistic level of this supposedly academic book has little historical value.

Even this is not always accurate. To take one small example: my name is cited inaccurately, though available in several works of reference. I am described as a 'Lib-Lab laureate' of Churchill, Keynes and Morrison. So far from being 'Lib-Lab', I detested the Liberal Party cluttering up the scene, serving no useful purpose; while admiration for Churchill, Keynes and Morrison needs no apology. So much simply for the historical record.

The quotations themselves in this book offer an appalling revelation of the quality of average run-of-the-mill politicians. On the formation of Churchill's government that eventually saved the country, in the mortal crisis of the fall of Western Europe before Hitler's Germany, Lord Davidson wrote to Baldwin, 'it is now quite clear that Winston is putting in the jackals and ousting even those who have done well of what I may call the respectable Rump of the Tory party'. This man was its Chairman and a supporter of Frank Buchman, Friend of Himmler.

We have reason to be grateful for Mr Cowling's rich harvest of quotations: they make clear who ruined this country, though that was not his intention.

NOTE

1.   M. Cowling, *The Impact of Hitler. British Politics and British Policy, 1933–1940.* (Cambridge U.P.).

GÖTTERDÄMMERUNG

Professor Hoffmann's History of the German Resistance to Hitler and Nazi rule has already been received as the fullest and most reliable account of the subject.[1] Indeed it is rather too full, for a cutting down of superabundant notes – two hundred and fifty pages of them, or one-third of the book, in the German academic manner – would have improved it. However, for facts and sources the book is indispensable; it remains to see the whole matter in proper perspective, for Professor Hoffmann's is a German one, and Germans are afflicted with myopia where other people are concerned.

His very first page betrays some uncertainty of historical judgement. For example:

> in 1649 the English followed the doctrine of sovereignty of the people to its extreme conclusion and beheaded their King, Charles I.

This was the act, not of the English people but of a tiny minority of Cromwell's Army; the overwhelming majority of the people, even of the King's enemies, were opposed to it. Other examples indicate some uncertainty of judgement as to foreign estimation of the Resistance within Germany, how much reliance might be placed on it, how far it offered an alternative to, or an alibi for, Hitler. These questions, and their consequences, do not affect the narrative, and we are grateful for new information.

On the side of the Appeasers in Britain we have the egregious busybody, Lord Lothian, in negotiation with my great friend, von Trott, whom Hitler executed (I now learn, with horror, after torture). In the columns of *The Times* I had a controversy with Lothian on the issue of Appeasement, reproduced in my book, *The End of an Epoch*. We now learn that Lothian told von Trott *after* the March on Prague in 1939, that 're-establishment of Bohemian and Moravian independence would disarm the British totally: this should not be too difficult for Hitler, he said, since he had achieved his strategic and essential purpose of destroying Czechoslovakia. If this principle were generally recognised in Eastern and South Eastern Europe and supported by Great Britain, then solution would also be found for the problems of

Danzig and the Polish Corridor. Chamberlain expressed himself similarly to Trott on 8 June'.

We should have woken up to find Germany in complete domination of Europe; these people, Chamberlain and Lothian, were in effect the enemies of their country. If Hitler had acted on their advice he would have had the game in his hands; thank God, the Foreign Office put its foot down at the last moment. Stalin's comment to Anthony Eden is very much to the point; he said, 'Hitler was a very remarkable man, only he had no sense of moderation'.

Were the leaders of the German Resistance much better? Their figurehead was the excellent Dr Goerdeler, the civilian Burgomaster of Leipzig, who was to have been Chancellor *if* Hitler had been overthrown. We learn, however, from Hoffmann what this moderate 'good' Germany's peace aims were, which the Allies were expected to accept: '1914 frontiers in the East [i.e. a considerable part of Poland], Austria [against Austrian wishes] and the Südetenland [i.e. a quarter of Czechoslovakia] to remain German, and also South Tyrol and Eupen-Malmédy'. That is, Germany was to remain in a position to dominate Europe, even after her defeat! A German-Swiss commented to me the other day that Europe cannot live with a united Germany – and the history of the past century proves it.

Professor Hoffmann at the outset wonders at the innumerable discussions in the past thirty years 'how it was possible for a world conflagration to be initiated in which over forty million men lost their lives and which ended in the dismemberment of Germany, the division of Europe, and Russian military hegemony on the Continent'. The answer is quite simple: the strongest people in Europe, its strategic centre, which should have been the keystone of the arch, never knew how to behave. All people are fools, but the Germans were criminal fools – as Hugh Dalton, a Labour man well informed in foreign affairs, used to call them, 'a race of carnivorous sheep'.

Hoffmann gives chapter and verse for the brutality inconceivable in any Western country (except during the Civil War in Spain) – the executions, murders, tortures, beatings-up by Nazis; but, remember, these were inflicted by Germans upon their own fellow Germans – apart from what they did to Russians, Poles, Jews, Dutch, Danes, French, Yugoslavs, Greeks, even their Italian allies, in fact everywhere they went. The delightful

Herrenvolk: the least qualified of all Europeans to lord it over others! Professor Hoffmann gives us the figures which tell the tale.

> It is estimated that between 1933 and 1945 some 32,600 persons were executed in Germany after pronunciation of a death-sentence. Based on files captured after the war, the British estimate at 4,980 the number of people executed for participation in the 20 July conspiracy alone . . . A glance at the suicide statistics for Germany will round off the picture. In the periods July to December 1942 and 1943, 7,862 and 7,379 persons respectively took their lives.

No wonder. 'Over six years [only] the regular courts alone sentenced 225,000 persons in *political* cases to terms of imprisonment.'

What a country! What a people! For it must be remembered that – in spite of the belated efforts of the generals and field marshals to get rid of Hitler, and Professor Hoffmann's well-meant explanations of their ineffectiveness and failure to do so – Hitler remained there with the support of the German people to the very end.

If one looked at the Resistance of the generals and diplomats, mostly aristocrats and army officers, from Hitler's point of view, one can understand his rage and revenge on them. After all, he had done an unparalleled job in preparing Germany, psychologically, politically and militarily, for the second round in its attempt to achieve the domination of Europe by force. He had re-militarised and rearmed the nation, given the army its head and a leading place in the state, expanded it a hundred times, given Germany its succession of triumphs over the democracies bemused by nitwits of Appeasers, and conniving stooges who fell for his propaganda against Communism. No wonder he thought that Britain was too decadent to fight, France worm-eaten with the sabotage of its upper classes (it was).

Hitler's preparation and conditioning of Germany for her second attempt was geared to the circumstances of demotic society, the brutal character of the people, the ghastly phenomena of mass credulity and average stupidity – not the residual relics of civilised decency that were not too evident even in pre-1914 Germany. Hence the savagery of the killings and murders, the concentration and death camps, the torture and extermination (see also Soviet Russia and Communist countries), characteristic of mass-civilisation and the people at large. Hitler, like Stalin, understood the people to his finger-tips, and how to treat them – unlike lily-livered, middle-class liberals. (Myself am liberal enough as to ends and aims, I should explain, but without suffering from liberal illusions.)

Why the utter failure of the German Resistance of all kinds to get rid of Hitler? – after all, the Czechs managed to kill their tormentor, the unspeakable Heydrich. (His successor ordered the killing of the entire male population down to babies of Lidice, where Heydrich got his comeuppance – a characteristic German reaction.) Hoffmann's answer is that 'the general picture is one of acquiescence, weakness, opportunism, delusion and error. Hundreds of German professors hastened to acclaim Hitler'. So, too, did political parties like the Catholic Centre Party and the churches; trade unions, liberals, social democrats, communists, were paralysed by the apparition. No one knew better than he did, except Stalin, what idiots humans are; he played cat-and-mouse with them to the end. The book provides plenty of evidence of the physical courage of Germans, all too recognisable, and equally of their appalling lack of moral courage and political sense.

Any number of these brave field-marshals and generals, colonel-generals and colonels, counts and *freiherren*, wavered to and fro according as Hitler appeared to be winning or losing. With Germans nothing succeeds like success – and nothing fails like failure. It was simply the fact that the war was obviously lost by 1943 that made up the minds of a section of the top brass – Kluge, Witzleben, Rommel among others – that Hitler and the Nazis must be got rid of, if Germany were to be saved from the wreckage. Even the brave Stauffenberg who planted the bomb at Hitler's map-table had wavered to and fro in admiration and detestation of 'the wall-paper-hanger'. What is new in the book is that Hitler's right-hand man in the extermination of the Jews, Himmler, made several treacherous attempts to come to terms with the Allies to save his own skin, at the expense of his colleagues in crime. (This man was the friend of Dr Buchman of the Oxford Group Movement, we recall.)

When the bomb went off, several were killed and wounded, the divine Führer was relatively unharmed: God looks after his own, as Hitler was able to claim shortly after, broadcasting to his people.

He exacted a terrible revenge upon the aristocrats of the army and diplomacy who had been behind the conspiracy. Those immediately involved – Colonel-General Beck, Count Stauffenberg and others – were immediately shot; their bodies buried that night 'in their uniforms with full medals and decoration. Next day Himmler had them exhumed and cremated, the ashes scattered'. Field-Marshal von Witzleben was publicly tried, minus his decorations, in an old pair of trousers without braces so that he could not keep them up – a typical example of the delicate German sense of humour. 'Hitler himself had prescribed hanging as the method of execution of the conspirators'. The Field-Marshal and his friends, the brave Count Yorck von Wartenberg, were hanged accordingly:

> sound-track film cameras were mounted to record the death of his victims for Hitler's benefit – they were naked, their trousers having been removed after hanging. The film was taken to the Führer's headquarters at once and shown there. Photographs of the hangings were still lying on Hitler's map-table on 18 August

– a month later: *pour encourager les autres*, no doubt.

Colonel-General Fromm, in a decisive position in Berlin, blew hot and cold, without committing himself; when the bomb attempt failed, he rallied to Hitler and sought protection from Goebbels. He was shot for cowardice. Rommel, the nation's hero, was forced to take poison, as several others did; in his case 'a state funeral was ordered, an embolism from the wounds being given out as the cause of his death' – by way of keeping the truth, as always, from the dear people. Admiral Canaris with his group were court-martialled; 'during the trial Canaris, if not others, was severely beaten as he had been previously. All were hanged in Flossenburg camp'. The Führer's birthday was celebrated by a last batch of twenty-eight executions in Brandenburg prison. Altogether some two hundred grandees were executed, hanged, shot or murdered for the impertinence of the attempt: the paperhanger was getting his own back with a vengeance on the aristos whose bacon he had saved, and given a career to with his renewal of the German war for domination of Europe. From 1933 on Hoffmann makes no difficulty – as English historians with muddled minds have done – in admitting that 'Hitler was bent on making himself dictator of Europe'. If he had succeeded, the German upper classes would have been with him. As it was, they committed suicide by conniving at Hitler's aggressions – he always intended the renewal of the war and the reversal of the verdict of 1914–1918, as they did. The British upper classes committed suicide by their connivance at Appeasement of Germany. Each of them can take that to heart as they survey the ruins of their world.

Would there have been any point in our coming to terms, if that had been possible, with the German Resistance to Hitler before the final catastrophe, with Hitler's suicide in his Bunker and the Russian capture of Berlin?

I am quite sure not, and that the Allies were right to insist on Unconditional Surrender. This was the Foreign Office view; the Foreign Office and Vansittart were right about Germany – as against Chamberlain, the Conservative Party, and the City of London – all along. And, ironically, it was a good thing that the Resistance and their attempts to railroad Hitler failed: a compromise peace would have been fatal, with a militarist Germany still intact, capable of a third attempt. It was even a good thing, though it is a bitter thing to have to say, that Hitler eliminated all these field-marshals and colonel-generals and their aristocratic friends, before the final *débacle* when Hitler, Goebbels, Himmler and Göring (later) took the poison-pills prepared for the eventuality. It was a useful clearance for the future.

The German historian Ranke – too much admired in his day – wrote a classic history of the long ding-dong struggle between the Latin and Teutonic nations. A comparable book might be written about the centuries-long warfare between Teuton and Slav. We can now see that, as the result of the German inability to behave decently and fulfil a proper role of pacific stability in the centre of Europe, accommodating themselves to the interests and well-being of others, the Germans have finally lost out to the Slavs. They are divided in two, from top to bottom and likely to remain so; they have nobody but themselves to blame.

NOTE

1. Peter Hoffmann, *The History of German Resistance, 1933–1945*, (Macdonald & Jane's).

DECLINE AND FALL OF THE LIBERAL PARTY

This book manages to convey a great deal of useful information in short, if costly, space; no less noticeable is its stolid accuracy, if written without elegance, and its admirable objectivity, without partisanship.[1] These qualities make it a reliable record, mostly of the decline and decay of the Liberal Party after the First German war of 1914–18. Mr Cook gives us a persuasive new reading of the Cabinet crisis of 1916, from which Lloyd George emerged as Prime Minister, and also of the 'Coupon' Election of 1918 which registered the split between the two wings of the Party. Another good point 'dispels the myth' that the great victory of 1906 'represented left-wing reforming radicalism. . . . The Party was dominated by centre Liberals. Its social composition [in Parliament] was preponderantly middle-aged men from the commercial and professional middle class. The real Radicals were few and far between.'

The story is that of the irresistible creeping tide of working-class representation in the Labour Party undermining and finally engulfing the historic party of Gladstone, Asquith and Lloyd George. Those three names conveniently sum up the rise, ascendancy and fall. What the historian notices is the (almost) inevitability and irreversibility of the general historic movement underneath all the surface phenomena of personalities, rivalries, conflicts not merely between individuals but over issues and policy. No doubt the prolonged conflict between Asquith and Lloyd George, between independent Liberals and Coalition Liberals, opened the way to decline and hastened the break-up; but underneath these considerations were the far more important social and economic factors, their movement and propulsion. It is curious that politicians, like so many Aesop's flies, caught up in the buzz of day-to-day events, do not seem to appreciate this, though their careers and fates are determined by it.

A Marxist could explain the decline of the Liberal Party fairly briefly, and significantly, if with some oversimplification. The social and class substructure of the Liberal Party collapsed with the fundamental economic trends of the twentieth century. Up to 1914 thousands of small independent businesses, family concerns, traders; tenant farmers and small-holders all over the country:

these provided the substructure, free-trade and cheap food in economics, middle and lower middle class socially, Nonconformist in religion, Liberal in politics. After 1918 business and trade moved towards monopoly and multiple concerns in every town, with a managerial and bureaucratic class mainly Conservative, and the mass of employees organised in trade Unions, mostly Labour politically.

The irresistible historic movement registers itself underneath the personal quarrels and the faction-fights. It is even registered *through* the personalities. Actually in the long duel between Asquith and Lloyd George, whatever one's sympathies or prejudices, the overriding fact remains – the necessity of more dynamic leadership in the war, which Asquith could not provide (actually he does not come out well in this book at several points), and Lloyd George could and did.

The inevitable decline shows in the numbers of Liberal MPs in Parliament. In 1906, 377; 1910, 270; 1918, 36 Independent Liberals, 127 Coalition Liberals; 1922, 60 Independent Liberals; 1923, 158 with the two wings united on Free Trade; then in 1924, 40; 1929, 59; 1931, 72 but divided again; 1945, 12; 1950, 9 – about which figure the Party has fluctuated ever since. The historian can only conclude that the Liberal Party came to an end as a political party in the decisive year 1931. There was no future after that.

The historic movement is no less obvious in the reverse figures for the Labour Party: from some forty MPs in 1910 to over 300 after the Second German War, around which order of magnitude it fluctuates (363 in 1966). There are, in fact, merely two political parties in Britain, whatever efforts at resuscitation are made by the Liberals. Not even if an archangel descended from heaven could it affect the figures. In 1945 it was thought that an archangel had descended in the shape of Sir William Beveridge, with his programme, *Full Employment in a Free Society*, which made a great noise in the newspapers. Mr Cook says, 'the Party placed great hopes on Beveridge' (so did Beveridge); it emerged from the Election with 12 seats. Not all the programmes excogitated by all the experts – Keynes, Walter Layton, Hubert Henderson, Beveridge – could ever make any difference. Why could they not see that? The answer is partly that they are not Marxists.

What constitutes, then, the apparently irreducible core – if that is the word for it – of the Liberal vote? Mr Cook tells us that the Nationalist upsurge in Scotland 'has achieved what may well be the end of Liberalism as the party of the Celtic fringe'. There remains only what remains of Nonconformity, the more conservative elements in which were recruited to Conservatism by Baldwin, with his Wesleyan descent and appeal. Disraeli described the Anglican Church in his day as 'the Conservative Party at prayer'; it looks as if the Liberal vote is coterminous with what remains of Nonconformity and has contracted with it. A politico-denominational-geographical map, such as André Siegfried compiled for some regions of France, might have brought this out well. And an Appendix giving the comparative numbers of MPs of the parties, along with the votes polled in this period, would have given the story at a glance. The story of decline and virtual extinction is the result, however, of the deeper historic movement in society which Mr Cook does not diagnose.

NOTE

1.   Chris Cook, *A Short History of the Liberal Party, 1900–1976* (Macmillan).

A. J. P. TAYLOR ON THE SECOND GERMAN WAR

This book has been the subject of acute controversy in Britain, and is probably explosive matter for a reviewer to touch. When it first appeared in April 1961, it was hailed by a chorus of praise from ingenuous publicists who knew little about the subject and had no faculty for criticism; on the second wave, it was subjected to scarifying comment by authorities who knew what they were talking about. The book was given a devastating analysis by H. R. Trevor-Roper in *Encounter*, leaving the author with not a leg to stand on. No serious attempt was made, since none was possible, to meet the criticisms; and now the book is published in the United States with no changes, so far as I can see, except for a 'Preface for the American Reader'.

A. J. P. Taylor is the *enfant terrible* of English intellectual and journalistic life. He is an Oxford don, regarded as a stimulating, provocative teacher. As a political figure, he is a man of the extreme Left, much to the fore in the unilateral Disarmament Campaign, though he combines this with writing regularly for the Beaverbrook press, for which he signalised himself by advocating the ending of the United Nations. In addition, he is a television performer with a vast and ignorant audience.

Now, for the historian, the prime necessity is for accuracy of statement: one must be able to rely on what the man says, or he is not any good as a historian. Almost equally necessary is responsibility of judgement.

Mr Taylor's 'Preface for the American Reader' contains a good many trenchant strictures on American policy before the war, and then says, 'The general moral of this book, so far as it has one, is that Great Britain and France dithered between resistance and appeasement, and so helped to make war more likely. American policy did much the same'. There is something in that, of course; but it is putting the cart before the horse. As if this were the primary cause of the war! The *primary* cause, as we all know, was Hitler's dynamic drive towards world power – to which Britain and France were merely reacting, insufficiently strongly.

Mr Taylor, however, makes his fortune by calling in question what we all know and going flat against common sense. He practically tells us that Hitler was not responsible for the war; then he, too, dithers and concludes, not until the last page, that 'Hitler *may* have projected a great war all along'. But there is no doubt what the book adds up to: by way of originality, out to affront, to shock, rather than to seek the truth and ensure it, it is a whitewashing of Hitler.

We are told, 'in principle and doctrine, Hitler was no more wicked and unscrupulous than many other contemporary statesmen. In wicked acts he outdid them all'. This is an entirely false disjunction. If a political leader inseminates and enforces the wicked racial rubbish of anti-Semitism, it will come to be carried out. But this historian lets Hitler off. He says, 'Everything which Hitler did against the Jews followed logically from the racial doctrines in which most Germans vaguely believed'. Here is another simple confusion of thought: whatever nonsense people may think, one must make a distinction between those who have not committed murder, and those who in fact have – and mass-murders on a terrible scale too.

This overwhelming fact is hardly mentioned throughout the

length of Mr Taylor's book. It might be pleaded that there is a technical reason for this: that this is diplomatic history, concerned with the foreign relations of the powers and their documentation. If that is so, then this is unilateral history, history in only one dimension, with the whole heart, soul and substance of the matter left out. How can one hope to understand or explain what happened by merely reading the surface of things in the diplomatic notes the powers exchanged with one another and without taking into account the full nature of the Nazi regime in all its barbarity? What is the point of it? What value is there in it?

Even so, Mr Taylor is at pains to whittle down Hitler's responsibility at every point. In the English edition, he gave the game away by saying that his is 'a story without heroes, and perhaps even without villains'. In both editions, speaking as a politician, I suppose, he tells us that putting the blame on Hitler 'satisfied the Germans, except for a few unrepentant Nazis'. Another half-truth. Again and again we are told that it was not Hitler who made this crisis or that, others did it for him. Over Czechoslovakia, 'even more than in the case of Austria, Hitler did not need to act. Others would do his work for him. The crisis over Czechoslovakia was provided for Hitler. He merely took advantage of it.'

He tells us with regard to Munich, that 'the settlement at Munich was a triumph for British policy, which had worked precisely to this end; not a triumph for Hitler, who had started with no such clear intention'. This is in complete contradiction to Sir Winston Churchill, who stated at the time that it was one of the gravest defeats that British policy had ever suffered.

Mr Taylor is very cocksure in his certainty as to Hitler's intentions: he might just have looked at the evidence plain for all to see in *Mein Kampf*. There we can see the objective made clear: *Lebensraum* in Eastern Europe, room for a population of 250 million Germans, a war of conquest against Russia, a German Army strong enough to achieve it and overthrow the West if necessary. He meant what he said, no political leader more so. Why deny the plain facts to titillate the gallery?

There is a simple intellectual confusion here also: that between strategy and tactics. Of course, Hitler was flexible as to tactics, prepared to wait for opportunities to come along and exploit them, but that does not mean that there was not a grand strategy as to which he was inflexible, with an overriding objective: the domination of Europe. Mr Taylor admits as much in passing, for his book is as full of self-contradictions as of misstatements.

One of the more innocent publicists in England greeted the book as 'a flawless masterpiece'; it is, in fact, flawed from top to bottom and offers an exemplary instance how history should not be written.

NOTE

1.   A. J. P. Taylor, *The Origins of the Second World War* (New York: Atheneum).

LADY OTTOLINE'S VANISHED WORLD

The first thing to be said about Lady Ottoline Morrell is that she created something: hers was a creative spirit, even if the creation were something of an *Ersatz*. She herself would have wished to be a writer; since she had not that gift, she did the next best thing – encouraged, boosted the confidence of, and devotedly boosted, those who were. Hers was a most generous spirit, giving, giving all the time. But she achieved something more. Her own personality and what she created around it were a work of art. Virginia Woolf saw this; Leonard Woolf called Ottoline 'a very silly woman': it shows the difference between Virginia and him, between a woman of genius and a mere intellectual.

I have been ordered to say something of what I saw of Garsington, through my own eyes, innocent enough, at the time.

There was the sheer beauty Ottoline fashioned around her. She and Philip Morrell rescued this exquisite old Oxfordshire manor from ruin and made something unforgettable of it: formal forecourt, cut yews, terraced gardens, statues and tritons, peacocks. Within were those panelled drawing rooms; one painted the colour of sealing wax, the other a pale sea-green, both perfect *décor* for Ottoline's Venetian red hair, the fantastic trailing silks and scarves, the pot-pourri and exotic perfumes, the mooing, murmuring voice with its suggestion of Italy, which Lawrence caught so well – and all too much else – in *Women in Love*.

When one thinks what the Edwardians – vulgar Philistines like Edward VII and Alexandra, to begin with – could have done with all their money! ... The art treasures they could have saved for the country, or divine houses like Kirby Hall they could have rescued from ruin – instead of pulling them down, as the Hamiltons pulled down Hamilton Palace. Or again, think of the arts they could have encouraged – as Ottoline did: the walls were covered with the paintings of young painters she helped, Mark Gertler, Stanley Spencer, Henry Lamb, Augustus John – the best of whose work it is both fashionable and foolish to decry – as she was generous in entertaining their persons within the walls.

She must have spent a mint of money on other people – fat lot of thanks she got for it! And the point here,[1] which the author gets wrong, is that Ottoline was *not* rich: she was merely comfortably provided for out of the Portland estate – all the more credit to her for what *she* did with the margin she had to dispose of. Of course, in those days things were cheap for the elect; today it is only bureaucrats, trade union or civil service, people provided for from public funds, who can travel first-class or entertain in hotels or restaurants. Then – what a vanished world! – it was the people who spoke the languages or appreciated the landscape who could go to Lausanne for their neuralgia, Marienbad for the cure (Edward VII needed the cure from over-eating), or Venice before it was submerged by the masses.

The second thing to be said is that Ottoline's was a deliberate revolt, not so much from her ducal background – she always remained more than a duchess herself – but from the Philistinism of Edwardian social life. (I can quite see her saying, 'But I *love* the people – I married into the people'.) I think she really did love people – I never understood that when I was young – in addition to being fascinated by them. David Garnet wrote a naughty lampoon about her, 'The Hue and Cry after Genius'; but she really had an extraordinary nose for genius, or talent of any kind, and a passionate desire to help.

For, again, what few understood: she was a religious woman, who wanted naturally to do good; and, what nobody could have guessed, underneath the fantastic aura, within the cocoon of the fantasy world she inhabited, was a woman humble of heart, not sure of herself or the way to good. Hence all those explorations with remarkable people like Russell, Strachey, Lawrence. Huxley, Yeats, Sassoon. Ottoline was not just a lion-hunter, like so many conductresses of *salons*; she was out to share as much as possible of their mind and spirit. That she managed to hold on to her own religious belief in an environment of such devastating unbelievers as Bertrand Russell and Lytton Strachey is tribute to her inner strength of mind as well as character. The clever second-rate who under-estimated her mentally revealed only themselves as usual (I think I was more frightened of her).

Ottoline took in a great deal of Lawrence the moment she set eyes on him:

> a slight man, lithe and delicately built, his pale face over-shadowed by his beard and his red hair falling over his forehead, his eyes blue and his hands delicate and very competent. He gave one the impression of someone who had been undernourished in youth, making his body fragile and his mind too active.

There is perception in that, as well as compassion; and also the capacity to express herself very well in writing, which Ottoline herself misdoubted. A woman capable of holding her own with these men whom she attached to her was obviously remarkable in her own right. Lawrence had a feminine intuition equal to her own; he at once perceived Ottoline's will-power, and that this led her to probe one's very soul, interfere with one's life. Usually this was benevolent in intention, sometimes beneficent in effect (I wasn't going to give it a chance: a little bird warned me to hold off). And the awful things these people said about each other, and about Ottoline! That kind of thing was not for me, I decided.

Nevertheless, this reliable book does provide corroboration for my distrust of people's getting so entangled with each other – not so much jumping in and out of each other's beds, a simple, external operation, as their penetrating each other entrails, too lovingly, and then turning nasty. A little proletarian common sense should have warned them. Here's Bertie Russell, plaguing Ottoline with his passion, pestering, beseeching – whatever sense he had was not common, and certainly not proletarian. For all his moral pretensions, he admitted that he did not consider Philip's feelings at all in seducing his wife, and doing all he could to break up the marriage, take Ottoline away from husband and child. Ottoline was overcome by him intellectually; physically, she found him unattractive, as indeed he was. She found great difficulty in enduring his overpowering halitosis. So like an insensitive heterosexual, he was totally unaware how offensive he was. (I have come to recognise halitosis as a sure sign of a heterosexual.) In Bertie it was exaggerated by pyorrhoea; in this case Ottoline's interference was in the public interest.

Did Bertie's first wife, Alys, never notice it? The poor lady had worse things to put up with; including, when Bertie fell out of love with her and in with Ottoline, his deliberate killing of Alys's love for him. He employed the same tactics with Ottoline when he fell in love with Constance Malleson. A just cause of pride for Ottoline was her massed red-gold hair; 'What a pity your hair is going grey!' said the moralist, who informed the world in his *Autobiography* that the grief of his life was the thought of giving pain to others.

Meanwhile, in America he had seduced an American girl, mind *and* body, who came over under the illusion that he loved her and would marry her. She found herself cold-shouldered on arrival. The apostle of truth wrote to Ottoline:

> I don't think she realises *quite* what you and I are to each other, and now there is no reason why she should. It would be very unfortunate if she thought you had anything to do with my change toward her.

The girl returned to America and ultimately became insane. So also did T. S. Eliot's first wife, Vivien. We must not hold Bertie guilty for these feminine derangements, but undoubtedly he was a disturbing influence. Eliot thought that Russell's playing round with his wife was an element in her disturbance of mind: 'He has wrought Evil'. Even the tolerant Ottoline was upset when she found Bertie using the same eloquent phrases with which he had seduced her to serve his purpose with the American girl.

The truth is, Bertrand Russell was a bloody humbug.

We need not concern ourselves here with his pacifist antics, though we may note his appallingly bad political judgement. On Germany's open aggression with her invasion of Belgium, Russell explained to Ottoline, 'For once Germany is wholly disinterested and guided by honour'. This inversion of sense and truth throws a dubious light on his kindly explanation to Ottoline, 'No woman's intellect is really good enough to give me pleasure as intellect'. It would give me pleasure to have Bertie described by the feeble intellect of Jane Austen.

The moral philosopher was not immune from mundane emotions like jealousy. Russell could not bear the thought of Ottoline sharing her bedroom with her husband – where I should have considered the emotion primitive, and in the circumstances positively *anthropologisch*. He was jealous too of Lytton Strachey:

> I think loathing for him quite pardonable. He is diseased and unnatural, and only a very high degree of civilisation enables a healthy person to stand him.

(Russell was always healthy.)

I should have thought that after all the adolescent tantrums Ottoline had to put up with from heteros like Russell, Henry Lamb and John, the company of a homo like Lytton was rather restful. (It is true she tried to convert him.) Lytton: 'I should love to come out and be your maid – I'm sure I'd make a very good one. I should arrange your petticoats most exquisitely, and only look through the crack of the door now and then'. Surely better than having Bertie's hands pawing one all over: Ottoline said that his hands were like the paws of a bear – to me they looked like the claws of a bird of prey. I can't think why Russell had such success with Americans, except that their charity is inexhaustible and they have little critical sense. What he thought of them he wrote to Ottoline, from Harvard:

> America produces a type of bore more virulent, I think, than the bore of any other country – they all give one exactly the same information, slowly, inexorably, undeterred by all one's efforts to stop them.

I can only say that Ottoline's prime qualification for sainthood was putting up with Bertie. I learn from this book that her daughter's name, Julian – rare for a woman – came from Ottoline's devotion to her spiritual adviser, Mother Julian, of the Community of the Epiphany in my own saintly vicinity in Cornwall. Mother Julian does not seem to have interfered in any disagreeable way with Mother Ottoline's variegated sex-life.

The Australian author gives a notably fair and balanced picture of the circle – Circe's circle, as Strachey called it behind

Ottoline's back– but without penetrating to her inner nature, or perhaps the inwardness of things. She finds it surprising that Eliot and Ottoline 'should have got on well together. His poetry was very complex. Also, Eliot himself was a pretty dry stick. [!] Yet, of all Ottoline's post-war friendships the one with Eliot was probably the closest and most genuine'. There is nothing surprising in this. Both had religious natures; Eliot was sincere and true, while underneath her exterior Ottoline was sincere, if not necessarily truthful (she was very feminine).

Some of those whom Ottoline helped were decidedly ugly ducklings. There was the Cambridge economist of the improbable name of Shove, a conscientious objector of course, whom Philip took in on the farm. The laziest of the lot, he formed a trade union among these slackers. A modern planner, he introduced a special feed into the henhouse, so that the egg-yield dropped and the hens decayed. When a foul fowl was produced for Christmas, Philip found that the hen-roosts hadn't been cleaned out and the hens wilted on top of 'accumulated droppings and rancid grain'. It seems a portent of the future of our economy, which was to owe so much to Cambridge economists.

The literary birds were apt to turn as nasty as the hens. Lawrence's Frieda was such a liability: at Garsington she felt she was 'a Hun and a nobody . . . the old Ottoline is rich and I am poor, and people will take such a mean advantage of one's poverty'. Frieda may be excused; after all she was a German. She was jealous in every direction, even of Lawrence. 'I am just as remarkable as Lorenzo'. Ottoline herself told me they fought like cat and dog in their bedroom – not out of an excess of love, I fancy. Then Lawrence wounded Ottoline deeply with his recognisable portrait of her as Hermione in *Women in Love*. Ottoline put that down largely to Frieda.

Aldous Huxley perpetrated similar breaches of friendship with his caricature of her and the circle in *Chrome Yellow* and *Those Barren Leaves*; W. J. Turner a more vicious onslaught in *The Aesthetes*: less distinguished a writer, he was never forgiven. Lytton Strachey was no less malicious behind her back, caddishly exposing her physical malfunctions of a rather delicate nature. What a lot they were! The only ones with decent impulses were the two ladies who, rather precariously feminine, insisted on being known as Brett and Carrington respectively. The latter spoke the truth when she said, 'What traitors all these people are! I think it's beastly of them to enjoy Ottoline's kindness and then laugh at her'.

Themselves were no laughing matter. Young and innocent, serious-minded and fanatical, I simply didn't want to know such people. I must be the only person who actually chose to drop Ottoline – now I am not only sorry but sad and grieved to think of it. Perhaps it was worse for me; but at least I was never malicious about her. I always recognised her kindness of heart, her generosity of mind. Julian tells me that she would say, 'My dear, he's a genius'. (I can only say there was nothing to show for it.) Too proud, I threw away my chances: think of all those interesting people I could have known, if I had wished. What a young fool I was; or perhaps, after all – considering what they were like – I wasn't?

NOTE

1. Sandra Jobson Darroch, *Ottoline. The Life of Lady Ottoline Morrell* (Chatto & Windus).

BERTRAND RUSSELL

I

Bertrand Russell has this in common with Byron that one could go on reading about him (almost) inexhaustibly. What does that quality come from? – for Russell's personality, unlike Byron's, never had much appeal for me. For one thing, Byron was beautiful; I found Russell physically unattractive, that stringy vibrancy, the harsh voice full of intellectual conceit, the gander-neck with very active Adam's apple. Young and innocent, I once said to Lady Ottoline at Garsington that I couldn't see what people saw so much in him. She murmured, in that sexy voice speaking English as if it were Italian (caricatured by Lawrence in *Women in Love*): 'Oh, my deah, you've no ideah how irre*sist*ible he is'.

Years later, after the Second German war – about which he

took a very different line from that over the First, in fact was more sensible – he was at a loose end for a job. I suggested him for a Research Fellowship at All Souls; but canny Scotch Warden Adams was taking no risks with such a bird. As Bertie stood in the gutter of the High in his shiny worn black suit, he said: 'the first £1,050 of my income every year goes to the upkeep of three women'. I was not very sympathetic to this misfortune: with an inadequate appreciation of the charms of these various ladies, I thought, 'You silly old fool, whose fault is that?'. However, I was sorry that All Souls did not annex him; his old friends at Trinity stepped in – particularly G. M. Trevelyan, then Master – and all was well. Russell was properly grateful for 'Trevy's' kindness; but Trevelyan used to say to me: 'he may be a genius at mathematics – as to that I am no judge; but he is a perfect goose about politics'.

This crisp judgement of the eminent historian every other page of this long book bears out.[1] Mr Clark has brought off a *tour de force*, but what is particularly admirable is the justice of mind with which he candidly admits Russell's mistakes and follies, his bad qualities, as well as his good. To answer my own question: what makes this book so readable is Russell's intellectual vivacity, always alive at every minute, brilliant or silly, when perceptive and convincing as also when unforgivably irresponsible. The book, as I can vouch, is an absolutely true and candid portrait of the man; the effect on me is to make me a bit more sympathetic to this extraordinary personality than perhaps before.

The dominant impression one gets is the extremism of the mixture: the brilliant gifts on one side, the perversity, folly and irresponsibility on the other. Santayana, with his humanist wisdom, summed up Russell better than any other has done. (Mr Clark may not know that Santayana was in love with Russell's brother Frank, the bigamist Earl, who is the anti-hero of *The Last Puritan*.) Santayana wrote:

> there is a strange mixture in him, of great ability and great disability; prodigious capacity, brilliance here – astonishing unconsciousness and want of perception there. They are like creatures of a species somewhat different from man.

In particular, there was the gulf between logico/mathematical acuteness, and lack of even ordinary understanding of human beings – but the latter is fatal to the understanding of politics or, for that matter, history. This was no bar to Russell laying down the law about everything. But why ever should people listen to him! Why ever did he have the influence, and the success, he had? There is the question. He was really a very lucky dog; all the messes he got into were of his own making – there was always somebody to pull, or bail, him out.

The epitaph for this book should have been Dryden's:

> Great wits are sure to madness near allied,
> And thin partitions do their bounds divide.

That was written about Shaftesbury, another genius of High Whiggery: how detestable it is, with its restless, feverish scheming, its intellectual conceit, its superficial rationalism, its reduction of everything and everybody to reason, when they are neither reasonable or rational themselves. And then their smug self-satisfaction, absolutely convinced that they are right, and as equally certain when they completely reverse engines. Russell's mental life was as inconstant and changeable as Shaftesbury's political life. The philosopher Broad said that Russell changed his philosophy every few years. We all know that; but what beats me is why people should follow such a weather-cock. Or, for that matter, take seriously the views on politics of someone who could advocate dropping a nuclear bomb on Moscow, and then say he had forgotten he had ever said it.

Surely, he was a great fool (Michael Foot's 'Man of the Century' – he would be!). His biographer shows that he was worse – a convicted liar. 'The real point is simply that Russell denied making certain statements he had certainly made, and accused his accusers of lies and distortions.' Then why regard a convicted liar as an authority on truth? I don't set up for a moral mentor, but I should be ashamed of such irresponsibility. Why take him seriously? – it only goes to show what gullible asses the bulk of humans are. (How well Hitler knew that! 'the German people have no idea how they have to be *gulled* in order to be led'.) Or, for that matter, why attach any importance to the views on marriage and morals of anyone who made such a mess of both as Russell did? Three failed marriages show what a fool Russell was about the one subject. The second most important woman in his life, Lady Constance Malleson, to whom he was not married – any more than he was to Ottoline, most important of them all – put her finger on the spot: 'I see now that your inability to care for anybody, with the whole of you, for longer than a short time, must be more painful to you than it is to those who are able to continue caring in spite of everything'. He was a colossal egoist.

But the man who wrote that fear of giving pain to anyone had been a dominant motive all through his life in fact didn't care. When seducing his friend, Philip Morrell's wife, Russell wrote: 'What Philip might think or feel was a matter of indifference to me'. When cold-shouldering an American girl he had seduced, and who loved him, he wrote to Ottoline: 'Never mind if she is hurt'. One might sympathise with Russell's view that all is fair in the sex-war, one cannot also accept the pretension to being in any way a moralist. Like all grand Whigs, he was in fact a humbug, and didn't know himself. It is the moral pretence that one cannot stand, even less than the cruelty. But the moral failure had no objection to telling other people how to live their lives.

Again, one finds this exemplar of morality disapproving of Keynes's and Wittgenstein's homosexuality. No doubt if Bertie had been at all that way inclined, instead of being helplessly heterosexual, that too would have been given the benefit of some absolute moral principle. One sees with this philosopher, even more than with most ordinary people of no pretensions, how their personal preferences rig themselves out in moral garments.

Was he any more conscientious about truth? Apparently not: one finds him lying easily enough, or 'making little of it', his usual phrase for a piece of disingenuousness at the expense of others. Though he liked history, and made an attempt (with his third wife) to write it, he was untrustworthy as to facts and remoulded events in his autobiography to make a better impression. Mr Clark tells us, of Russell's account of his affair with Lady Constance Malleson, 'at its best, this is an urbane example of his ability to make the best of his own story. The truth is very different'. And there are other urbane examples. To the historian, lying is even worse than cruelty. No wonder an American sociologist, an acquaintance of mine, who owns a portrait of Russell by Roger Fry, making him look evil, thinks he was an evil man. Russell certainly had demonic energy; perhaps he was also a bit diabolical.

To complicate the picture, this man who thought and uttered so much nonsense could occasionally deviate into sense. As a young man he thought that an egalitarian society, with socialist taxation to reduce everyone to the same level, would 'cut off all the flowers of civilisation'. If the Shelleys and Darwins had had to work for their living they would never have produced what they did – 'and surely one Darwin is more important than 30 million working men and women'. Or again: 'what can a charwoman know of the spirits of great men or the records of falling empires or the haunting visions of art and reason? Let us not delude ourselves with the hope that the best is within the reach of all'.

Even on education one finds him subscribing to commonsense. He was in favour of competitive examination for the universities and special schools for exceptionally gifted children. 'A great deal of needless pain and friction would be saved to clever children if they were not compelled to associate intimately with stupid contemporaries.' One hardly recognises in this piece of common-sense Michael Foot's 'Man of the Century'.

One may recognise him better in the shocking irresponsibility of his pronouncements, and the equally shocking irresponsibility of his contradictions. In *Marriage and Morals* he had written, 'it seems on the whole fair to regard negroes as on the average inferior to white men'. After some protest, presumably from America, he instructed his publishers to substitute for the words, 'It seems on the whole fair', the words 'There is no sound reason'. The effortless (and disingenuous) irresponsibility takes one's breath away. But it is all of a piece with his changing his mind about an important philosophical issue in the middle of a lecture; or his idiotic words about Macmillan and Kennedy being fifty times worse than Hitler or Stalin; or that the way to end the First German war was to assassinate Sir Edward Grey. After 1939 he blithely admitted that he had been wrong to be an Appeaser of Germany; the same holds good (or rather bad) of his attitude to the 1914 war, along with the rest of that Cambridge crowd, hopelessly wrong as they were, and as conceited as they were ignorant.

Russell changed his mind quite as much on the problems of philosophy. He made his reputation by his work on mathematical logic; but that did not qualify him to hold forth on anything other than mathematical logic. The sagacious (and angelic) Mrs Whitehead advised him to stick to his last and work away at what he was qualified for. He wasn't qualified to do anything in the least practical; hardly competent to brew a cup of tea, he was no good at all at practical science, still less was he competent to lay down the law about the practical problems of government.

No philosopher myself, I am assailed by the horrid thought of the uselessness of all this palaver about philosophy. Russell himself tells us that, after Einstein, hardly any of his *Principles of Mathematics* remained valid. Wittgenstein put the whole of *Principia Mathematica* out of court, and went on to demonstrate the nullity, or at least, futility of philosophy. Russell reversed his position on fundamentals again and again. All to what point? A young Oxford critic observed that he left no philosophic masterpiece, 'but, instead, umpteen flawed and superseded books'. Quite unresolved and uncertain in the realm which he knew about, he should have been less cocksure in the realms he knew little about and was not prepared to learn or be told. He admitted, candidly enough, that his motive was the love of power, especially power over men's minds.

Difficult as it is to appreciate how men could have been such fools as to take the celebrated buffoon seriously, his hold over women was still more extraordinary: I suppose intellectual vivacity goes to their – hearts. The person who comes best out of this book is, after all, Ottoline: reluctant to become Bertie's mistress, she remained always a faithful and wise counsellor. Religious herself, she had a good effect in making him aware of more things in heaven and earth than were dreamt of in his philosophy. With the influence of his second marriage, Bertie became bitterly anti-Christian; but fancy succumbing to the influence of a Dora Black! The account Mr Clark gives of the first wife, Alys Pearsall Smith, makes one sympathise with Bertie: life with an earnest, Philadelphian Quaker, relentlessly ethical, hopelessly gone to the good, given to good works and emotional blackmail, must have been unbearable. I suppose she had some redeeming features.

Still, when one reflects what all those women had to put up with, one way and another, one reflects that the charity of women is inexhaustible.

2

Much as all sensible people must disapprove of Bertrand Russell's political antics, his crazy political irresponsibility, candour compels me to admit that I find *The Autobiography of Bertrand Russell*² fascinating to read. For one thing, it is beautifully written, in English sharp and precise, clear as crystal. For another, his has been a remarkable life on two counts. He was born into the elect circle of the governing class at its Victorian apogee, with Prime Minister Lord John Russell for his grandfather, so that the figures of history – names to most of us – flit easily in and out of the family story. Then he became a member of the most distinguished intellectual circle in Britain, with its American affiliations through his first marriage, with Pearsall Smiths, Berensons and William (rather than Henry) James.

It was natural enough that Russell should have become a rebel against the grand Whig priggery he was born into – though it is rather adolescent to keep up the stance of a rebel into one's nineties. And the joke is that he has not ceased to be a Victorian. This book, however, was written before his dotage: from internal evidence it appears that it was written in 1949, when he was seventy-six. It is the first volume of two; whatever one thinks of the author, it will be one of the significant autobiographies of our time.

He tells us in a prologue what he has lived for: 'Three passions, simple but overwhelmingly strong, have governed my life: the longing for love, the search for knowledge, and unbearable pity for the suffering of mankind'.

'Unbearable'? – he has been able to bear it very well, longer than most, to his ninety-fifth year.

As for love, he first fell in love with the Pennsylvanian Quakeress, Alys Pearsall Smith, and married her. One afternoon 'I went out bicycling and suddenly, as I was riding along a country road, I realized that I no longer loved Alys'. Then, 'so long as I lived in the same house with Alys she would every now and then come down to me in her dressing gown after she had gone to bed, and beseech me to spend the night with her. Sometimes I did so, but the result was utterly unsatisfactory'.

Next, Russell fell passionately in love with Lady Ottoline, the wife of his friend, Philip Morrell. 'My feeling was overwhelmingly strong, and I did not care what might be involved. I wanted to leave Alys, and to have her (Ottoline) leave Philip. What Philip might think or feel was a matter of indifference to me.'

There is a third, more shocking, example. At an American college where Russell was a visiting lecturer, he proceeded to seduce a girl of undergraduate age, while her sister kept watch on the door for the copulating couple. Well, all is fair in love and war – and I am no prig about people's sexual affairs: sex makes fools of us all, the one realm where human equality is real. But sex creates obligations, and the girl fell in love with Russell. When she came over to England, he cold-shouldered her and brushed her off. (She went back miserable to America and eventually committed suicide.)

I am afraid I cannot take seriously his claim to excessive pity for the suffering of mankind – it is, in part, self-delusion, and for the rest, when one considers those three crucial examples, heartless humbug.

People are fools to take him as any guide in the realm of morals.

What then about politics? What value, if any, has he had as a political guide?

G. M. Trevelyan, the historian, was an intimate member of the exclusive (and also supercilious) Cambridge circle to which Russell belonged. One of the last things Trevelyan said to me about Russell was, 'he may be a genius about mathematics – as to that I am incapable of judging – but he has always been a goose about politics'.

The truth about Russell is best summed up by George Santayana, who knew him intimately, in his 'Letters'. He points out the striking contrast between acute intellectual perception about abstract matters, logical analysis and argument, and obtuseness where human beings and their affairs are concerned. And Russell carries forward his arrogance generated by his undoubted superiority in one sphere into the other, where he is astonishingly defective. Proficiency in mathematical logic is no qualification to pronounce about politics; rather is it a disqualification, as William James sensibly saw: 'Say good-bye to mathematical logic if you wish to preserve your relations with concrete realities'.

Candour and sincerity are characteristic of this remarkable book. As a young man at Cambridge, Russell tells us, 'having been reading pantheism, I announced to my friends that I was God. They placed candles on each side of me and proceeded to acts of mock worship'. When one reflects on the reverence with which this irreverent philosopher is regarded by Left intellectuals around the world, anyone with any sense of psychology should perceive how revealing this is of the inner man: his latent megalomania, released in old age for all to see, if not for all to worship. Russell places the highest point of his life intellectually in the year 1900: he has lived another sixty-seven active years in decline from that point.

What is it then, that makes the book nevertheless enjoyable reading? There is its intellectual (if not moral) distinction, its vitality, sheer high spirits and amusement. We can allow that Russell has been a liberator so far as Victorianism about sex is concerned. And we are introduced to all the brilliant people he has known, about whom he writes entertainingly, and who themselves contribute their gaiety and amusement to the book. Some of the best things in it are the letters exchanged among these friends: Gilbert Murray, Logan Pearsall Smith, Sir Edward Marsh, Lytton Strachey. They were all well aware of their superior gifts and talents: it is rather refreshing, when we are all supposed to be so equal, to see that some people still regard themselves as more equal than others, and comic to find that these are usually Left intellectuals.

3

The second volume of Bertrand Russell's *Autobiography*[3] has been regarded as inferior to the first, on the ground that it is shorter, scrappier and filled out with letters, both his and other people's. Actually it is all of a piece with the first, making one big fat book with an addendum of letters which are fascinating to read in themselves. I find this section of as compelling interest as the first – perhaps for a personal reason more so: one knew quite a number of the characters who appear in the story, Russell himself, T. S. Eliot, G. M. Trevelyan, Lady Ottoline Morrell, Gilbert Murray, even if one did not know D. H. Lawrence, George Santayana (how I wish I had!), and Bertrand's naughty, bigamous brother, Frank, who for the rest shows a great deal more commonsense than Bertie.

What an absorbingly interesting career Russell's has been – aristocratic society in Victorian England in her prime; then pre-1914 Cambridge at *her* intellectual prime; the London of the brilliant (and unregenerate) Bloomsbury circle; in Russia conversing with Lenin himself; the China of the Nationalist Revolution; America during the Second World War, entanglements with the universities and with Dr Barnes of the Barnes Foundation.

There are two more marriages, in addition to the dissolution of the first; though the book ends with Russell on the threshold of his seventies, the fourth marriage is not yet on the horizon.

This volume covers 1914–1944, from the beginning of the First German war to the end of the Second. The book brings home at the end how completely wrong Russell had been all along about the First German war, 1914–1918. One of his intellectual virtues is candour and now he admits how wrong he had been. He describes his attitudes of conscientious objection during the first war as having become 'unconsciously insincere. I had been able to view with reluctant acquiescence the possibility of the supremacy of the Kaiser's Germany'. But, 'when, in 1940, England was threatened with invasion, I realised that, throughout the First War, I had never seriously envisaged the possibility of utter defeat'. QED. Lack of imagination along with intolerable intellectual arrogance.

Russell and his fellow conscientious objectors were just battening on the resistance to German militarism being borne by millions of their fellow-countrymen. I find their posturings as moral heroes – which we were called upon to admire when young – cruelly insincere. The real heroes were the poor fellows who died in hundreds of thousands in order that this elect minority might go on making their pretentious gestures. (They would have got short shrift if German militarism *had* won!) But there is no word of apology for this worse-than-wrongheadedness, no word of reparation to the men who laid down their lives that German militarism might not prevail.

This leads me to a theme that is brought home to one again and again in this book, as in Russell's life. Several times over he confesses himself to have been completely wrong – yet it never leads him to be any less cocksure the next time round. It is the certainty about things in themselves uncertain that is so childish. Why has he never learned? The reason is what Santayana, who knew him well, saw long ago: a combination of intellectual arrogance with an aristocratic lack of ordinary commonsense. He should have shut up about politics long ago, and confined himself to philosophy and mathematics.

Having confessed that he had been wrong about the Germans and their war, he yet retains his condemnation of the people who disagreed with him – that is, had been right all the time. Here he is on the young T. S. Eliot in October 1914. Russell writes, 'I naturally asked him what he thought of the war. "I don't know", he replied, "I only know that I am not a pacifist"'. On this Russell comments, 'That is to say he considered any excuse good enough for homicide'. I consider that a disgraceful misrepresentation: I suppose it is yet another example of Russell's 'passion for truth', on which he so prides himself. He really ought to be ashamed, setting up as a moralist, and then misrepresenting anyone so cruelly, let alone a personal friend.

But it is representative of another intellectual trait which I diagnose with distaste in this eminent intellectual. He says much the same disingenuous thing about Sir Edward Grey's vain attempts to restrain Germany from her headlong course. Russell describes Grey's qualified assurances to France as 'lying' to the English public. Now this comes, like the comment about Eliot, from Russell's habit of isolating people's statements from the context that gives them their proper meaning and validity. No doubt this is all very well in mathematics, but it puts him out of court in the real world of politics and history, which deals with human beings and the necessary conditions of human action.

It is difficult to see why people have taken him seriously on these matters. Of course, serious people do not, those carrying the burdens and responsibilities of politics.

He confesses himself now to have been wrong about the education of children – about which he wrote a best-seller. He set up a school, to educate his children with others, with a minimum of discipline – and found, to his surprise, that 'whatever may have been the cause, many of the children were cruel and destructive. To let the children go free was to establish a reign of terror, in which the strong kept the weak trembling and miserable'. Did Bertie learn nothing from that experience? The school had eventually to be abandoned; he now regards himself as a failure as a parent, and 'in retrospect, I feel that several things were mistaken in the principles upon which the school was conducted'. Many people make mistakes, but few are so confident that they are right in the first place.

Wrongheaded as Russell so often is, why does one find him such good reading? Well – intellectual vigour, high spirits, candour, fun, naughtiness, jokes, all keep the book tingling. And he passed much of his life with such interesting people. T. S. Eliot was his pupil briefly at Harvard, and there is much information about Eliot, who was so deeply reticent about his personal life – about Eliot's disastrous first marriage, for example, which inflicted such a deep wound and made him so miserable most of his life. Over this Russell was kind and helpful, but ambivalent about Eliot's wife. (Trust Bertie! – but one couldn't trust Bertie with the women.) Vivien Eliot was a psychopathic dancer of talent and beauty, and Eliot blamed himself for her misery. He should never have married her – and, the moment he did, knew it was a mistake. 'The fact that living with me has done her so much damage does not help me to come to any decision. I find her still perpetually baffling and deceptive. She seems to me like a child of six with an immensely clever and precocious mind. She writes *extremely* well (stories, etc.) and has great originality. And I can never escape from the spell of her persuasive (even coercive) gift of argument. I feel quite desperate.' Then, Eliot realised and wrote of Russell: 'He has wrought Evil'.

In the end she went off the rails, and ruined Eliot's happiness – he was so gentle and long-suffering. He never let the public into the secret of his life, though it is evident in all his work and in fact his work owed much to it: he would never have written as he did but for it. I happen to know that before his second marriage, that brought him so much happiness only ten years before he died, Eliot destroyed a whole chest of papers and evidences relating to the first. It is curious how close Russell and Eliot were at one time, though at opposite poles in every way. When one reads through *The Criterion*, which Eliot edited, one sees what an intellectual *bête-noire* Russell became for him. I cannot but think that Eliot was right every time.

There is an amusing exchange with Eliot's mother, expressing her 'absolute faith' that her son's future was in his philosophy, 'but not in the *vers libres*'. It shows how touchingly wrong mothers can be about their gifted sons: the reference is to *The Waste Land*, into which Eliot put a dream of Russell's, by the way.

From Eliot we move to Lenin, who rather disappointed Russell. 'I do not think that I should have guessed him to be a great man. In the course of our conversation I was chiefly conscious of his intellectual limitations, and his rather narrow Marxian ortho-doxy, as well as a distinct vein of impish cruelty.' No doubt that hits the mark well enough; Russell's disillusion with Bolshevik Russia was complete. He should never have entertained expecta-tions of any revolution – Eliot would never have been such a fool. Over D. H. Lawrence one's sympathies are divided: something to be said on both sides. Lawrence was right enough in his detestation of the Left intellectuals, only Bertie felt that Lawrence did not want to do anything to improve the state of the world, merely talk about it. Perhaps Lawrence was right in thinking that more harm is done by interfering do-gooders after all. It is difficult to see what actual good Russell has done in the world, for all his interfering and protesting about this and that, except for the brilliant and amusing books he has written.

NOTES

1. Ronald W. Clark, *The Life of Bertrand Russell* (Weidenfeld & Nicolson).
2. *The Autobiography of Bertrand Russell* Vol. I: *1872–1914*.
3. *The Autobiography of Bertrand Russell* Vol. II: *1914–1944*.

THE SOUL OF KING'S

Lowes Dickinson's Autobiography[1] has had an exceptionally friendly, if uncritical, reception; it makes most interesting reading, if only for its transparent honesty, a rare quality, especially in an autobiography. Then, too, it is a symptomatic book, for it is dominated by the theme of homosexuality. Twenty years ago it could not have been published; the really original thing is that Lowes Dickinson should have written it, the only original book he ever did write.

Many distinguished dons are homos, or have homosexual tendencies, even if they do not act on them; and often they make the best teachers, inspiring and suggestive, for young men, for they are at least interested in their subjects. Goldie, as they all called him, realised this perfectly well. He writes, 'the homosexual temperament must, I think, be regarded as a misfortune, though it is possible with that temperament, to have a better, more passionate and more noble life than most men of normal temperament achieve'.

In that case, why a misfortune? – better than living the life of a clod anyway, if it makes a man more sensitive, more intuitive, more aware, doubling his gifts so that he has both feminine and masculine within himself. Now that the wet blanket of humbug and hypocrisy has recently been removed, we can appreciate how true this is of so many leading figures in the contemporary arts, of music, ballet, painting, poetry, what not. And why not?

Of course, in Lowes Dickinson's time there were the pressures of society and its forceful disapprobation. But fancy taking seriously the disapprobation of any humans, when one knows how stupid, foolish and cruel they are. It is true that the lives of hundreds of thousands of useful citizens have been ruined by an attitude essentially infantile and silly. But why respect human silliness?

In these circumstances, two different reactions were exemplified in two of the most celebrated Cambridge figures of their day. Lowes Dickinson, like his friend E. M. Forster, reacted into sentimentalism, an exaggerated cult of the beauty of personal relations – in which they found intimations of immortality. In fact they went to the good, with a great deal of self-pity. There was self-pity in A. E. Housman, too; but there was also iron: he reacted with contempt for humans, not only for their foolery and cruelty, but for their unsatisfactoriness – they never (or so very rarely) come up to expectations, they are such poor stuff. This reaction justified itself in both better scholarship and better poetry, on an altogether higher level: Lowes Dickinson's was second-rate all through.

A third reaction was adumbrated, but not practised, by Wilde – it would have been better for him if he had: 'To be in love with oneself is the beginning of a lifelong romance'. To that I add: 'and in every way more satisfactory, and safer'.

The practical point is to turn what the unintelligent regard as defects into positive advantages. The French say that everyone has the defects of his qualities; but equally one has the qualities of one's defects – without the defects one wouldn't have the advantages: one should make the most of them. To act on this should diminish the self-pity which used to be the most regrettable characteristic of the homosexual temperament – witness T. E. Lawrence, even more than Lowes Dickinson – and mitigate the suffering, which, in so far as inflicted by others, is hard to forgive.

On the whole, Lowes Dickinson did achieve this and made himself into a fine teacher and inspirer of young men. That was the best side of him.

By the same token I think much less well of what he wrote and thought. He knew what horrors men are in the aggregate: then why the Liberal illusions? I never respect them – so superficial and untrue. Indeed at one point he goes even too far in his despair of men, 'for the springs of action lie deep in ignorance and madness'. Not madness, simply unreason – though to that one must add racial aggression, for man is a most aggressive animal.

This being so, why so insistent an appeal to sweet reason? Here once more is the cant of that Cambridge group – that the Germans were not responsible for the war of 1914, that it was all due to 'The International Anarchy', about which Lowes Dickinson wrote his largest book; that the League of Nations 'consolidated by the entry of Germany is bound to make a great difference', etc. I am reminded of an old joke of the Cecil family, about Lord Robert, at the time – that these people thought the League of Nations existed to support the League of Nations Union.

A far truer grasp of the situation was that of a hardened realist in politics, Leo Amery: 'Germany so nearly brought if off the first time, she was bound to have a second try.' All these well-intentioned Liberals, with their denunciation of the Treaty of Versailles, only weakened their own country's will and helped Germany to try it all over again. Lowes Dickinson's friend, Leonard Woolf, diagnosed 'in Goldie . . . a weakness, a looseness of fibre, in his thought and writing, which was subtly related to his gentleness and highmindedness'. I suppose I detest high-mindedness – I much prefer it low – partly because of its priggery; and Goldie admitted to his priggishness. He also admitted to an extraordinary imperceptiveness with regard to environment. With those acute disqualifications, why the itch to influence affairs, with so imperfect a grasp of the facts of (political) life?

Yet this was his aim: 'I never wanted to write learned and scholarly works. I wanted to influence opinion and the course of events.' In the end, 'I have spent most of my life in writing and thinking and inquiring into political facts and tendencies; with no result, I imagine!' In so far as it had any effect at all, it was deleterious; for Goldie was as mixed-up in these matters as he was mixed-up in himself.'Whether I have been at all successful I doubt. Events can be influenced by thought, but only if the thought is more original than mine has ever been, and the personality behind it more massive.'

In the event Lowes Dickinson has been totally forgotten – and this is the only book by which he is likely to live. In his day he was a much respected figure on the Left, regarded as a sage. But I never could read a single one of his books – Platonic dialogues on *The Meaning of Good* (Ugh!), *Justice and Liberty* (Grr!), *A Modern Symposium* (Plato again), *The Greek View of Life* (with all the fun left out). Anyway we know now why Plato meant so much to him, though I don't remember in Plato any of Goldie's absurd boot-fetishism, and all the fuss about masturbation and wanting his friends to tread him.

With my working-class background I fear I was somewhat uncultivated ethically, unappreciative of the middle-class moral exquisiteness of this Cambridge group, and inclined to the opinion expressed at one point in this book, 'what a lot of fuss about nothing'. In any case I preferred the real world of history and politics, and the heaven of music and the arts, to the twilight world of fussing about ethics, the Liberal conscience, the 'true and beautiful' exemplified in the activity of Quakers, G. E. Moore's infallibility on the absoluteness of personal relations. Moore convicted Goldie of 'the naturalistic fallacy' in *The Meaning of Good*; Goldie replies peaceably. 'I expect it is there, and also that it doesn't much matter,' and, more to the point, 'Moore has probably long ago altered his position, on this as on other matters'. Like Bertrand Russell on metaphysics. Then what's the point?

What a lucky lot they were at King's and Trinity in that halcyon world of pre-1914, before civilisation broke down! There were 'the long talks in our rooms or, in the summer, pacing the grounds of King's, still, as I think, one of the loveliest spots in the world.' There was the garden with its memories of tennis with those golden youths, 'sitting there with Roger and Ferdinand', the ghost of the boy 'I used to see seated in the summer house, and who, for me, will sit there still, till I visit the place no more. He was killed in the first weeks of the war'. Others, Goldie's friends, recall the radiance of those years, the gardens, the chestnuts and the limes in the Backs, bicycling about the Cambridgeshire countryside, before traffic became intolerable, coming back to see the moonlight falling along the windows of that marvellous Chapel. (No appreciation of the music or the services echoing within those vaults, however.)

Indeed Goldie seems to have been ungratefully ambivalent about Cambridge, with no generous appreciation of how lucky his lot was to have been cast in that beautiful place. 'Cambridge was not then, and never has been, altogether congenial to me.' It is

doubtful whether he would have found Oxford more to his taste –
I should have thought him of the essence of Cambridge, or at any
rate King's. If Keynes was its brains, E. M. Forster its voice,
Goldie perhaps was its soul!

When I was young and promising, Lady Ottoline Morrell,
whose kindness was not entirely disinterested, purposed to present me on a platter to Goldie: I was to go to Garsington for
confirmation. Think what a career I might have had if I had
become one of Goldie's boys! But Providence, who has so often
interfered in my affairs with a flaming sword at the gate, struck me
down with peritonitis so that the presentation at the temple never
took place. It was as well, for I was not really his type, and I fear
that my aggressive innocence would have disappointed his somewhat eccentric expectations.

NOTE

1.   Dennis Proctor (ed), *The Autobiography of G. Lowes Dickinson* (Duckworth).

DISENCHANTMENT WITH COMMUNISM

Here is a book[1] that illuminates the most ghastly issue of our time,
the mentality of Communism, the hold it establishes over the
minds of its followers, the deformation of character that is apt to
follow, the cult of lying, the Machiavellianism, the deliberate
breaking of spirit of those who do not conform, the 'disciplining'
not stopping short of murder; and then, the disillusionment, the
despair and sense of utter loneliness of those who break with 'the
party,' marked by it for life.

It is the spiritual terrorisation that stands out like the Counter-
Reformation and Inquisition all over again. Those who understand the ferocious ideological conflicts of the sixteenth century
will recognise the atmosphere: the obsessive, twisted psychology
of an antinomian sect, only directed to secular objectives, and the
remorseless pursuit of power-politics in the modern world. It is a
ghastly spectacle, and a most revealing book.

In it we watch the impact of the malign thing upon the minds of half a dozen intelligent, sensitive men, all of them writers. Crossman had the good idea of collecting the stories of their conversion, experience, disillusionment, awakening to truth and the facts as they are. Three of the contributions are first rate, those of Arthur Koestler, Ignazio Silone and Richard Wright, an American negro writer. It is noticeable that these were real Communists who had a life in 'the party'; the other near-Communists are nothing like so interesting.

Koestler's essay is the most damaging. Here are two of his conclusions: 'The necessary lie, the necessary slander; the necessary intimidation of the masses to preserve them from shortsighted errors; the necessary liquidation of oppositional groups and hostile classes; the necessary sacrifice of a whole generation in the interest of the next – it may all sound monstrous and yet it was so easy to accept while rolling along the single track of faith.' 'The moral of this story is that Joliot-Curie, Blackett and the rest of our nuclear Marxists cannot claim starry-eyed ignorance of the murderous happenings in Russia. . . . How our voices boomed with righteous indignation, denouncing flaws in the procedure of justice in our comfortable democracies; and how silent we were when our comrades, without trial and conviction, were liquidated in the Socialist sixth of the earth. Each of us carries a skeleton in the cupboard of his conscience. . . . At no time and in no country have more revolutionaries been killed or reduced to slavery than in Soviet Russia.'

It is symptomatic of them all that Koestler should have started from the standpoint that contemporary society is 'deformed', 'moribund', a 'polluted civilisation'. They all thought like that – until they discovered something far worse. What they needed was to know a little anthropology, or possess a little common sense: they would then have realised that what was wrong was something to do with themselves, that they were the misfits.

Their underlying assumption was an adolescent perfectionism, and what strikes one was the jejuneness of their outlook on the world. In addition to the arrogance and conceit of the intellectual, the astonishing ignorance. It never seems to strike them that they need to learn rather than to instruct – particularly from this country, more mature than most political societies, more experienced, at least, easy-going and tolerant. They have no idea of what England stands for: Moscow via Berlin was their Mecca –

and what a Mecca! It is noticeable how little English this book is – Mr Crossman is about the most English of its contributors, and no one could regard him as very typical.

NOTE

1. *The God That Failed. Six Studies in Communism.* With an Introduction by Richard Crossman (Hamish Hamilton).

R. H. TAWNEY'S INFLUENCE

R. H. Tawney was a name to conjure with in the Labour movement in my young days. He held a unique position as not only its mentor but, in a sense, its conscience. All section and almost all individuals in the snake-pit of the Labour party had confidence in him: a sage and a good deal of a secular saint, he was above factions, let alone ambition, a natural conciliator though a fearless and upright man. He was perhaps a great man as well as a good man, Hugh Gaitskell said the best man he had ever known.

R. H. Tawney and His Times[1] regards him as the greatest Englishman of his time; but that title must go to Winston Churchill (whom Tawney admired): their personalities stand in fascinating contrast. Ross Terrill is hardly the ideal biographer for Tawney – but who could do justice to his manysidedness? A contemporary English historian is called for; in default of that Mr Terrill, a young Harvard man who writes on politics, has done a conscientious job in the manner of American researchers.

Though some of the subtleties of the English social and intellectual scene escape him, and there are some appalling deformations of the language, he has gone to immense pains and consulted all the sources, people as well as papers. The first and shorter part of the book, the biography, is the more interesting; the second half, discussing Tawney's ideas – 'Socialism as Fellowship' – could well be shorter.

Tawney influenced social thought in Britain probably more than any man of his time – particularly in regard to education, where he pushed through the campaigns for 'Secondary Education for All'. His attack on the 'Acquisitive Society', his lifelong denunciation of capitalism, his incessant propaganda for 'Equality', had a large part in transforming society to what we see it today.

His chosen instrument was the Workers' Educational Association – his beloved WEA, of which he was all his life the creative and directing figure. He was a seminal influence at the London School of Economics – which he characteristically but absurdly preferred to Oxford and Cambridge – and also as an historian of eminence, though flawed by his social bias.

He was very much a product of Rugby and Balliol, the next generation on from T. H. Green and Arnold Toynbee (senior), with the socialist tinge which they gave to their Victorian liberalism. Tawney carried their ideal of 'plain living and high thinking' to an extreme: clothes out of an old junk-shop, household arrangements that were chaotic, positively dirty – the cult of squalor went too far.

It was really inverted snobbery – the refusal to take his MA at Oxford, or to become a Labour peer when he could have done good with the House of Lords as a platform. As for his peasant appearance, Mrs Tawney said to me proudly at their hen-house of a Rose Cottage: 'Doesn't he look like a duke?'.

A real man of the people, who had had great difficulty in emancipating himself from this squalor, would have less sympathy with this conception of life – it was, after all, merely a form of slumming. And for an eminent historian to have no appreciation whatever for the country's historic heritage, the monuments of a distinguished culture – Hatfield or Hardwick, Penshurst or Wilton, Chatsworth or Houghton or Woburn – was not only a deprivation but a deformation of history.

Tawney's cult of the peasant, proper enough in its place, was an easier option. We should take our sanitation for granted: the higher achievements of the mind in art, culture and science are immeasurably more valuable. Not much evidence of concern for these in the mass of Tawney's work; no aesthete – except for a distinguished style – with him it was ethics, ethics, all the time. He got a second in Greats.

I never had much sympathy with his conception of life – partly because I had seen too much of it at first-hand in my working-class environment: I did not need to go slumming, to learn about it from an upper middle-class background. And from the point of view of an historian, when today demotic prejudices prevail and a younger generation of historians are all too ready to follow in Tawney's footsteps in writing about the People – it amuses me to reflect that uninteresting people are less interesting than interesting ones. No wonder they are so unreadable.

Then how do Tawney's ideas – so influential in our own time – stand up?

His fundamental concern was with social equality as the basis for a Socialism of Fellowship. There is not much evidence of Fellowship in the Labour movement today, or in the society so much influenced by Tawney's thought – unthinkingly. His view that equality must be right because men are of equal worth is assumed, rather than thought out. A violent criminal, murderer or rapist, is not of equal worth to society with an air-pilot or coal-miner, an oil-rig man, a composer or mechanic or teacher. Tawney's confused socialising idea was not based on a true view of human nature.

The consequences are now plain for all to see. The emphasis on equality has been bad, (a) for work – in undermining the incentive to work; (b) for character – in disseminating slackness and releasing envy throughout society; and (c) for culture in every respect.

Tawney asked 'by what right is the control of industry vested in the hands of those who control it today?' – as if there was no answer to the question. But the answer is simple; simply by right of *effectively operating* it. Tawney's followers in all post-war governments – not Labour alone – have made industry almost impossible to operate, while totally incapable of operating it themselves.

Just look round at the appalling scene industry presents today. Just look at British Leyland! Tawney would be heart-broken at the spectacle of sheer selfishness, lack of consideration for others, for their own poorer people, the disgrace of egalitarian society. It shows up how wrong psychologically his highminded idealism was. Dean Inge was quite right about him: he didn't know what ordinary humans are like.

Tawney held that there were 'two basic possible dynamic principles of industry': one was the profit motive, the other the motive of service. Service as a motive? We can see today that the idea was a complete delusion, while they have mortally damaged the only incentive that effectively operates the economy. The result is that the whole thing is jammed up and visibly breaking down.

Even in Tawney's chosen field of education, by which his life's work largely stands or falls, he became rather disillusioned with the WEA before the end: it had, of course, outlived its utility. With regard to schools, particularly the comprehensives so much in question, there is a phrase that gives the whole case away: 'To the end he agitated for better and more egalitarian schools'. Here is another unfounded assumption, for the more egalitarian they are socially, the less good they are educationally. As for his rosy preference for the London School of Economics, he should have lived to see it in action in the past few years!

Tawney was certainly a good man – I always thought of him as rather far gone to the good; but I am forced to the conclusion that his ideas have done more harm than good in the upshot.

NOTE

1.   Ross Terrill, *R. H. Tawney and his Times: Socialism as Fellowship*.

PRIESTLEY'S ENGLAND

There should be something a little piquant about a Cornishman reviewing a book about the English by J. B. Priestley.[1] For Priestley is very much an Englishman, with a recognisable York-shire inflexion: upstanding and big-hearted, independent-minded and generous, fair-minded and tolerant, fundamentally demo-cratic if a bit insensitive. By education and intellectually I am English, but by temperament and heredity a complete Celt. My temperament gives me as much trouble with the English as Aneurin Bevan's gave him – but then there are things about the English that I don't like: their laziness and slackness, for one thing. (If the Anglo-Saxons hadn't been so slack the Normans – so few of them – would never have conquered them.)

However, I am a tremendous admirer of the English achieve-ment in history in the past four centuries – quite wonderful for a small island people: no other European people can compare with the record from the Elizabethan Age to 1914–18. But the achievement was that of the upper classes, in particular of the gentry and middle-class; for the showing of the English today I have less than no admiration, little indeed but contempt. *In the past half-century they have thrown everything away that their forbears won for them by effort and hard work, imagination and enterprise.*

That said, it is consoling to find that I am largely in agreement with Priestley on the subject: from these two wings, together we can hardly be wrong. His approach, as becomes a follower of Jung, is largely psychological: 'in the English psyche the barrier between consciousness and the unconscious is not fixed, and indeed is not really complete, so that the conscious and the unconscious often merge as if they were two English counties sharing irregular misty boundaries.' Good – as it were two Midland counties, even the boundary between Yorkshire and Lancashire is not all that clear: nothing of that between the Tamar boundary and the rest of England!

Hence the reasonableness as against doctrinaire rationalism, with the Latins; hence the reliance on instinct and the intuitive, the practical imagination, as against the theoretical as with Germans – evidence of their inadequate grasp of external reality. I am in agreement, too, with Priestley's emphasis on affection rather than passion in the emotional life of the *modern* English. Indeed I go further than he does in stressing the essential kindliness of English social life – all foreigners notice this; this is why they find England the most pleasant country to live in. There is an easy-goingness and a tolerance here: 'what could begin to look like a murderous encounter in France or America, or it might be a bloody street-battle in Japan, would in England end at the worst in a few scuffles and arrests.'

This is borne out by history – after all the history of a people gives you its long-reel portrait, as its philosophy and religion reveal its soul. It is here that Priestley is inconsistent with himself: he describes it as 'a piece of self-deception that the English are kinder, altogether more tender-hearted . . . and are inclined to be too soft with their enemies'; and the British Empire, 'now fading from memory, wasn't exactly held together by daisy-chains.' Here Priestley is wrong, from an inadequate sense of history. The British Empire was, in fact, held together by sea-power, which hurt no-one. Compare the record of the British with other Empires in history – the Roman, Spanish rule in the Netherlands, Philip II or Louis XIV or Napoleon, the German domination of Europe, or the Russian record – and he, or anybody else, ought to be able to see the difference.

All this tosh comes from the *New Statesman* view of history, which is long overdue for the trash-bin. Several evidences of it remain like fossils in this book – the over-estimation of an aristocratic irresponsible like Charles James Fox, who was lyrical about the French Revolution though he opposed Pitt's enlightened commercial treaty with France, on rabidly anti-French grounds. Fox's patroness, Georgiana Duchess of Devonshire, was *not* 'a woman of good sense': she had hardly any sense at all – what she had was sex-appeal. She cost the Devonshire estate something like a million in gambling debts. She and Fox were both compulsive gamblers: he gambled away a fortune of £300,000 – I quite sympathise with poor old George III who did not wish to see the Treasury in such hands.

Mr Priestley in the last decade has fallen, quite rightly, for history: then why not get it right? To say that 'the last truly English king was the much-maligned Richard III, the victim of Tudor propaganda, Shakespeare and a succession of actor-managers' is utterly silly. Apart from the fact that Shakespeare and Sir Thomas More and all historians know the truth about Richard III better than Mr Priestley, there is also the fact that the Tudors were on the whole more English than their predecessors or successors. The Plantagenets were dominantly French, the Stuarts Scots-French, the Hanoverians German. Henry VII's mother was English; Henry VIII's grand-parents were dominantly English, so were Edward VI's and Elizabeth I's, the daughter of Anne Bullen.

I am in agreement with Priestley's view of Oliver Cromwell as a man, one of the greatest of Englishmen; again the historical judgement is at fault: 'what Cromwell was trying to do – and he might have succeeded if he had lived longer – was to create an England far closer to ours.' All historians know that this is nonsense: Oliver's rule was a military dictatorship, against ninety per cent of the country, it was bound to collapse when the great man died.

Again I agree with Priestley in regarding Ernest Bevin as the big man he was, but to say that he should never have been made Foreign Secretary is another piece of *New Statesman* history, on its way out. People who know better – Dean Acheson, for example – know that Bevin was quite as considerable a figure in foreign as in home affairs. And Wellington certainly had genius as a soldier, nor was he playing, like an Irishman, a character-part: he was the soul of integrity, with an inspired common-sense. Oddly enough, Palmerston is given a better write-up than he deserves: his jingoism was a liability.

Mr Priestley doesn't get these historical estimates right, any more than I would know about actresses. (But, then, I know when I don't know.) I am charmed by his portraits of actresses, and learn all the time when he is writing about the theatre (then why doesn't he learn from an historian about history? – odd that people should think they know about history when they don't.) As against this, he has the advantage of a novelist in appreciating demotic social life: his sympathies are popular rather than middle-class, and never aristocratic. Thus his treatment of marriage is hardly in keeping with sociology: in almost all societies it is bound up with property. No point in sentimentalising the subject: does the relaxation of the rules today lead to any great stability or satisfaction?

Priestley's sympathies are those of a large-hearted man, and he covers a wide range of national sports and entertainments. He proscribes hunting, however. Now I am the last person in the world to be a hunting man, but I can at least see the point of it, and the beauty of it. Not to be able to do so omits quite a tract in the English experience, in literature and the arts as well. Choices are sometimes eccentrically personal: to choose Delius is a good piece of Bradford patriotism, because he happened to be born there, like Priestley, but he was a German, his music – as Priestley allows – essentially rootless. But he is one hundred per cent right about Elgar, and salutarily scornful of silly denigrators of his music. ('Bitter regret' is a bit insensitive for the Cello Concerto, however; the mood is nostalgia, grief and farewell.) The Englishness of Vaughan Williams' music I allow, in spite of the Welsh name – it is, if anything, too English. But fancy omitting Byrd, both very English and the greatest of English composers. What happened to English music after the Golden Age? – that is something the Puritans have to answer for. These middle-class philistines won twice over, in the seventeenth century and in the nineteenth, clamping down on the free expression of the spirit, and spirits too, for that matter.

What curious omissions there are here! Religion, for example: the English invented the Quakers, the Methodists, the Salvation Army, each of which has had its influence all round the world. (Do Boy Scouts come under the heading of religion and morals, or sport and entertainment?) The grandest contribution of the English intellectually and practically has been in the realm of science; yet Newton and Darwin are barely mentioned. (We are given a portrait of Sir Humphrey Davy, but he was a Cornishman.) To eighteenth-century Europe England meant Newton and Locke. A people's philosophy mirrors its mind: crazy, limitless transcendental idealism that of the Germans; practical empiricism that of the English. An outsider myself – like Santayana, Mr Priestley's enthusiasm for whom I share – I fear that the Yorkshireman has not searched deeply enough: the wicket is stickier than he thinks, he has perhaps taken it a little too easily.

And what odd choices for his portrait gallery of Englishmen! The Middle Ages might have been represented by Chaucer, so recognisable in his Englishry today. Certainly not Sir Walter Ralegh: a man of genius, he was not at all a nice man – if only Priestley knew – an absorbed egoist and a congenital liar, not to be trusted. Now John Hampden would have been the man to choose, a far more representative figure. Among writers, Dr Johnson is right; but surely not Lamb? I should have said Fielding, most English of writers with his essential qualities – good temper, tolerance, width of sympathies, with his massive good sense, his rich and down-to-earth humour. Priestley is admirable about Dickens, who bears out his theme very well too: his novels 'represent a huge explosion of Englishness, with the barrier between the unconscious and consciousness in tatters.' But what about Trollope, what about Hardy? – there is a fundamental Englishness though of very different kind and quality, in each of them: solid realism and fidelity to fact in the one, poetry, compassion *and* humour (*pace* Mr Priestley) in the other.

What about the language as reflecting the character of the people? – both Teutonic and Romance, flexible, lax, lazy (with little grammar), rich, practical and idiomatic. The English *are* kinder than other peoples: there is no equivalent for the word 'kindness' in French or German; any more than there is a word in English for the horrid German 'Schadenfreude' – so characteristic of them, taking pleasure in the ills of others. The English are romantic in the arts, not classical like the Latins – though that is no reason for excluding Reynolds: people recognised the English element in his sanity and balance, his generous nature. And why should the English, the most practical of peoples in industry and trade, have achieved the most *poetic* of European literatures? I think that is but another aspect of the working of the practical imagination.

I am glad that Priestley gives Wordsworth his due, most English of poets, if *very* North Country. But, when choosing women, why choose the ludicrous Annie Besant, most unrepresentative of Englishwomen, instead of, say, Mary Kingsley, that wonderful woman in all she stood for and did?

'Live and let live' is the proper motto of the English – like Shakespeare and Fielding, not the odious Puritans. And this makes a good motto for Mr Priestley, with his width of sympathies, his broad, warm humanity. What an admirable figure on the English scene he has for so long been, with his fertility and his prolific output in plays, novels, essays, secular sermons – and now taking to history! (A mere Celt and accepted as a historian, I am not allowed to write poetry, let alone stories.) It would be churlish not to pay tribute to the sheer enjoyability of Mr Priestley's book.

To this the brilliant illustrations add a whole dimension. They are admirably chosen, many of them familiar, some of them gratefully new – Cotman's 'Landscape in Blue', for example, the magical Samuel Palmer of a Shoreham Garden, and the splendid self-portrait of Charles Keene, as good as a French Impressionist and totally unknown to me. Among the familiar, we could have done without Mary Fitton, who never was a starter for Shakespeare's Dark Lady, with her auburn hair and blue eyes; but what a wonderful Gainsborough of the founder of Truman's Brewery, a solid John Bull in a romantic landscape – it might be taken for a parable.

NOTE

1.   J. B. Priestley, *The English* (Heinemann).

VANISHING BRITAIN

It is ironical, though perhaps understandable, that as more of Britain is destroyed with every year, every month, that passes – towns, villages, countryside, country houses, churches – the more books are written about the diminishing subject. It is true that there are some gains to set against the losses, and Mr Christian's informative book tells us fairly what they are.[1]

In some areas the land itself is receding, in East Anglia, for example. But there they have on their doorstep an area for reclamation as large as a county – the Wash: if that were in Holland it would have been reclaimed, like the Zuyder Zee. Then Morecambe Bay in Lancashire, turned into a great freshwater reservoir, would solve the problem of water-supply for the North-West, without drowning any more dales and swamping good agricultural land. Mr Christian tells us that there is more derelict land in Cornwall than in any other country. There is room for much more afforestation there – it could do with more woods and trees. The South-West Water Authority has created several lakes, in that lakeless land, to keep up the level of the denuded rivers. There certainly should be another lake on Bodmin Moor – Colliford Downs is the proper place – to accompany beautiful, sickle-shaped Sibleyback, created since the war.

Mr Christian is strong on the credit side to the account, the admirable work of rehabilitation in many areas – notably the Potteries which used to be so ghastly, now much improved, or various derelict industrial districts in Nottinghamshire, Derbyshire, or South Wales. He is keen about the disused gravel-pits that have been linked up to make lakes for the sailing and water-sports of the people. I note that these are demotic gains, characteristic of our brave new society; the losses – country- and town-houses, churches and historic monuments, townscape and countryside – were the creation of an elect society and are naturally mourned by the elect. I recall a conversation at the luncheon-table at Oxford about the ruining of seaside resorts, when I dared to say that the solution was quite simple: 'Select places for select people; popular places for popular people'. There was a shocked silence, as if I had said something improper, for ordinary people prefer humbug to honesty.

In fact the principle is the right one: the people are much

happier in places like Bournemouth and Southport, Blackpool or Southend, where the entertainments are in keeping. The best plan is to concentrate the horrors. In Cornwall, Newquay and Perranporth, St Ives and Looe are ruined: very well, let them go. On the bay at St Austell, at Duporth, is a Butlin's Camp: invisible, away to itself, it does no damage. That is the best principle: concentrate the damage, screen off the nastiness – for, of course, the idiots leave their mark, litter, vandalism, the hedges and moors alight from their filthy cigarettes, etc. – with shrubs, bushes, fences, wire-netting – anything to keep them in their proper place, where they are happiest, in their caravan-sites, etc.

Of course, the motor-car is the source of much of the trouble. Mr Christian tells us that ten thousand cars enter the Lake District on a fine Sunday. Myself, I see no reason why anybody should have a car unless he needs one for his business: four hundred people in one train are better for the landscape, fuel, etc., than four hundred people in separate cars. There are far too many people anyway in an overcrowded island – fancy importing more, simply because the whites won't work, and here people have 'never had it so good', in that revealing phrase. With too many people there is naturally pollution of every kind – in the air, the rivers and streams, around the coasts, with consequent destruction to bird and animal-life. I am less concerned about the disappearance of the natterjack toad than I am about the destruction of sea-birds, and the recession of wild-flowers from the hedges within miles of towns – the motor-car again. Mr Christian rightly notices the diminishing primroses. When I was a boy the hedges all round my native town were starred with them in spring – not so today, for the hundreds of idiots picking them. (Why must they do it? Answer: because people *are* idiots.)

I am not so much moved by the demolition of working-class streets from the Industrial Revolution as Mr Christian is – they are not beautiful anyway. One must discriminate; an historian's heart is much more wrung by the hundreds of country-houses going down every year, their contents – furniture, pictures, books – dispersed and going abroad in an ever-increasing stream. These were the creations of Britain in her great days, and represented a balanced way of life unsurpassed in history. The destruction in historic towns is no less shocking: Mr Christian cites the horrid cases of Gloucester and Worcester, Derby and Manchester (which miserably failed to take advantage of the opportunities

opened up by German bombing). In my heart of hearts, I don't
expect any other in our contemptible society. The explanation is
quite simple, and a social one: the lower middle-class bureaucrats
who run our society – this *is* the social revolution – have no taste.
Taste is the product of an aristocracy, which at its apogee, in the
eighteenth century, imposed its standards from the top downwards.

Mr Christian is wrong to say that 'beauty lies in the eye of the
beholder', i.e. that anybody's opinion is as good as anybody else's.
It is not. Standards of taste, criteria of beauty, excellence in the
arts or works of intellect, are known to and set by those who know
about the subject, not by those who do not.

The emphasis in *The Landscapes of Britain*[2] is largely archaeological, and the book offers a useful guide to the remarkable sites and
remains in this island from the prehistoric past to the present.
Britain is exceptionally rich in these – partly because the island
was such a melting-pot for races, peoples and cultures, partly on
account of its (comparative) insular security. Stonehenge and
Avebury – the second appears to be missing here – are unsurpassed prehistoric monuments, hardly paralleled in Europe.

I confess that I do not share the Gothick taste for ruins, 'bare
ruined choirs': I prefer to see the roofs on the walls which these
were intended to support. It gives me pleasure to see from an
illustration here the good work done at Iona in replacing roofs on
church and monastic buildings. The roof should have been
restored on Holyrood, as was proposed for a Scottish National
Memorial after the 1914–1918 war. I am delighted to learn that
Haddington parish church has had its choir restored since the war
– ruined, I suppose, at the Reformation. It is heartening to see a
stretch of the Roman Wall reconstructed from a scatter of stones –
I should like to see more of the great lintels replaced at
Stonehenge, and fallen stones re-erected in the upright position.

The authors begin quite rightly by emphasising the extraordinary variety of landscapes in these islands – they might have
added their beauty too, in which the country is not inferior to any
in Europe. This makes its erosion and destruction all the more
unforgivable – too many people crowded into it! The authors
reflect the fashionable inflexion for industrial archaeology, which
one can easily have too much of. I prefer to be instructed about
such an astonishing megalithic monument as the standing stones
at Callanish in the Isle of Lewis – a kind of northern Stonehenge –

which I had never heard of. (But then I am regrettably ignorant of Scotland – so far away.)

The West Country is my home-ground, in the restricted sense of Devon and Cornwall. Mr Kay-Robinson gives us an admirable account of these two counties,[3] representatively illustrated and well informed – for all that he begins with a mistake. Devon till 1974 was not the second in size of English counties, after Yorkshire, but the fourth. Lincolnshire was second; I am not sure which came third – Lancashire, Northumberland, or Norfolk? He surprises me by saying that Devon is not three times the size of Cornwall: he says wrongly that it is not quite twice.

His Preface opens up the complex question of the similarities and differences between Devon and Cornwall. As an outsider to both he underrates the differences, in my view. Geographically they are similar enough; but Devonshire and Cornish folk are distinguishable and recognisably different. The outsider thinks that we over-emphasise this, but surely we know better than any outsider about the truth of the matter? Devon was mostly populated by West Saxons pushing west – more so than Dorset, for example. The Cornish descry dominantly English characteristics among Devon folk: they are more placid and easy to get on with, less mercurial and more stolid than Celts, less clannish and not so individualistic and touchy. A great deal more might be said on this head.

Mr Kay-Robinson (neither a Devon nor Cornish name, by the way) gives brief introductory sketches to the history and characteristics of each county, followed by a fairly representative gazetteer of interesting places worth seeing.

With Messrs Binding and Stevens' *Minehead: A New History*[4] we move into Somerset. We learn at the outset that the name does not mean what one would take it to mean, but is cognate with the Welsh *mynydd*, meaning hill – is it not therefore Celtic? – and gets it from the North Hill behind which the town shelters. With the Norman Conquest the land herabouts came into the possession of the Norman Mohun family, who dominated it from their stronghold nearby, Dunster Castle, that wonderful rose-red building on its hill, the most memorably sited of all houses in the West Country, except for St Michael's Mount. There is something of medieval France about its appearance, with the historic little town of immense charm nestling at its feet.

Dunster's unspoiled appearance is entirely owing to its having been in the hands of the Luttrells, the Mohun successors, for centuries. One knows what it will look like once the people have their own sweet way, with their liking for the hideous: one can see from what its next-door neighbour, Minehead, looks like. Its prosperity as a port was owing to the Luttrells, who alone had the resources to build a quay and make a harbour. In Elizabeth I's reign they got the little place incorporated as a borough, but afterwards repented and had it de-corporated, since the burgesses were but 'simple and rude handicraftsmen who are fitter to be governed than to govern others'. No doubt.

The right to return two MPs was retained, however. In the eighteenth century the convenient arrangement obtained by which the Tory Luttrells returned one member, and Whig governments the other. From 1802 to the Reform Bill of 1832 the representation was entirely in the pocket of the family and it was therefore suppressed as a so-called 'pocket borough'. 'As early as 1723 the Luttrells' election expenses amounted to £459.4.7. One hundred voters were paid 2 guineas; fifteen sailors £1 each for loss of voyages. By 1761 the usual gift to a voter had risen to 3 guineas.' I do not see why not: it was all that they had to sell, poor souls. I cannot think that Reform can have been popular with the inhabitants of Minehead, robbing them of their expectations of cash and their fun into the bargain. Nor can we think that the average ability returned to Parliament was any lower than in our own reformed days. Come to that, are we so very reformed? One might consider safe Trade Unions seats as the pocket boroughs of today.

Minehead, like most towns, was Parliamentarian in the Civil War, and oddly enough Dunster Castle was held for Parliament by a Luttrell wife who was a Parliamentarian Popham, while the Luttrells were Royalist. It must be harder for the family, so generous and public spirited, kindly and hospitable, to hold out today in that turreted and walled fastness – a loss to the country if anything happened to disperse those treasures of family portraits, rarities and possessions which have been so devotedly cared for by its châtelaine!

With Leo Tregenza's *Harbour Village*[5] we reach Land's End, or almost; for his village is Mousehole (pronounced Mowzel) near Penzance. The enviable name Tregenza means the homestead of the first or foremost man; the book is published by Kimber, another Cornish name, which means the meeting of two streams, as in Quimper in Brittany. And indeed in this most characteristic

– or once was – of our fishing villages Breton fishermen and onion-sellers were familiar figures. Once we were intelligible to each other in our common Celtic language. Mr Tregenza's family moved from Mousehole to Paul, the whole of two miles away, where the old fish-wife Dolly Pentreath was the last native speaker of the language. Now we are learning it up again. You see, Mr Kay-Robinson, how different we are from Devon?

This little autobiography is true to Cornish life in the easy-going days early this century: fishing, swimming, going to local school and chapel, for Mousehole was characteristically Methodist. 'Architecturally Mousehole is the typical fishing village.' Then, 'nowadays much of the hillside at the back has been used for new "estates", built in concrete and with composition roof-tiles'. Of course: everywhere is like everywhere else: no distinctive character, hideously expressive of a hideous society.

NOTES

1. Roy Christian, *Vanishing Britain*, (David & Charles).
2. Roy Millward and Adrian Robinson, *Landscapes of Britain*, (David & Charles).
3. Denis Kay-Robinson, *Devon and Cornwall*, (Bartholomew).
4. Hilary Binding and Douglas Stevens, *Minehead. A New History*, (Exmoor Press).
5. Leo Tregenza, *Harbour Village. Yesterday in Cornwall*, (William Kimber).

INDEX